GETTING A JOB IN
PRIVATE EQUITY

BEHIND-THE-SCENES INSIGHT INTO HOW PRIVATE EQUITY FIRMS HIRE

BRIAN KORB and AARON FINKEL

WILEY

John Wiley & Sons, Inc.

For general information on our other products and services or for technical support, please contact our Customer Care Department within the United States at (800) 762-2974, outside the United States at (317) 572-3993 or fax (317) 572-4002.

Wiley also publishes its books in a variety of electronic formats. Some content that appears in print may not be available in electronic books. For more information about Wiley products, visit our web site at www.wiley.com.

ISBN-13 978-0-470-29262-4

Printed in the United States of America

10 9 8 7 6 5 4 3 2 1

CONTENTS

PREFACE

When we sat down to write this guide, our goal was to paint an accurate picture of career prospects in the private equity industry. We wanted to excite candidates about the industry and encourage them to pursue their dream job. At the same time, however, we didn't want to give anyone false hopes. For most, finding a position in private equity will be difficult, as the number of candidates pursuing private equity opportunities has always far outpaced the number of available positions.

Perhaps never before has the private equity profession wielded such power or played as important a role in the financial markets as it does at present. The appeal of working in the industry is obvious: Private equity is about investing millions (sometimes billions) of dollars into companies and helping determine their fate by exerting influence on operations and strategy, and in today's market that includes some of the most prominent companies in the world. Private equity investors work with companies from the initial investment to the time they are taken public or sold. They are passionate about investing and have the ability to create tremendous value.

If you've already looked into getting a position at a private equity fund, you may have been warned that the challenge could be daunting and the competition fierce. This guide will give you a better understanding of the career path in private equity and how the hiring process works. However, we do not profess to offer surefire, can't-miss strategies for securing a position, because there simply aren't any! Remember, too, as in other industries, there can be timing issues and natural business cycles that are out of your control. Instead, our aim is to give you insight into the elements that are in your control so you can put your best foot forward during your pursuit of a job. This guide also does not take a textbook look at private equity, give a detailed history of the industry, or explain how funds are raised and deals are done. You can get that information from many other sources (some of which are listed in Appendix A).

We segment candidates seeking positions in private equity by where they are in their professional careers, and thus we have chapters on the most common entry points: out of undergrad, pre-MBA (which, as you will see, often means being hired out of an investment banking or consulting analyst program as these are typical initial feeders into private equity jobs), from business school and postgraduate school. We devote a separate chapter to venture capital (earlier-stage investing) because the skill sets that venture funds look for, the timing of the opportunities to break in, and the career track can all differ significantly from later-stage private equity funds. There is also a chapter on private equity fund of funds, hybrid funds, and secondary funds, as those run slightly different recruiting processes and hire different types of candidates.

This guide focuses primarily on junior and senior (non-partner) roles at mid- and later-stage private equity and leveraged buyout (LBO) funds. When we use the traditional term *private equity* (PE), we are referring to the entire spectrum of early- to later-stage investing. When discussing a specific portion of the market, for example venture capital or buyouts, we will note it by name.

Most candidates target a long-term career in private equity by following what we call the *traditional path*, which starts early in their career. We also call this the *2-2-2 route* because it usually involves spending two years in an analyst training program (usually investment banking or consulting), followed by two years in a private equity firm and then two years in business school before securing a career-track opportunity. As you read this guide, you will learn that it is increasingly difficult to enter the process later in your career to make up for missed experiences. If you didn't land in an investment banking or consulting analyst program after graduating from college, it will be more difficult to secure a pre-MBA position at a PE/LBO fund; and if you wake up one day in business school (or several years later) and have an epiphany that PE investing is your true calling but you lack prior PE experience, the battle is likely to be even more challenging.

We will outline the traditional path and refer to it throughout this guide, but it is not the *only* way to get into PE. There are those who break in via other ways, and we make certain to give attention to them as well.

REAL-LIFE STORIES

As recruiters who specialize in private equity, we are well-positioned to offer career advice: We know what the hiring firms demand and we are intimately aware of the experiences of candidates who have successfully found positions. Thus, in addition to our own guidance, we believe a great way for you to *really* get a grasp of the private equity search process is to read insight from those on both sides of the equation who have experienced it firsthand. For the hiring firms, we include insight (Insider Tips) throughout the book from PE professionals, some of whom are in positions where they make hiring decisions.

On the candidate side, we have firsthand accounts (case studies) of 36 individuals who went through the search process, and we have included resumes from 15 of them. The experiences outlined in the case studies run the gamut from those who broke into PE the more traditional way to those who lacked the usual requirements but were still able to secure a position in a less traditional way. We have case studies from pre-MBAs, current MBAs, and professionals up to several years out of graduate school. What the authors of all the case studies have in common is that they were top performers and high achievers both academically and professionally and had a burning desire to succeed.

By reading the case studies you will quickly see that, in most instances, to secure a position in private equity you must be willing to commit early, put in the work, get the best education/training, and do whatever else it takes to excel—and that's true whether you eventually break in via the traditional or nontraditional path. Are we saying that many of our readers will find a position without the traditional background? No, but if you follow the advice of those who were the exceptions, and if you, too, have a stellar reputation and are willing to work hard, you can improve your chances of being an exception as well.

We believe the competitiveness, intensity, pace, and even the potential for compensation in the private equity industry parallels the sports world; therefore, at times we use professional sports analogies to describe various aspects of the job market. In fact, sports terms are commonly used by private equity professionals, so you may find being familiar with them a useful asset going forward. For example, funds hiring at the more senior level may tell us they are looking for someone who can *quarterback* a deal. When targeting junior level staff, the same funds say they want people who can *block and tackle* for their deal teams. Mid-market funds often want *utility fielders* who can take on many roles, given that they are smaller, less structured organizations.

We view the process of finding a position in private equity as similar to that of reaching the pinnacle of professional sports; thus, as someone striving to make it, we think you should tackle your search in a similar way as someone training to be a pro athlete. Think of working in private equity as the major leagues. To succeed in either athletics or private equity you need to have a high level of natural ability and work overtime to make up for areas in which you are deficient. In baseball, if a pitcher can't throw a 90-mile-per-hour fastball he will have a tough time making it to the majors. And even if he *can* throw 90 mph, there is no guarantee he will make it. You may have everything that it takes to eventually work in private equity, but for a variety of reasons could still find yourself on the short end of the stick. We hope this guide will also help you reduce the chances of that happening to you.

If you want to be a big earner and a superstar in this industry, you are going to have to do the work to get there—but you will have to do the right work. Anyone can work hard. Getting ahead in PE is about working smarter and getting on track early. We wish you luck!

ACKNOWLEDGMENTS

The authors would like to acknowledge the following members of Glocap's Executive Search team who were instrumental in helping put this book together: Joanna Albright, Pamela Harrington, Katherine Sorensen, and Sarah Woods. We would also like to thank the many industry executives whose views (though anonymous) we believe will provide readers with unique insight into the private equity hiring process; and we thank the authors of the case studies, who shared with us their stories of how they secured positions in private equity.

ABOUT THE AUTHORS

Brian Korb is a co-founder of Glocap and is the head of the private equity practice. Brian also oversees several aspects of the Executive Recruiting division and personally focuses on placing experienced principal and partner-level investment professionals into venture capital and LBO funds. From his experience over the past decade covering the private equity industry, Brian has developed a deep insight on emerging compensation and hiring trends, and he is frequently quoted in industry publications and mainstream media. In addition to this book, Brian oversees Glocap's annual *Private Equity Compensation Report*.

Before joining Glocap, Brian worked at Deutsche Morgan Grenfell, focusing mainly on corporate finance transactions. He graduated with a B.S. in economics from The Wharton School with concentrations in finance and accounting.

Aaron Finkel is vice president and head of publications at Glocap. In addition to coauthoring this book, Aaron coauthored Glocap's *Guide to Getting a Job in Hedge Funds*. He also coordinates the research, analysis, and production of Glocap's annual *Private Equity and Hedge Fund Compensation Reports* and handles all media relations. Aaron has over 17 years of experience in financial journalism, 11 years of which were spent at Institutional Investor's newsletters, where he worked as a reporter, editor, and publisher. Aaron has covered various topics throughout his career, including emerging markets, corporate finance, and asset management. Prior to his time at Institutional Investor, Aaron lived and worked in Venezuela for five years. He is a graduate of Brandeis University.

GLOCAP SEARCH

Glocap Search (www.glocap.com) is an executive search firm focused on the alternative asset industry and has a global practice placing investment professionals at all levels, from general partners to analysts, into private equity funds. It also has substantial practices placing CFOs, controllers, and COOs, as well as admin/support, IT, and marketing professionals, into these same funds.

With over 100 recruiters and offices in the United States and abroad, Glocap is one of the leading search firms serving the alternative asset community. Glocap's dedicated, specialized teams of search consultants have all worked in the industry into which they place or from which they draw their candidates and have similar educational pedigree. This insider position, and the level of knowledge that comes with it, gives us the ability to work in close partnership with clients to understand in depth their needs, culture, and internal processes. In many cases, in addition to placing professionals for our clients, we act as a trusted adviser on compensation trends, optimal organizational structure, and competitive landscape.

Chapter 1

GETTING STARTED

The private equity market has gone through a major transformation over the past two decades, with many of the most dramatic changes occurring over the past few years. As you are likely aware, you are attempting to enter one of the highest profile sectors of the financial markets—one that is wielding significant influence on the economy while at the same time creating great wealth for its investors. The wealth that has been amassed has played a significant role in increasing the attractiveness of the sector and thereby further fueling the competitive environment to enter. This chapter begins with a brief overview of the current state of the private equity market giving particular attention to how recent changes have affected hiring. It also provides a basic introduction to private equity.

THE MARKET TODAY

Notwithstanding the 2008 credit crunch and general market turbulence, it's safe to say that today's private equity (PE) industry is still a major force in the financial world and that it bears little resemblance to the fledgling market of nearly 30 years ago when there were just a few practitioners. Perhaps nowhere is the magnitude of the industry more apparent than in the size of today's buyout funds. In 1980, Kohlberg Kravis Roberts & Co. (KKR) ran the world's largest buyout fund at $135 million. In today's buyout world, in which firms compete to one-up each other, $1 billion funds are commonplace and the $20 billion barrier has been broken.

The clout of individual PE firms was pointed out in more detail in a November 2004 article in the *Economist* titled "The New Kings of Capitalism." The article pointed out that The Blackstone Group alone had equity stakes in about 40 portfolio companies which, combined, had over 300,000 employees and annual revenue

1

of more than $50 billion. If they were a single unit, the holdings would have made Blackstone one of the top 20 Fortune 500 firms.

In the same article, the *Economist* noted that in 2004, Texas Pacific Group's portfolio companies had over 255,000 employees and revenue of $41 billion, while The Carlyle Group's portfolio companies had 150,000 employees and revenue of $31 billion. With their recent deals, the portfolios of Blackstone, Texas Pacific Group (TPG), and Carlyle are even bigger and, along with Apollo Advisors LP, Bain Capital, Kohlberg Kravis Roberts & Co. (KKR), Warburg Pincus LLC, and others, are part of an elite group of funds that oversee billions of dollars of capital. Table 1.1 lists the largest PE-backed leveraged buyouts (LBOs) ever, in which many of these firms were participants. These funds are pioneers of the industry, and anyone looking to break into private equity must

Table 1.1   Ten Largest Closed PE-Backed LBOs

RANK	FIRM NAME	TARGET	VALUE ($ BILLION)	SECTOR	CLOSING DATE
1	Kohlberg Kravis Roberts & Co/TPG/Goldman Sachs	TXU Corp.	$44.30	Utilities	Oct-07
2	The Blackstone Group	Equity Office Properties Trust	$37.70	Real estate	Feb-07
3	Bain Capital/Kohlberg Kravis Roberts & Co./Merrill Lynch Global Private Equity	HCA Inc.	$32.10	Hospitals	Nov-06
4	Kohlberg Kravis Roberts & Co.	RJR Nabisco Inc.	$30.20	Consumer products	Apr-89
5	Goldman Sachs/Carlyle Group/Riverstone/AIG Management	Kinder Morgan Inc.	$27.50	Energy	May-07
6	Kohlberg Kravis Roberts & Co.	First Data Corp.	$27.00	Data processing	Sep-07
7	TPG/Goldman Sachs	Alltel Corp.	$26.90	Telecom	Nov-07
8	The Blackstone Group	Hilton Hotels Corp.	$26.70	Hotels	Oct-07
9	Kohlberg Kravis Roberts & Co./Management	Alliance Boots PLC	$19.40	Drug stores	Jun-07
10	The Blackstone Group/ Carlyle Group/Permira/ Texas Pacific Group	Freescale Semiconductor Inc.	$17.50	Semiconductors	Dec-06

Source: Thomson Financial's *Buyouts* magazine. Data accurate as of December 31, 2007

be familiar with them and the impact they have on the market. Many of these large funds have also diversified their activities. In addition to its LBO funds, Blackstone manages mezzanine, real estate, hedge funds, and private equity fund of funds. Carlyle runs leveraged finance, buyout, venture and growth capital, and real estate funds.

Private equity's higher profile has also put the industry under an additional spotlight—that of government regulators which have been scrutinizing tax issues, governance, and reporting, among other things. Although the large funds get a lot of attention, there are still many smaller PE funds impacting the market, and it is not uncommon to find one run by just a handful of investment professionals that are successful in their own right.

Despite the slowdown of 2008, the private equity market remains stronger by many measures than it has ever been. Indeed, up until 2008, the industry was enjoying one of its most dynamic periods, with unprecedented growth in assets and a surge in overall prominence; 2007 was a banner year, with U.S. buyout funds raising a record $228 billion, 29 percent more than the previous mark of $177.1 billion set in 2006, according to *Private Equity Analyst* data. Venture capital and fund of funds have also been attracting new money. In 2007 firms in those two asset classes brought in $32.2 billion and $26.3 billion, respectively, representing increases of 19 percent and 20 percent over 2006. Figure 1.1 presents a breakdown of annual fund-raising by buyout, venture capital (VC) and fund of funds.

Another indication of the prominence of the private equity industry is the well-known business leaders, celebrities, and former politicians who have joined its ranks, including Jack Welch (Clayton, Dubilier & Rice), Lou Gerstner and Arthur Levitt (Carlyle), the U2 rocker Bono (Elevation Partners), former senator Bill Frist (Cressey & Company), and former U.S. Treasury Secretary Paul O'Neill (Blackstone). Al Gore is also a partner at venture capital firm Kleiner Perkins Caufield & Byers. Table 1.2 lists the most active VC investors of 2007.

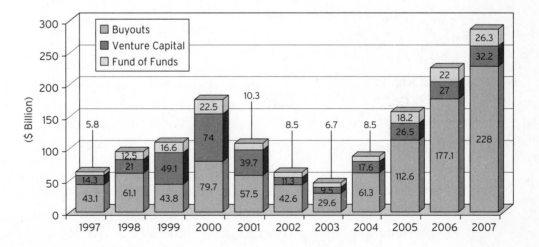

Figure 1.1 **Private Equity Fund-Raising, 1997–2007**

Source: *Private Equity Analyst*

Table 1.2   Top 25 Most Active Venture Capital Investors of 2007

2007 RANK	FIRM NAME	NUMBER OF DEALS 2007	NUMBER OF DEALS 2006
1	Draper Fisher Jurvetson (Draper Associates)	129	99
2	Intel Capital	112	108
3	New Enterprise Associates	105	93
4	Atlas Venture, Ltd.	103	81
5	Warburg Pincus LLC	89	80
6	Polaris Venture Partners	74	69
7	Accel Partners	71	55
8	Sequoia Capital	71	82
9	Kleiner Perkins Caufield & Byers	70	80
10	Menlo Ventures	67	41
11	U.S. Venture Partners	67	76
12	The Carlyle Group	66	99
13	Highland Capital Partners, LLC	65	48
14	Oak Investment Partners	62	86
15	Foundation Capital	60	46
16	Alta Partners	58	42
17	Bessemer Venture Partners	58	44
18	Canaan Partners	58	46
19	Austin Ventures, L.P.	57	61
20	InterWest Partners	57	50
21	Benchmark Capital	56	54
22	Venrock Associates	56	57
23	3i Group PLC	53	75
24	Trident Capital	53	39
25	Domain Associates, LLC	52	35

Source: Thomson Financial's *Venture Capital Journal*

A Global Market

Over the past several years the private equity market has continued to grow into a global industry, both in terms of where funds are investing and in the profile of the Limited Partners (LPs). Pools of capital have also become more sophisticated, with PE firms adding new asset classes to their stable of investment vehicles (some added fixed-income, hedge fund, and other products). Underscoring the maturation of the industry, one firm (Blackstone) led a groundbreaking initial public offering and others are expected to follow suit.

There are large global firms that oversee investments in many different countries, and major firms such as Advent International, Apax Partners, Bain Capital, Blackstone, Carlyle, KKR, TPG, and Warburg have offices outside of the United States to monitor those investments and to source new ones. While companies in China and India continue to attract significant interest, funds are also investing in companies in other emerging regions including Eastern Europe (specifically Russia), other areas of Asia (Vietnam has seen strong growth), the Middle East and Latin America (Brazil, in particular). Many well-known firms have launched new funds specifically to invest in many of these countries.

Sovereign investment funds, which invest the capital of non-U.S. governments, are expected to continue to invest in U.S.-based private equity funds as they look for higher rates of return than can typically be made by investing directly in stocks and bonds. One noteworthy example is GIC Special Investments, which manages private equity investments for the government of Singapore and has been a longtime investor in KKR. In fact, a report by McKinsey & Co. estimated that through 2012, sovereign funds in oil-exporting countries alone would invest about $300 billion in alternative assets, a figure that is about equal to the amount raised by all U.S. PE firms in 2007, according to *PE Analyst*. The same McKinsey report notes that the Abu Dhabi Investment Authority earmarks 10 percent of its $875 billion for private equity. In addition to being investors, some sovereign funds have become owners of PE funds. Most notably, the China Investment Corp. paid $3 billion for a 10 percent stake in Blackstone, the Mubadala Development Corp. (Abu Dhabi) paid $1.35 billion for a 7.5 percent piece of the Carlyle Group, and the Abu Dhabi Investment Authority bought 9 percent of Apollo Management LP.

Not to be outdone by their foreign counterparts, U.S. institutions are still major players, with the California Public Employees' Retirement System (CalPERs) and the California State Teacher's Retirement System (CalSTRS) being two of the largest. As of February 29, 2008, CalPERs had $241.7 billion in assets, of which $22.8 billion was in private equity, while CalSTRS had committed $12.7 billion of its $171.9 billion to PE. Other major investors include the Canada Pension Plan Investment Board, the New Mexico Public Employees' Retirement Fund, the New York State Teachers' Retirement System, the Oregon Investment Council, the Pennsylvania State Employees' Retirement System, Teachers' Retirement System of Illinois, the Teacher Retirement System of Texas, and the Washington State Investment Board. University endowments, including those run by Harvard and Yale, have been consistent investors in PE funds. Newcomers such as the Kentucky Retirement Systems and the New Jersey State Investment Council made recent investments.

Employment Scene

It's not surprising that as the size and scope of private equity funds have expanded over the years, so, too, have their hiring habits. Although we've seen some effects from recent market turbulence, the pace of hiring and the corresponding demand for highly capable professionals remains strong. In any given year, we continue to see many firms bringing on multiple new hires.

As recruiters, we analyze the hiring market in terms of supply and demand—the supply of candidates looking for jobs versus the demand from firms looking to hire. Although in private equity the demand never *technically* exceeds the supply (meaning there are always more qualified candidates seeking positions), on an absolute basis there are more positions available in the past few years than ever before. And even on a relative basis, the competitive environment has shown improvement, particularly for pre-MBAs finishing their investment banking and consulting programs and for graduating MBAs. A lot of the improvement is due to the spectacular fund-raising in 2006 and 2007, which, has led to the need for more investment professionals to help put the money to work.

Looking at how the private equity market has evolved over the past decade gives further evidence that the overall hiring has not matched one-for-one the capital that has been raised. Table 1.3 shows that over the past 13 years the amount of capital under management has increased by more than six times, the number of professionals working in the industry has nearly tripled, and thus the amount of capital per professional has increased over time (it would be incorrect to conclude that the industry is severely understaffed, but it probably means there is some room for growth). In terms of geography, New York City is far and away home to the largest private equity workforce, according to the *2008 Global Private Equity Review* published by Private Equity Intelligence. Following New York are London and the San Francisco Bay area. The top 10 cities for private equity employment account for nearly half of the global total, with Boston, Chicago, Los Angeles, Dallas, Paris, Stockholm, and Tokyo rounding out the list.

Some of the most notable changes to the private equity hiring market are being driven by the tactics of the mega-funds (those funds with several billion dollars in

Table 1.3 Evolution of the Buyout Market

	1994	2006	2007
Number of LBO firms in existence	347	593	614
Number of LBO funds in existence	512	1,040	1,095
Number of professionals	3,706	9,057	1,0398
Number of first-time LBO funds raised	27	38	44
Number of LBO funds raising money	110	179	206
LBO capital under management ($B)	113.6	636.5	729.7
Average LBO capital under management per firm ($M)	327.4	1,073.3	1,188.4
Average LBO fund size to date ($M)	199.7	442.7	473.9
Average LBO fund size raised ($M)	247.7	1,114.8	1,434.2

Source: Thomson Financial's *Buyouts* magazine

assets under management). Over the past few years the number of mega-funds has increased significantly, which means that as a group they have an even greater impact on the hiring behavior and compensation structures of most other funds, regardless of their size, geographic location, and/or the stage of a company in which they invest. By virtue of their size the mega-funds need more junior investment professionals. Each year they set the tone for hiring by beginning their annual recruiting earlier than most other funds and offering higher compensation packages. Over the past few years, hedge funds have also emerged as a force to be reckoned with. In spite of the recent market turbulence, hedge funds have grown into an asset class that increasingly competes with private equity funds for top talent (we go into more detail about the effect hedge funds have on the hiring market in Chapters III and IV).

PRIVATE EQUITY 101

Before initiating your job search, there are a few things about private equity with which you should be thoroughly familiar. Even if you think you know the nuts and bolts, this section could serve as a helpful brush-up on PE basics, including how various funds and roles differ. We also explain some basic hiring terms used throughout this book.

While we want to avoid sounding like a textbook, we still think it is important to discuss the basics of what private equity funds are and how they are structured. The term *private equity fund* may sound like it would be a stand-alone entity, but it usually is not. Even though someone may say they are an associate, senior associate, or vice president working at Fund ABC, they really work for a management company that has a fee agreement with Fund ABC. For example, Chicago-based Madison Dearborn Partners, LLC is the management company for five funds: the Madison Dearborn Capital Partners, L.P. (a $550 million fund raised in 1992); the Madison Dearborn Capital Partners II, L.P. (a $925 million fund raised in 1996), the Madison Dearborn Capital Partners III, L.P. (a $2.2 billion fund raised in 1999); the Madison Dearborn Capital Partners IV, L.P. (a $4 billion fund raised in 2000); and the Madison Dearborn Capital Partners V, L.P. (a $6.5 billion investment fund raised in 2006).

Most private equity funds are set up as limited partnerships. As such, they have a general partner (GP) in charge of making decisions for the partnership, and limited partners (LPs) who are the investors in the fund. Typical LPs are institutional investors including public and private pension funds, endowments, other large financial institutions, wealthy individuals, and the partners of the fund themselves.

The GPs make money two different ways: through an annual management fee paid by LPs and a carried interest (called *carry*)—a percent of profit. The annual management fee is usually 1.5 to 2.5 percent of total capital commitments to the fund, while the carry has historically been 20 percent of profits. You will often hear the term *2 and*

20 to describe this fee structure. Under such a structure, a $1 billion fund would have a 2 percent management fee and a 20 percent incentive fee. The management fee alone will provide the fund with $20 million in fees each year to pay salaries and overhead. If the fund doubles over the course of its lifetime to $2 billion (a 100 percent profit), the management company will reap $200 million based on an incentive fee of 20 percent, with that sum split among the partners and anyone else with a piece of the carry at the fund. A very select group of venture capital or leveraged buyout firms can even take home 25 to 30 percent of profits.

Don't get ahead of yourself here: If you join in a junior role you will not likely get a large percentage of the carry, but some of the fund's carry can filter down to you. If, however, you stay on for several years, you can be in a position to build real wealth as your percentage of the carry pool grows significantly (see Chapter XII for a more detailed discussion on compensation).

Characteristics of Private Equity Investments

In its simplest form, a private equity investment is a privately negotiated transaction involving an equity ownership stake. By their nature, private equity investments are less correlated to the public equity markets and are thus less subject to stock market cycles. Private equity funds offer the possibility of greater returns than investing in public equities; however, the trade-off is that they are relatively less illiquid. So if an investment in a fund is underperforming, it's not easy to exit. Although many of the large LBOs that have made headlines over the past several years were buyouts of public companies (if a public company is taken over entirely it is said to be *going private*), PE funds most often invest in private companies whose stock is not listed on a public exchange.

What the Funds Do

Throughout your interview process you will be asked numerous times why you want to work in private equity. The basis for your answer lies in understanding exactly what funds do. A PE fund earns its money based on the appreciation of its equity ownership stake in the operating companies in which it invests. Of course, not all investments lead to profits. A typical $1 billion fund will make multiple investments, and while some may only produce modest profits, a few big successes could be enough to provide significant returns for the entire fund.

The vast majority of investment professionals' time and effort at PE funds is spent working on actual transactions, which includes finding, reviewing, evaluating, negotiating, and structuring deals. Once investments are made, many funds dedicate a significant amount of time to monitoring and adding value to portfolio companies before exiting the investment. Generally, PE funds buy controlling or highly influential interests in companies. This element of control/influence is an essential ingredient in firms' ability to add value to their investments. Private equity firms add value in multiple ways:

- Provide capital and guidance in the form of financing strategies to grow the company.
- Actively guide operational and business strategy.
- Help make add-on acquisitions to grow the company.
- Sell various (sometimes nonessential) parts of a business.
- Replace management and/or restructure operations if necessary.

The typical cycle for a PE fund is:

- Raise money from investors (LPs).
- Invest that money in companies that fit their strategy.
- Use a predetermined strategy to add value to those companies.
- Exit (sell) the investment.
- Split the profit with investors (LPs).

The Different Types of Funds

Knowing the various funds or investment types will help you understand the industry and determine where you want to work and, just as relevant, the best fit for your skills. There are several types of private equity funds; the main characteristic that distinguishes them is the stage of a company's life at which a fund invests. As stated earlier, this guide will focus primarily on mid- to later-stage PE, which includes leveraged buyout (LBO) and growth equity funds. We also include a chapter on early-stage venture capital (VC) and private equity funds of funds. Some firms may have multiple fund types. For example, Bain Capital has both venture capital and LBO funds.

Buyout Funds

Leveraged buyout or simply *buyout* funds invest in more mature, later-stage companies that are almost always cash flow positive. As their name suggests, LBO funds purchase, or buy out, an entire company or a controlling interest in a corporation's equity. Leveraged buyouts are structured using a combination of debt and equity. The word *leverage* indicates that debt is used (as a lever) to enhance the fund's equity investment, allowing for a larger total purchase (and related larger financial return on the initial equity). In a similar fashion, a mortgage allows for the purchase of a larger home than would straight equity (a down payment). Table 1.4 lists the largest buyout funds ever raised.

The universe of LBO funds is divided into multiple groupings mainly based on the size of their funds (and thus the size of the deals in which they invest). We group

Table 1.4   Largest Global Buyout Funds Ever Raised

RANK	FUND NAME	FIRM NAME	LOCATION	YEAR	AMOUNT ($BILLION)
1	Blackstone Capital Partners V LP	Blackstone Group	New York	2007	$21.70
2	GS Capital Partners VI LP	GS Capital Partners	New York	2007	$20.30
3	KKR 2006 Fund LP*	Kohlberg Kravis Roberts & Co.	New York	2006	$16.6
4	TPG Partners V LP	Texas Pacific Group Inc.	Fort Worth, Texas	2006	$15.0
5	Permira IV	Permira Advisers LLP	London	2006	$13.95**
6	Apax Europe VII LP	Apax Partners Worldwide LLP	London	2007	13.82
7	Providence Equity Partners VI LP	Providence Equity Partners Inc.	Providence, R.I.	2006	$12.1
8	Carlyle Partners V LP*	Carlyle Group LP	Washington	2007	$12.0
9	Thomas H. Lee Equity Partners VI LP + Parallel Fund	Thomas H. Lee Partners LP	Boston	2007	$10.1
10	Apollo Investment Fund VI LP	Apollo Advisors LP	New York	2005	$10.0
11	Bain Capital IX LP + Co-Investment Fund	Bain Capital Inc.	Boston	2006	$10.0
12	Bain Capital X LP*	Bain Capital Inc.	Boston	2007	$10.0
13	Silver Lake Partners III LP	Silver Lake Partners LLC	Menlo Park, Calif.	2007	$9.0
14	Warburg Pincus Private Equity X LP*	Warburg Pincus LLC	New York	2007	$9.0
15	GS Capital Partners V LP	GS Capital Partners Inc.	New York	2005	$8.5

Source: Private Equity Analyst

*Fund still open as of early 2008.

**Converted from euros using 2006 currency averages.

funds into five categories—small, small-mid, mid-sized, large and mega-funds. The large and mega-funds (those with upwards of $2 billion or more in assets) typically invest in multi-billion dollar transactions often through an auction process (run by investment banks) and may do so in partnership with other large funds if the deal size warrants it. Middle-market funds (those with $2 billion or less) invest in smaller deals and frequently look to source those through more proprietary means.

- Beyond the firms listed in Table 1.4, some other noteworthy firms that have mega buyout funds are Cerberus Capital Management, Fortress Investment Group, Hellman & Friedman, JC Flowers & Co., Leonard Green & Partners, Madison Dearborn Partners, Thomas H. Lee Partners, and Sun Capital Partners.
- Examples of firms that have funds that are more mid-market focused are Aurora Capital Group, Brazos Private Equity Partners, Brentwood Associates, Bruckmann Rosser Sherrill, Catterton Partners, Centre Partners, Charlesbank Capital Partners, Gryphon Investors, Genstar Capital, H.I.G. Capital, KRG Capital Partners, and Wind Point Partners.

Venture Capital Funds

Venture capital funds are very different from LBO funds, not only in how they invest, but also how they hire, pay, and promote their investment professionals (we discuss venture capital in more detail in Chapter VII). In brief, traditional early-stage venture capital funds invest in companies that are not yet profitable and, in fact, are often cash flow negative, or "burning cash." The companies often don't have revenue and may not even have a product yet.

Venture funds are looking for the next great product or company that will revolutionize a specific industry. They usually target industries within information technology (including semiconductors, Internet, communications, and software), health care (biotech, medical devices, and health care services), and increasingly clean technology, with some funds targeting all three areas. For example, Kleiner Perkins, one of the original backers of Google, invests in technology components, systems and software, and health care. Kleiner Perkins also has a Greentech team that invests in clean technologies.

- Some well-known firms with VC funds include Accel Partners, Battery Ventures, Benchmark Capital, Bessemer Venture Partners, Charles River Ventures, Draper Fisher Jurvetson, Greylock Partners, Kleiner Perkins, Mayfield Fund, Menlo Ventures, New Enterprise Associates, Sequoia Capital, and Sutter Hill Ventures.

Growth Equity Funds

Whereas venture capital funds target early-stage companies and LBO funds seek out more mature, profitable, and cash-producing businesses, growth equity funds invest in companies that lie somewhere in between. Specifically, these companies are more mature than those in which venture funds invest. Growth equity funds target companies that are usually profitable (and cash flow positive) or close to it. They generally have proven business models but may need capital to continue to grow.

Transactions done by growth equity funds less frequently involve leverage, as many of these growing businesses have yet to amass the assets and/or are not producing enough cash against which to borrow. The transactions usually involve purchasing significant ownership (but not necessarily full control) in portfolio companies.

- Some larger, well-known examples of firms with growth equity funds are General Atlantic Partners, Spectrum Equity Investors, Summit Partners, and TA Associates.

Fund of Funds/Hybrid Funds

Private equity fund of funds invest primarily in a selection of PE funds rather than directly into operating companies (although many larger hybrid funds will frequently co-invest in companies alongside private equity funds with which they have a relationship). Fund of funds are a way for some investors, particularly smaller institutions, high-net-worth individuals, or family offices, to diversify their PE investment risk. By investing in dozens of PE funds, a fund of funds could have indirect exposure to hundreds of companies.

Because the skills involved can differ in many aspects, working at a fund of funds is usually not considered a stepping-stone to working at an LBO fund. (See Chapter VIII for a more detailed discussion of fund of funds and a list of top fund of funds managers.)

- Well-known managers of private equity fund of funds include Adams Street Partners, AlpInvest Partners, HarbourVest Partners, and Horsley Bridge Partners.

Secondary Funds

Secondary funds do not invest directly in businesses and/or do not involve traditional equity investment. Rather, secondary funds primarily purchase part or all of an LP's interest in an existing fund. For example, pension fund A may have invested, or committed to invest, $50 million in LBO fund I two years ago and now decides that it doesn't want to be an investor in LBO fund I. Secondary fund X comes in and offers pension fund A $35 million for its $50 million interest in LBO fund I. Pension fund A sells its interest in LBO fund I with the consent of the PE fund.

The valuation that takes place in secondary funds is of portfolios of investments and not so much individual companies. Therefore, as with fund of funds, it is also less common for someone to move from a secondary to a traditional PE fund (see Chapter VIII for a more detailed discussion of secondary funds).

- Firms that manage secondary funds include Lexington Partners, Landmark Partners, Coller Capital, Pomona Capital, and Paul Capital.

Mezzanine Funds

Mezzanine funds invest in private debt (i.e., mezzanine debt) frequently as part of LBO deals. The capital can come from private and/or public sources and can be used to invest in public or private companies. Mezzanine debt is the middle layer of debt used in leveraged buyouts—subordinated to the senior debt layer but above the equity layer. This type of hybrid structure often incorporates equity-based options, such as warrants, with a lower-priority debt. Mezzanine debt is often used to finance buyouts where it can give new owners priority over existing ones in the event of a bankruptcy.

Mezzanine level financing can take the form of preferred stock or convertible bonds. It can also provide late (bridge) financing for venture-backed companies immediately prior to a company's IPO. In some cases people who have worked at mezzanine funds have moved into traditional PE funds, but it doesn't happen that often. In addition, some well-known firms—Audax Group and TA Associates in Boston, for instance—have both mezzanine and PE funds, so some of the roles can involve both types of investing.

A few stand-alone firms with mezzanine funds are Golub Capital; Northstar Capital Partners, and Peninsula Capital Partners.

WHO IS WHO AT THE FUNDS

In addition to knowing the differences between fund types, it's important that you become fluent in the different roles at PE and VC funds. As well as knowing the appropriate level at which you are attempting to enter a fund, you should be able to distinguish between the different levels of professionals you are meeting. To sound informed you need to know what each of these roles is and how it fits into the investment process. Following are some definitions we give for different titles. We believe these are the most commonly accepted titles, but they can refer to different professional levels depending on the fund. For example, some funds use the title associate, senior associate, VP, or even principal for the same role immediately out of business school. So it's always worth paying attention to specific funds' individual classifications. Table 1.5 lists the top 50 fund managers in the world.

Analyst

Based on how we define analysts (see the following list), hiring at this level is not common in the industry. However, there are cases where hiring occurs more consistently, including at more institutional/mature funds (this can include the private equity groups within some investment banks). At these firms analysts can be brought on for two- to three-year programs. Some hiring also happens at later-stage venture capital and growth equity funds that are hiring analysts for deal-sourcing roles. In each case, after completing these programs, analysts may transition to another fund as an associate before possibly going to business school.

- Analysts are the most junior professionals at funds.
- They are typically hired directly out of undergrad, though some may have initial work experience.

- Those that are hired with more experience are still always pre-MBA and typically have three years or less of total work experience. That experience may be from an investment banking/consulting program but could also include finance roles in accounting or industry, etc.
- Analysts generally work on basic deal support, including research, analysis, financial modeling, and valuation. At smaller funds a significant portion of the role can also include providing operational support. Some analysts may also have the title *deal analyst* and focus more on research and support and less on deal execution.

Associate

Although we have seen the associate title used at both the pre- and post-MBA levels, the majority of firms use it to designate pre-MBA professionals, and that is the classification we adhere to.

- Associates generally have five or less years of total work experience, most frequently from a traditional two- to three-year investment banking or consulting program.
- Associate is the most common initial entry point into the various types of private equity funds.
- Associates are usually the most junior professionals (or second most junior at funds with analysts) and are typically hired out of the two- to three-year investment banking or consulting programs, many times for another two- to three-year commitment.
- They have more interaction with senior professionals than do analysts and, in some funds, may even oversee analysts.

Senior Associate

The title of senior associate is the most common designation for recent MBA graduates.

- Senior associates can be current MBAs or professionals with up to two years of post-MBA or equivalent experience (very commonly hired directly out of business school) and usually between four and seven years of total work experience.
- They go beyond supporting deals to overseeing some aspects of execution and increased involvement in deal negotiations and managing portfolio companies.
- They are typically not the most junior person at a fund. In fact, they could be the number two person on some deal teams.
- Compensation usually includes a portion of carried interest.

Vice President

- Vice presidents typically have three to six years of post-MBA or equivalent work experience and usually six to nine years of total work experience.

- They are typically the number two person on deal teams.
- They begin to lead more senior execution tasks and some initial deal negotiations.
- Compensation almost always includes a portion of the carried interest.

Principal

- Principals have four to nine years of post-MBA or equivalent work experience and usually eight to thirteen years of total work experience.
- They typically run the day-to-day deal process and manage a team of investment professionals.
- They earn more significant carried interest.

Partner

Partners can have the title of partner, general partner, or managing partner, and are among the most senior professionals at the firm.

- Partners generally have at least seven years experience post-MBA and often much more.
- A partner may be one of the founders or original partners in the fund.
- Partners are responsible for managing their own deals.
- They are usually involved in fund management and operational issues, including fund-raising, hiring decisions, and overall fund strategy.
- Partners earn a substantial portion of the carried interest.

Table 1.5   Top 50 Fund Managers

Rank	Firm	Location	Assets under management ($ Billion)	Firm Type
1	GS Capital Partners Inc.	New York	$58.70	Diversified PE
2	Carlyle Group LP	Washington, DC	$46.00	Diversified PE
3	Blackstone Group	New York	$41.70	Diversified PE
4	Kohlberg Kravis Roberts & Co.	New York	$38.10	Diversified PE
5	Bain Capital	Boston	$37.00	Diversified PE
6	TPG Inc	Fort Worth, TX	$32.50	Diversified PE
7	Permira Advisers LLP	London	$32.00	Diversified PE
8	CVC Capital Partners	London	$26.29	Diversified PE
9	Cerberus Capital Management LLC	New York	$25.00	Primarily distressed
10	Warburg Pincus LLC	New York	$24.00	Diversified PE
11	Providence Equity Partners Inc.	Providence, RI	$21.06	Diversified PE

(continued)

Table 1.5 (*continued*)

Rank	Firm	Location	Assets under management ($ Billion)	Firm Type
12	Apax Partners Worldwide LLP	London	$22.00	Diversified PE
13	Apollo Advisors LP	New York	$19.25	Diversified PE
14	Hellman & Friedman LLC	San Francisco	$16.90	Diversified PE
15	Welsh Carson Anderson & Stowe	New York	$16.00	Diversified PE
16	3i Group PLC	London	$15.12	Diversified PE
17	General Atlantic LLC	Greenwich, CT	$15.00	Diversified PE
18	Angelo Gordon & Co.	New York	$14.75	Diversified PE
19	AXA Private Equity	Paris	$14.40	Diversified PE
20	EQT Partners AB	Stockholm	$13.82	Diversified PE
21	Candover Partners Ltd.	London	$13.61	Primarily buyouts
22	Silver Lake Partners	Menlo Park, CA	$13.40	Technology-focused PE
23	First Reserve Corp.	Greenwich, CT	$12.70	Energy
24	Terra Firma Capital Partners	London	$12.69	Primarily buyouts
25	Partners Group	Baar-Zug, Switzerland	$12.61	Diversified PE
26	Cinven Ltd.	London	$12.20	Primarily buyouts
27	Lexington Partners Inc.	New York	$12.00	Secondaries
28	Fortress Investment Group LLC	New York	$11.20	Diversified PE
29	Avenue Capital Group	New York	$11.15	Primarily distressed
30	BC Partners	London	$11.00	Primarily buyouts
31	Madison Dearborn Partners LLC	Chicago	$10.50	Primarily buyouts
32	CCMP Capital Advisors	New York	$10.00	Primarily buyouts
33	TA Associates	Boston	$10.00	Growth equity
34	Sun Capital Partners	Boca Raton, FL	$9.60	Buyouts and distressed
35	Leonard Green & Partners	Los Angeles	$9.00	Primarily buyouts
36	PAI Partners	Paris	$9.00	Primarily buyouts
37	Summit Partners	Boston	$9.00	Diversified PE
38	Thomas H. Lee Partners	Boston	$9.00	Primarily buyouts
39	New Enterprise Associates	Baltimore	$8.50	Primarily venture

Table 1.5 (*continued*)

Rank	Firm	Location	Assets under Management ($ Billion)	Firm Type
40	Oak Investment Partners	Westport, CT	$8.40	Growth equity and venture
41	Coller Capital	London	$8.30	Secondaries
42	Credit Suisse Private Equity	New York	$8.30	Diversified PE
43	Oaktree Capital Management LLC	Los Angeles	$8.28	Primarily distressed
44	Horsley Bridge Partners Inc.	San Francisco	$8.15	Diversified PE
45	GTCR Golder Rauner LLC	Chicago	$8.00	Primarily buyouts
46	JC Flowers & Co.	New York	$7.90	Distressed and buyouts
47	Intermediate Capital Group PLC	London	$7.88	Debt and mezzanine
48	Technology Crossover Ventures	Palo Alto, CA	$7.70	Growth equity and venture
49	Berkshire Partners LLC	Boston	$7.60	Primarily buyouts
50	Eurazeo	Paris	$7.54	Primarily buyouts

Source: Galante's *Venture Capital and Private Equity Directory*, 2007 edition, as reported by the firms

HIRING TERMS YOU SHOULD KNOW

Throughout this guide you will see references to the *traditional path*, *pre-MBA*, and *post-MBA* positions and the *on-cycle* and *off-cycle*. These are terms that we use to describe various aspects of the hiring process.

The Traditional Path

As mentioned in the Preface, we call the traditional path for someone looking to become a long-term player in private equity *2-2-2*—two years in an investment banking or consulting program after undergrad, two years in a private equity/LBO firm, and then two years in business school. If all goes well, the next step after business school would be a full-time partner track position at a PE firm. Once again, this guide addresses those people who have followed or are currently immersed in that traditional path, but it also takes an in-depth look at those people who were able to get into private equity without following the *2-2-2* path.

Pre-MBA versus Post-MBA

Pre- and *post*-MBA are terms we use to categorize different positions and are not meant to imply that a candidate has to (or did) attend business school; thus, they should not be taken literally. We separate jobs into pre-MBA and post-MBA to distinguish between the experience needed to get the jobs and the type of work that will be done. We define pre-MBAs as those people who have generally been out of undergraduate school for five years or less, regardless of whether they plan to go to business school. It may be easier to think of this simply as a more junior role at a private equity fund. Post-MBAs are those candidates with anywhere from 5 to 15 years of total work experience and could include individuals who never went to graduate school but are still on a promotional track.

The Hiring Cycle

On-cycle and *off-cycle* are the terms most often used to describe the timing of pre-MBA and current MBA hiring cycles. As we explain in Chapters III and IV, private equity firms have been making offers to analysts in investment banking and consulting programs and to business school students as early as the end of their first year. If a pre-MBA analyst is interviewing anytime from late spring to late summer after his first year for a position that begins the following summer, he/she is considered on-cycle. A candidate who is interviewing for a position that starts before the natural end of their current commitment (usually July for analyst programs) is said to be interviewing for an off-cycle start date. *Off-cycle* can also refer to the timing of a firm that interviews for immediate hires (they are looking to pull someone out of their program early).

Chapter II

OUT OF UNDERGRAD

As a college student it is inevitable that at some point you have to think about your professional career. Although you may still be far from deciding what business profession to pursue, something may have piqued your interest about private equity and you likely have questions about how to break into the industry and what the optimal path is.

Although the hiring of analysts (the most common title given to candidates hired directly out of undergraduate school or with some initial work experience) is less common, there are some firms open to hiring at this level. From our experience, any hiring that does happen occurs more consistently at the more institutional/mature firms (this can include the private equity groups within some investment banks). At these firms, analysts typically enter with a class for two- to three-year training programs in which they will be exposed to different investment processes. After completing such a program, analysts may transition to another fund as an associate before possibly going to business school. Some hiring also occurs at later-stage venture capital/growth equity funds that hire analysts for deal-sourcing roles.

THE TRADITIONAL PATH

As we noted in the previous chapter, when hiring at the most junior level, the large majority of private equity funds focus on candidates in quality, structured two- to three-year investment banking or management consulting programs. These candidates bring a level of deal/project experience, financial skills, and maturity that someone right out of college would not. If you ask private equity veterans whether you should pursue a position with a private equity fund directly out of undergrad, they would most likely recommend against it and we would tend to agree. While a small number of quality PE funds do hire at this level, the vast majority don't, so we recommend being careful about spending too much time pursuing jobs that can distract you from the traditional path.

19

For someone still in college, the best way to pursue a career in private equity is thus to get on the most common path. Trying to take a different track can sometimes work against you later in your career (see Chapter IV for case studies of people who struggled to enter PE after following a nontraditional path earlier). Now is the time in which you are ideally positioned to take the best first step.

Although we introduce you to two candidates who landed jobs straight from undergrad (Case Studies 9 and 10 in Chapter III), both are exceptions. The bulk of our advice to undergrads focuses on the merits of following the traditional path, which commences in an analyst program. These programs are the PE world's version of field training, in which analysts get extensive deal and/or project exposure that will provide the foundation for working in PE. Most funds view both types of programs as part of the hands-on training necessary to make the transition from college into the coveted PE job. (Think of this as PE's version of the residency program that doctors must go through.) Both will also provide you with contacts that will be invaluable to your long-term career.

POSITIONING YOURSELF FOR AN ANALYST PROGRAM

The choices you make coming out of college will have an effect on your future ability to get into private equity. While each year we see bankers and consultants landing PE positions out of their respective programs, there are definitely more bankers hired (we discuss more specifics about consultants in Chapter III). Thus, you should think about whether you have what it takes to get into an elite training program at a bulge-bracket firm (as the largest or most elite investment banks and consulting firms are typically called), and even whether you have the strong desire to do so. If you don't think you have what it takes or if your desire is less (but you still want to gain the skills to eventually work in PE), then maybe you should target a middle-market/boutique firm. Both firm types have merits.

It's up to you to choose which path is best suited for you. As you will read later, many larger PE funds look to recruit the top-performing analysts from leading programs, and some funds will target banks even more specifically by the deals on which they focus (i.e., large versus middle-market).

Insider Tip ▷	**From a Managing Director at a Major LBO Fund** I would not hire someone without deal experience. I did it once and it was a disaster. I wouldn't do it again at any level. We look for smart people with quantitative skills who are tenacious and aggressive and can model financials. A good investment banking analyst can be a good PE analyst.

Getting into a prestigious banking/consulting program is like going to a university with a powerhouse Division I sports program: It will give you the most visibility to be drafted by a professional team, or in this case a top-flight PE fund. We estimate about 2,500 to 3,000 undergrads are hired each year into mid to large investment banking and consulting programs in the United States. All the bulge-bracket investment banks have analyst training programs, as do most of the regional and middle-market banks and the major consulting firms. Our research shows that in 2008 the leading investment banks, including Citigroup, Credit Suisse, Goldman Sachs, JPMorgan Chase, Lehman Brothers, Merrill Lynch, Morgan Stanley, and UBS, combined had about 1,000 first-year analysts in their North American offices. On the consulting side, firms including Bain & Company, Boston Consulting Group, McKinsey & Company, and the Monitor Group had over 400 first-year analysts on their payrolls.

Securing a spot in one of these analyst programs may not be easy, especially if those banks and/or consulting firms do not recruit on your campus, but there are steps you can take to improve your chances of receiving an offer. Perhaps the most useful is to focus on getting a formal banking/consulting internship during the summer after your junior year of college. As we pointed out in the preface to this guide, committing early to a PE career is essential. The same is true when looking for a summer internship. If you are a sophomore, this is the best time to begin planning your path.

Insider
Tip ▷

From a Principal at a PE Fund

The advice I would give to people coming out of college looking to get into PE would be to get into a banking program. Once in the program you should do what you can to get exposure to LBO shops. The leveraged finance and M&A groups are the best ones to be in. You should also develop a good rapport with your managing directors (MDs) because partners from the large shops will call them when they are recruiting and ask who their top analysts are. Those interested in PE should of course get as much deal experience as they can, but on top of that they should also try and develop an investment mind-set. As you are doing deals, you should think to yourself, "What are the merits of this company as a long-term investment? What are the major risks? Do I want to live with this company for five years?" Because that is that you will do when you are on the principal side.

For the few fortunate ones, the right summer experience between your sophomore and junior years will give you a leg up to secure the coveted investment-banking/consulting internship before your senior year, which in turn will help you get into an analyst program at an investment bank or consulting firm when you graduate. For others it will be a matter of using your summers to get whatever formal finance or accounting exposure you can. Your friends may be off to the beach, but for you, getting the most out of your summer will be the first step to differentiating yourself and demonstrating your commitment to a PE career. While these summer jobs are not necessary requirements, they are extremely helpful because banking/consulting programs look favorably on those who use their summers wisely. If you are a senior and did not use the summer to your advantage, you may have to play catch-up by widening your search of investment banks or nonbank alternatives that will accept you.

> **Glocap Insight**
>
> Think of a summer banking/consulting internship in the same way a young baseball player would view going to a summer baseball camp to improve his chances of playing at a major university. Just as the ballplayer will learn new skills, fine-tune existing ones, and meet coaches with connections, so too will the banking/consulting internship help you hone your talents and meet people who can help you along the way.

Assuming you land an analyst position after college, if at any point you have a choice of which group to work in, you should choose one that will give you the skills most transferable to private equity. The groups within an investment bank that most closely meet those criteria are the leveraged finance, private equity (not private placements), financial sponsors, or mergers and acquisitions (M&A) groups, and some industry groups that integrate those functions. Private equity funds that have an industry focus such as media or health care will find additional value in candidates who have worked in those specific groups. Some well-known consulting firms have private equity, corporate finance, or valuation groups that teach some of these same skills.

OTHER OPTIONS

If you don't get into a traditional analyst training program, all hope is not lost. Accounting firms have transaction and valuation groups that also involve heavy financial modeling and can be a good lead-in to PE (see Case Study 8). Doing internal corporate M&A at a major corporation (such as GE or Microsoft) can sometimes provide many similar skills sought by PE funds. Some other options include working in a commercial bank (corporate lending); at a rating agency (in a credit training program); in a management rotation program at a large corporation or insurance company; and/or in sell-side research, of which technology and health care coverage can be attractive to a venture capital firm. Working in a business development role at a service provider or even a provider of financial information services could provide skills that are applicable to a deal-sourcing role, which requires good business generation skills and a strong ability to network.

WHAT IF I'M OFFERED A JOB STRAIGHT AFTER GRADUATION?

If you come across a more mature fund and get a job offer, it may be worth taking as it could potentially put you on a faster track to a long-term career in PE. That being said, since very few large, quality, stand-alone funds hire out of undergrad, you should question whether the opportunities that may be available to you directly out of college are the ones that you should be pursuing to best prepare for a long-term career in PE.

If you end up at a fund that, by its nature, offers less structured training compared to that offered by investment banks and consulting firms, you could very likely work on only one or two deals that close (or even none!) during your first couple of years there, so learning could be spotty. You could also join a PE/LBO fund and focus mainly on doing research and prospecting for deals over the phone. Although those are valued skills for some growth equity funds where they can lead to successful career paths, they are not as applicable across all types of funds and do not always replace hands-on deal execution experience.

If you get an offer from a fund that is not a well-known name, we would advise that you proceed with caution. Working at such a fund may not allow you to build the platform of necessary skills and make the contacts that you will need if you want to build a long-term career in private equity. If you feel the offer is a golden opportunity, you should at least ask what you will be doing at that fund because, depending on your role (such as one that involves predominantly cold-calling, like the person in Case Study 9 discusses), you may or may not get what you want out of the experience, which should be to work toward best positioning yourself for the longer-term PE career you want.

Chapter III

PRE-MBA

As someone who is still new to the workforce, you should be starting to think about the career track of your chosen profession. If you are in some type of business training program, you may be learning general concepts of corporate finance and/or strategy. Or you may have been exposed to private equity deals and could at least know of someone who has secured a position at a PE fund. Either way, you've decided to explore private equity as a career. While you may be acquiring some of the essential skills to become a PE investor, taking the first step toward your goal will be challenging. This chapter outlines how PE funds hire at the pre-MBA level, where they hire from, and what you can do to better position yourself to secure a coveted role, which for some could be a stepping-stone to a career-track opportunity.

As mentioned in the previous chapter, most private equity funds focus their pre-MBA hiring on candidates in investment banking and, to a lesser degree, consulting training programs. Thus, if you are in one of these programs you have most likely seen some of your predecessors secure positions in private equity, and you may be familiar with the hiring process. What you may not know is that hiring at the pre-MBA, or associate, level is the most active segment of the market for private equity professionals. Over the past few years the demand for top candidates has reached new heights, driven primarily by the record amounts of capital that have poured into the industry and the ensuing demand for resources to invest that money, most notably at mega buyout funds (see Figure 1.1 in Chapter I). Despite the rising demand, there are still far more high quality candidates looking for opportunities than there are positions available (remember, even though we call them pre-MBA, this does not imply that they all go to business school.)

To show you what you are up against, let's review some statistics. As we stated in Chapter II, about 2,500 to 3,000 undergrads are hired each year into mid-size to large investment-banking and consulting programs in the United States. Whereas 10 years ago there might have been 20 to 30 firms that consistently hired at the pre-MBA level, we now estimate that over 300 firms hire roughly 500 to 600 pre-MBA analysts each year, however this does not include the exceptions who are hired out of the smaller firms or who have backgrounds other than banking or consulting. Thus, if PE funds only hired pre-MBA bankers and consultants from the most recognizable firms, there would still only be positions for about 20 percent of them. It goes without saying that those who make the cut are top performers.

While this chapter focuses on the traditional path, there are definitely candidates who secure pre-MBA positions with a diverse range of backgrounds (although, as the preceding figures show, the challenge is formidable). As we said, there are more than enough analysts with banking or consulting experience to satisfy the needs of hiring firms, so for someone outside of that pool to make it they will have to beat out someone with a more traditional background. If you believe you are developing the requisite deal skills (possibly by working in a transaction/valuation group of an accounting firm; doing internal corporate M&A; working in a commercial bank, at a rating agency, as a sell-side or buy-side equity researcher, or filling a comparable role in financial services), you may have what it takes to work at a PE fund, but you will more than likely have to blaze your own path because funds and recruiters are not likely to reach out to you. Later in this chapter we give more advice for candidates without the traditional banking or consulting backgrounds, and there are also case studies of people who secured roles with these less traditional backgrounds as well.

THE ROLE

Nearly all private equity funds hire junior professionals as analysts or associates in support roles and expect them to work hard and contribute, but frequently these funds do not leave much room for a longer-term role. Instead, most initial private equity jobs are two- to three-year commitments, with the large majority of funds holding fast to the idea that junior professionals must move on after that initial commitment ends—potentially to business school or another opportunity. Of course there are exceptions, meaning some funds do allow those analysts or associates who they believe will be true stars to remain with the fund instead of going to business school. There are even funds that commit to bringing analysts or associates back after they attend business school, with some going as far as paying their tuition in exchange for a commitment to return.

We cannot emphasize enough that private equity firms want superior individuals who are mature, driven, hardworking, and possess top analytical skills. Private equity funds are not in the business of teaching junior professionals how to construct a discounted cash flow or LBO model (see *Expect Minimal Training* Chapter XIV). Not only do they expect you to be able to put together a model, they want you to be able to flawlessly analyze complex and challenging transactions and use your business judgment to develop conclusions about the analysis. Additionally, they require effective and polished communications skills. No matter where you are now, it should go without saying that you should be striving to stand out as one of the highest achievers among your peers.

HIRING

In today's pre-MBA hiring market we have observed two major waves of hiring in a given cycle. The first wave mainly includes the larger, multibillion-dollar funds which have annual hiring needs and often hire multiple candidates. These funds tend to begin their recruiting earlier in the cycle and look to lock in top-tier analysts at bulge-bracket banks to positions that start after they complete their two-year commitment. The next wave of recruiting comes later in the cycle and is comprised mostly of mid-size and smaller funds. In addition to targeting analysts at bulge-bracket firms, these funds also recruit from mid-market and regional banking programs, often in the same cities where their firms are located. It is during this wave that firms may also start to consider exceptional talent outside of traditional banking and consulting programs.

From a Banking/Consulting Program

If you are in an investment banking or consulting program, you are entrenched in the first step of the traditional 2-2-2 path and are heading toward step two. Nevertheless, given the numbers stated earlier, now is not the time to take anything for granted. With that in mind, your course of action should not be dissimilar from the process of applying to analyst programs described in the previous chapter. Just as the undergrad process began as far back as your sophomore year, you must plan early if you want to successfully move on to the next phase of a career in private equity. The case studies in this section further emphasize the importance of getting an early start. In addition to those stories, we also recommend you read Case Studies 14 through 16 from MBAs in Chapter IV, as these applicants, too, went through the pre-MBA process and offer useful insight into how they succeeded.

The First Wave of Hiring—The Race for the Best

As stated earlier, private equity funds compete each year for the top pre-MBA talent. If you're one of these analysts you usually know it—you're probably in a top group at a top firm; you have been invited to work on high-profile projects, have helped represent the firm in meetings with clients, and received a positive mid-year review. In fact, if you are in this group it will be tough not to know it because you will also most likely be pursued aggressively by the leading buyout firms as well as by recruiters.

Over the past few years the competition for the leading banking analysts has picked up in intensity due to the tightened market (caused by the record amount of capital that has flowed into the industry and also the continued growing competition from hedge funds). Indicative of the competition for top talent, many funds (especially large ones that make multiple annual hires for each analyst class) are starting their searches earlier each year to ensure they are able to preview all of the best analysts before they make other commitments. The accelerated hiring has been led by the mega funds, and there has been a trickle-down effect on hiring by all funds that want to secure the best talent available. Whereas a few years ago the mega funds might have extended offers in September for start dates the following summer, they now make their offers in June or even earlier (before candidates even start the second year of their analyst programs), for start dates more than a year out. Mid-sized funds that used to make offers in February are now extending offers to candidates five months earlier, in September (still about 10 months before their expected start date).

| Glocap Insight | We estimate that approximately 80 percent of the analysts in investment banks and consulting firms who choose to leave after two years receive offers from PE funds by the 18-month mark of their analyst programs, although this percentage has increased in each of the past several years. |

As we said, if you are fortunate enough to be a top analyst from a prestigious program, the opportunities will come your way and you should be able to choose where you want to work. To be ready, however, for when private equity firms and recruiters approach you, we recommend beginning your preparations in the first six months of your training program. That means getting your resume together early into your first year. You should also start to familiarize yourself with the different types of PE funds— what they do and how you might fit in. It may sound early, but that is how competitive it has become. Your decision on which fund to join will be based on which is the best fit for you (see the section titled *Evaluating Your Choices* in Chapter IX).

| Glocap Insight | In addition to competing with their peers for top candidates, private equity firms also have to contend with hedge funds which, as their own hiring process has matured, continue to target some of the same candidates as private equity funds. In today's market, the effect of hedge fund hiring is particularly noticeable at the pre-MBA, or associate, level. Hedge funds now compete head-to-head with the buyout/growth equity funds during the peak of the hiring cycle. Some hedge funds begin their recruiting efforts just as early as the buyout/growth equity funds (and in some cases earlier) and have used aggressive compensation packages to one-up the mega funds and land candidates who would have traditionally been destined for private equity. |

The Second Wave

To us, the process of getting into a private equity fund out of an analyst training program is like a professional sports draft. In this case it is funds, not sports teams, that go after the obvious star talent. Not all funds, however, target only these top pedigreed candidates from the premier investment banks and consulting firms. Each year there are hundreds of other highly qualified analysts who complete investment-banking and consulting training programs at bulge-bracket and boutique firms across the country. For them, there is a second wave of recruiting that occurs and, from our experience, analysts who secure positions during this period can move up and shine as bright as anyone else (see Case Study 4).

This second wave of hiring typically begins once many of the top analysts from the leading banks and consulting firms accept offers and are out of the market—which is usually by the end of the summer. It's at this point that hiring firms that have not filled all their needs sit down with their internal teams and recruiters to review how many openings they still have and then may begin looking at the candidates who were not initially considered. This is also when many funds enter the market that may not have a clear picture of their hiring needs until closer to the end of your analyst program (meaning they are hiring later in the cycle). In both cases, the funds expect there will be future stars in this group of candidates as well.

We have found that some funds are absolutely open to hiring analysts from middle-market and regional investment banks (in some cases, funds may even prefer to hire a mid-market banker over one from a bulge-bracket bank). So, if you're a top performer from one of those types of banks, opportunities should be available for you. From our experience, there are always some hiring firms that say, "I need someone who can crunch numbers and think on their feet—a great 'deal' athlete. I'm indifferent as to

Insider Tip ▷

From a Senior Investment Professional

I would say, don't even think of working at a private equity firm unless you can think on your feet and can make decisions with sometimes limited input. To me, the most important attributes/skills of a private equity analyst/associate are the ability to quickly understand what drives a business; strong analytical capability (beyond quantitative skills); and being able to think and act outside a structured environment (outside the box).

I felt I was best prepared for my career in private equity because of my love for math and engineering, and having worked in various businesses beginning at a young age. To me, it is very important that a candidate fit in with the personality of my firm. When hiring someone I also take into consideration the reason why they want to do it. If it is to prove something or for the money, then they are wrong candidates. Someone who feels passionate will almost always succeed.

which school or firm they come from." Given the choice between a B+ candidate from a bulge-bracket banking program and an A+ candidate from a boutique/less-mainstream investment bank, the fund will often take the A+ person, many times referred to in the industry as the "better athlete." Consider the specific example of a $300 million fund, not in a major financial center, that concentrates its investments in smaller companies in that same proximate geography. More often than not these types of funds can be targeting closely held or even family businesses and will look for a person who specifically understands businesses of this size and can relate to the local culture of the targeted investment companies.

Overall, our advice for those in this group is to take a practical approach by focusing on the firms that will be more interested in you. These can include some larger funds, but most, not surprisingly, will be more middle-market and/or regional ones. Recruiters may still call you for these positions, but usually not as early in the cycle. That doesn't mean you should limit your opportunity set by not starting as early as you can. The strategy is similar to when you were a senior in high school and you divided the colleges to which you were applying into *reach* schools and *safety* schools. You should do the same with PE funds—have your reach funds, but have your safer funds as well and target them specifically.

Glocap Insight	People like to hire what they know. Mid-market PE funds will target people from mid-market investment banks, while alumni like to hire people from their previous firms or schools.

Even though the path you will follow differs from that of the analysts hired in the first wave, you should understand their hiring cycle and expect to work within a similar framework. If their job search is a sprint, yours might be more of a marathon that can stretch from August to January or beyond. You, too, should get your resume ready early; however, you should pace yourself. You may have to work harder and be more creative, and you will have to be more convincing about why private equity is for you. You will be grilled harder and scrutinized more in interviews by partners who wonder if you can help them and their investors make money. The partners will examine you to see if you are who they want representing their firm at the highest level.

AN ADDITIONAL WORD ON CONSULTANTS

While there has historically been a preference for pre-MBA candidates with investment banking training, there are some firms that consistently hire consultants, and that trend appears to be growing steadily. Private equity funds have been increasingly highlighting strategies and methods to both diligence opportunities prior to invest-ment and add more to their portfolio companies after their initial investments. This includes improving operations and focusing more attention on their overall busi-ness strategies. Both of those play more to the training of consultants than that of bankers.

More specifically, for example we have noticed that increasingly funds that used to fill four pre-MBA positions with investment banking analysts are now more open to bring-ing on three bankers and one consultant to balance the hard-core financial analytics with some strategy/operations training. There are even a handful of funds that have expressed a strong *preference* to hire only consultants, and a smaller group that, as a rule, *exclusively* hire consultants over bankers.

Alumni from consulting firms probably make up 10 to 20 percent of the PE indus-try, and it is no surprise that firms with former consultants value that training and skill set. If you are coming out of a consulting program, it could make the most sense to first target those firms. To improve your chances even more, we'd recommend enroll-ing in a Wall Street training program that teaches some of the financial modeling skills sought by such firms (see Case Study 3 for the story of someone who got into private equity out of a consulting program).

OTHER CANDIDATES

If you are currently working in a non-banking/non-consulting role, you still have options. Each year we see candidates land positions after acquiring the requisite skills in a nontraditional setting. As we pointed out in the previous chapter, working in the transaction or valuation groups of an accounting firm can also be a stepping-stone into PE. Additionally, those who have done internal corporate M&A at a major cor-poration or worked in a commercial bank (perhaps doing corporate lending), in a credit training program at a rating agency, in a management program at an insurance company, at a sell-side or buy-side firm doing equity research, and so on, can also have acquired the skills to work in a PE fund.

As someone with a less traditional background, it's less likely that opportunities will come to you; therefore you will have to be more proactive and utilize anything at your disposal to better your odds of securing an offer. This includes researching and identifying those firms that have hired professionals with similar backgrounds and/or even alumni from your current firm or undergrad school, and then reaching out to them. It may take some digging and may lead to many dead ends and turndowns, but it could be worth the effort. We'd also recommend focusing on firms outside of the major financial centers, since there are usually fewer candidates targeting them.

Remember, for you to secure a position, you will have to beat out someone who may have the traditional experiences sought by PE funds. Your goal, therefore, is to convince PE firms to look past any deficiencies in your background to see what you bring to the table that will make them want you on their team. Expanding your search to include sourcing roles at growth equity funds (see Case Study 13) and/or working at a private equity fund of funds (see Chapter VIII) could also increase your chances. Neither of these focuses as much on hard-core financial modeling skills; however, both can provide a bonafide entry into the world of private equity.

CASE STUDIES

Following are case studies of candidates who secured pre-MBA positions. The first seven are from candidates who landed with their PE funds the traditional way—out of banking/consulting programs. We also have an example of someone who secured a pre-MBA position with an accounting background. And finally, we include the stories of five exceptions—two who got in directly out of undergrad, two who benefited from specialized technology and health care industry experience, and one who landed at a growth equity fund with a background in business development. All of these candidates had stellar professional backgrounds and records of strong academic achievement. Whether they were first-round draft picks or later selections, the authors of the case studies paint a good picture of how they conducted their job searches while at the same time working the long hours to maintain their day jobs.

You, too, will have to squeeze in phone interviews and day trips to different cities for face-to-face interviews (Chapter XI goes over what to do once you get an interview). The analysts from bulge-bracket banks may find that their firms are more accommodating (especially if it is during the real sprint times described earlier), as they might view your getting hired into a top fund as a good reflection on them. Others may have to deal with banks and consulting firms that are less accommodating, making the search that much more taxing. Either way, it was a grind for these people and could be for you as well. Pay careful attention to the advice each person gives and how they describe their interviews and their job search process. The resumes that correspond to some of these case studies and others that appear later in the book can be found in Appendix B.

Case Study 1: Bulge-Bracket Hire

This person went from an analyst training program at a bulge-bracket investment bank to a buyout shop. This is an example of an on-cycle candidate who went through more of a summer sprint. He knew early on that he wanted private equity, excelled at all levels, and landed a top job.

■ ■ ■

I started looking into getting a job in private equity well before the end of my first year of analyst training. I had my resume ready by mid-July because I had heard from people in prior years that the hiring market would heat up by the end of the summer. Unfortunately, I got a bit crushed at work and my search didn't really take hold until late August (although I was contacted by a recruiter in July), when I got my resume out. I interviewed at five firms during a three-week stretch beginning in mid-September. I went to the first round at two places, the second round at two other places, and into a fifth round at the firm that eventually extended me an offer.

When I graduated in 2004 with a degree in economics I was not thinking private equity. My thoughts going into the analyst program were that I would do as well as I could, hopefully enjoy it, and maybe make a career out of it. I didn't want to look past it. I was randomly placed in the natural resources group at my bank, which was good and bad—good because with oil prices soaring, there were a ton of deals and I was working on nonstop live deals from the beginning; bad because I was absolutely overwhelmed by the work load. I liked what I was doing but knew I would need a change. I had pitched some deals to PE funds and also talked with a lot of friends and other analysts as the year went on, about the merits of working in PE.

I definitely feel lucky that I started when I did and found a job so early into the process. Having an offer early into my second year has made things a lot more relaxed for me. I can see the light at the end of the tunnel.

I would advise other banking analysts interested in PE to be sure they want this career well before the recruiting period comes up. You've got to go after it hard, so you better want it and do your homework, especially when it comes to preparing for interviews. It sounds obvious to say that you better know your LBO models and your deals inside and out, but it's true. On my interviews I was grilled pretty hard by the partners.

Of course, I'd recommend others start as early as possible for the sheer value of not missing out on an interview at a place you'd be interested in.

The firm that eventually extended me an offer had me meet just about everyone that I would be working with, which meant about 12 to 15 people. About half of them asked me about my work and the others just wanted to get to know me and see if I would fit in with the firm. All the other firms asked me pretty technical questions. They asked me to walk them through an LBO model. Some would show me an LBO model and say, "Let's say the depreciation changes by $1 million—talk about how every line in your model changes."

Of course, I'd recommend others start as early as possible for the sheer value of not missing out on an interview at a place you'd be interested in. Personally, I wasn't interested in working at a large shop like a KKR or a Blackstone. I've heard they're the ones that are pushing the process earlier and earlier as they go after the number one guys in the leveraged finance groups. I knew I wanted a smaller, more collegial shop and didn't target a specific style of investing. The firm I ended up with was in the market for three people, and I was the first they hired.

(See Resume 1 in Appendix B.)

Case Study 2: Bulge-Bracket Banker—With a Late Start

This person grew up knowing about private equity and achieved a successful transition into PE by going to a top banking program.

■ ■ ■

Growing up in Silicon Valley, I was exposed to the venture capital (VC) world early on. I knew I wanted to go into VC and began moving in that direction as a senior in college, when I focused on getting into a banking program. I knew the program would be a great experience and give me skills in finance and be a good launching pad for me.

I came out of undergrad with a degree in business administration. I also knew I wanted to join the tech group of whichever analyst program I went to. I took advantage of the on-campus interviews, was offered a spot in a top banking program, and accepted. Since I was allowed to state my preferred industry, I listed technology.

I was first approached by headhunters and some PE funds that don't use headhunters just after I finished the first year of my analyst program. The funds try to get you to commit before you get offered, and possibly accept, a position as a third-year analyst. I wasn't looking to get into buyouts as I was still interested in VC, but had to be realistic. There were simply less venture opportunities out there. I ended up interviewing at a buyout/growth equity shop.

Even though I knew that some PE funds were beginning the hiring process very early, I wasn't concerned that I didn't have an offer until well into my second year.

My first interview wasn't until late November or early December of my second year. A headhunter pointed me to the fund and someone from my bank also had a contact at the firm. I interviewed with five firms, and for me the process went very fast. I was already in the process with other funds when this one contacted me. I think the banking program really gave me the skills and industry knowledge that opened a lot of doors for me in the world of private equity. Many funds like to hire ex-bankers, but a good number of people hired come from consulting or other backgrounds, as long as they have the necessary skills and experience.

The entire search process was pretty grueling and time consuming as you have to do your day job at the same time as you are managing your search. Luckily, my bank was very supportive (as I suspect are others). They know how the process works and were good about letting me go on interviews. The toughest part was trying to figure out what you want to do and differentiating between firms because there are so many of them. I'd advise candidates to do their homework. I wouldn't have been able to see all of what is out there without a recruiter. I would also advise people to leverage their networks and not to be afraid to ask senior people at their banks for help.

If I could do it all over, one additional thing I would have done is to try to explore more. There are so many funds out there, you want to make sure you are focusing on the ones where you will enjoy working. Sometimes you are in the middle of your search and then a fund gives you an offer and they want a quick answer. There is no time to delay.

Even though I knew that some PE funds were beginning the hiring process very early, I wasn't concerned that I didn't have an offer until well into my second year. It was the big shops that have a strict recruiting schedule and were extending offers by Labor Day. I wasn't interested in going to one of those places. I knew they work you hard and I had done that in my banking program. I was looking for a better work/life balance. And there were still plenty of jobs coming through.

Case Study 3: Getting In from a Consulting Program

This person didn't focus on PE early, but leveraged consulting and industry experience.

■ ■ ■

After graduating with a degree in engineering and a summer banking internship at a leading Wall Street bank, I co-founded a software company where I worked for a year and a half. I subsequently returned to university to pursue a master's degree in engineering. Upon receiving my master's in 2002, I considered opportunities in industry, banking, and consulting. I had not really even thought about private equity and did not have a great sense for what it was all about. I joined a top-tier consulting firm and worked hard developing my skills around market analysis and corporate strategy. During my time there, I had the opportunity to lead a tech and telecom project team.

I had no master plan of working in private equity, but began to look for various opportunities at the beginning of my second year as a consultant. I considered a wide variety of options, including venture capital, industry, and private equity. In each of these positions, I would be able to leverage my background in technology and strategy to be a value-added member of the team. For me, the decision to move into PE was more of an evolution of the things I had done. It was helpful during the process to talk with friends of mine who also worked in each of these industries.

In my search, I didn't target big, late-stage buyout funds. Instead, I focused more on technology as an industry and sought out opportunities in that vertical. My approach was to take advantage of my technology and strategy background. I realized that I lacked formal finance training, so I didn't look too deeply into generalist firms where I had no advantage. Moreover, I was a little late to the game. While some people started in August or September, I didn't begin until late September or early October. My consulting job kept me on the road four days each week. And, while my firm was understanding, the process of working and searching for a job was grueling. As a backup, I also considered staying on with my firm for a third year. Eventually, I landed a job with a technology-focused private equity fund that valued my consulting and technology experience.

For me, consulting prepared me very well for private equity. Bankers come into private equity with more muscles in finance, but consultants know the competitive dynamics of particular industries. I also benefited from a track record of doing good work, in school and at my various subsequent jobs. Additionally, the graduate work that I had done in engineering helped to differentiate me from other candidates.

I would advise those looking for a job in PE to know your strengths and weaknesses and figure out where you are positioned well. Know the culture of the funds and come across as an engaging person. Go into interviews with confidence and determination.

I would advise those looking for a job in PE to know your strengths and weaknesses and figure out where you are positioned well. Know the culture of the funds and come across as an engaging person. Go into interviews with confidence and determination. Show them that you know *why* you want to be in private equity and, more specifically, *why* you want to work for them. These are all extremely small organizations where every person is an important member of the team. It's similar to an athletic team with only a handful of members: Come draft day, they want to know that you will be a good draft pick for them (See Resume 2 in Appendix B.)

Case Study 4: Getting In from a Regional Bank

This is an example of someone who got into PE from a non-bulge-bracket bank and who secured a job late in the hiring cycle, proving that PE funds do come back for top candidates. Note how this person says being later in the cycle was actually a benefit.

■ ■ ■

I did little during my undergrad years to prepare for a career in private equity. I got out of college in 2002 with an Ivy League degree in American history and didn't know what I wanted to do. I played baseball in college and was drawn to consulting and investment banking because some of my past teammates had gone that route. Unfortunately, I had two hurdles in my way—my timing and my major. I began looking for my post-undergrad job in the fall of 2001, a time when the job market was tough and not many companies were visiting college campuses. With a major in American history I had no economics, no math, and no finance.

I was able to interview with some of the New York banks (some of my interviews were pretty embarrassing as I had no idea what some of the basics were, like EBITDA), but I ended up getting an offer and taking it with a more regional bank in a smaller city. I think I was one of the last people they hired; fortunately, they saw potential in me.

I had no clue what leveraged finance was, but that was where I was placed and it turned out to be a stroke of luck. My first six to nine months were pretty painful, getting up to speed on leveraged finance—I had never learned Excel or PowerPoint, and that is what I lived and breathed. Looking back, it was good that I was in a small city. I had no problem working late into the night: There were no distractions and I had no school buddies around tugging at me.

I was accepted for a third year, but in the spring of my second year I started looking around and targeted private equity. Banking was getting routine. At a small firm there were only three people on each deal team so I got great deal experience. I knew there were a lot of bright and motivated people in private equity and I liked the life/ work balance. I knew I was not on cycle, so I focused my search on three to five firms and used geography as a guide, staying away from larger cities. For me, headhunters were critical. My firm didn't focus much on helping me find a job. The headhunters got me the first contacts and got me in the door.

I ended up at a late-stage buyout shop with several billion dollars under investment. I believe the two main reasons why I was considered at this firm were (1) my leveraged finance background (model-intensive and credit-focused), and (2) my deal experience (closing several transactions with M&A components). I don't think I was treated any differently in my interviews because of where I did my training—once you're in the room, everyone focuses on your modeling skills, deal experience, critical thinking ability, and your personality.

Overall, I found that interviewers usually look highly on people who have been successful at each level of their life—high school, college, extracurriculars, first job, and so on. But in terms of doing anything differently or recommending my way, it's a tough call. I would guess the hit rate for New York City banks is much higher for PE versus a regional bank. The key is to learn as much as you can where you are, and grab for responsibility.

I think two things helped me get into PE: I was coming out of leveraged finance, which is very model-intensive and credit-oriented. And I was off-cycle, so I wasn't competing against every single Goldman and Blackstone second-year. I didn't look during my first year because I didn't know what I wanted and I wasn't that good. I was probably average during my first year (it took me nine months to learn Excel). By my second year, I was at the top of my class and felt I was in a position to look. I knew where I stood vis-à-vis the analysts from the higher-profile banking programs and I didn't feel like I was overlooked by the PE firms. I saw it more as I had job security with the third year offer (I made sure to put that on my resume).

Being in a smaller city hurt me during the search process, as I couldn't just hop over to see someone during lunch the way people can in larger cities where the funds are concentrated. I was limited to phone interviews at first. Being off-cycle benefited me in another way because later in the cycle the hiring firms seem to make quicker decisions. For me the entire process from first interview to final offer lasted about four weeks.

My job search became a type of second job and a secret life. It's a skill to balance your current obligations and not be able to talk about it with most people due to confidentiality. It is always stressful to interview and have your life on review, but I found that the more practice I got through phone interviews and with firms that I was less excited about, the more my story was honed and sharpened. I became comfortable speaking and talking about myself. Yes, there may be times when you'll need to get on a flight on short notice, but if you're paying yourself, usually you'll have about two weeks notice. The toughest part is juggling your current job responsibilities and traveling. I'd recommend talking and entrusting your job search with an associate or VP with whom you feel comfortable, so they can give you advice and cover for you when you'll need it.

Although my path was unique in the sense that I did not get into PE through a New York City I-bank, I think everyone's path is somewhat different from others. You may hit the perfect time in a recruiting cycle where they need a consultant-type person, or you may interview with a former athlete who understands the discipline and is impressed with your balance of school and sports in college, for example. Overall, I found that interviewers usually look highly on people who have been successful at each level of their life—high school, college, extracurriculars, first job, and so on. But in terms of doing anything differently or recommending my way, it's a tough call. I would guess the hit rate for New York City banks is much higher for PE versus a regional bank. The key is to learn as much as you can where you are, and grab for responsibility.

My advice to pre-MBA candidates would be to put together a one-page cheat sheet of your deals so you are ready for interviews. It should have revenue and EBITDA figures as well as any multiples and key factors that you can talk about. A lot of interviews honed in on deals so you should know the deal terms. I would also say, in addition to doing well in college, shining at your first job is critical. All firms are definitely looking for the top guys, no matter where they did their training.

I also interviewed at a lot of smaller firms for practice. I even did this with a few hedge funds and funds of funds. When they ask you, "Why do you want to go into private equity?" you'd better have an answer ready. Basically, all the interviews ask the same questions: Why do you want to go into private equity? Walk me through a deal you did. What was your role? If you were an investor, would you have made this investment? Why? What was the industry landscape like? You should have answers ready for all of these questions.

(See Resume 3 in Appendix B.)

Case Study 5: Going from a Regional Bank to a Regional Fund

Here is an example of someone who joined a mid-market bank after graduating from college and then joined a smaller PE fund.

■   ■   ■

I graduated in 2004 from a large public university with a strong undergraduate business program with a concentration in finance. At the time I was not thinking of private equity. My father is an entrepreneur who runs his own contracting company, and in working for him the summer after my freshman year I became intrigued by business and knew I wanted to pursue finance (I enjoy diving into numbers). The next summer I worked for a local real estate services company, and following my junior year I interned at a regional mid-market investment bank. The internship had a one-week training program that taught modeling skills, although I was learning this in school as well. At the end of the summer I got an exploding offer to return after graduation.

I liked the investment banking process, but still didn't know what I wanted to do. Although my school was far from the major financial centers, the business program was a strong one and most bulge-bracket banks recruited on campus. Unfortunately for me, my offer expired before the on-campus recruiting was set to begin in the first semester of my senior year. Rather than risk losing a sure thing, I accepted the offer with the mid-market I-bank. Also, in some ways, I was a bit intimidated about working in New York and had heard horror stories about the lifestyle of a bulge-bracket banker.

One of the advantages of working at a smaller, regional firm was that I had the opportunity to work on many aspects of mid-market merger and acquisition (M&A) deals. On most occasions I was part of a three-person deal team, and I often interfaced directly with our clients and private equity funds. By six months into the program I knew I wanted to get into private equity and decided to work as hard as I could and to do whatever it took to make that happen. I also knew that I would be facing an uphill battle because recruiters wouldn't come to firms like mine.

Knowing that I would be on my own, I got out the Capital IQ database and began to research regional private equity firms. Even though I felt I had the skills to work in a larger fund, on a personal level I was still hesitant about my fit with one. My approach to sending out resumes and cover letters was more rifle shot than shotgun. In fact, I only targeted three firms. (I had been offered the chance to stay on with my I-bank on an associate track and knew I could fall back on that. I also knew I could have tried to go back out to the PE market during my third year as an analyst.)

The position I was most passionate about was listed on an online job site specializing in PE positions (not Glocap). After sending in my resume, I called the headhunter at the online job site and was told the hiring firm initially passed on me. Upon learning that, I urged the headhunter to contact the hiring firm again and highlight my relevant transaction experience. After not hearing back from the firm a second time, I felt it was best to take matters in my own hands. I e-mailed a cover letter to one of the partners, asked for a phone interview, and followed up my correspondence with a phone call (which went to voice mail). Fortunately for me, he was receptive. I think I benefited from a combination of my persistence, initiative, and good timing—the firm had raised its second fund with a few hundred million in capital commitments and was in need of people.

My courtship with this firm began in January 2006. The first step was a 30-minute phone interview during which I was mostly questioned about my background and had to walk through my resume and deal experience. I was also asked why I wanted to work in private equity. I was able to point out that as an entrepreneur my father played a part in my interest. Further, aspiring to potentially be an entrepreneur myself one day, I felt that the hands-on nature of buy-side deals and exposure to other business founders/owners would provide a unique looking glass into what it takes to succeed as an entrepreneur. I also spoke about how the lower- to middle-market experience opened my eyes to all aspects of transactions that I may not have had at a bulge-bracket bank. I was also asked some leveraged finance/technical questions and presented with the following situation: You get a deal book for a non-asset-based services company, and talk about how much debt it could take on and what kind of covenants it would have.

The next round of interviews was on-site. I met with three partners and two vice presidents with whom I would be working. While the senior partners focused on character questions, the junior ones were interested in my raw horsepower—whether I could crunch the numbers. The VPs wanted to know if I would fit in with the team and if I was polished as the person they would hire would represent the firm by working very closely with numerous stakeholders (i.e., portfolio companies, lenders, and investors).

I remember being asked a twist on the proverbial "What's your weakness?" question. This firm phrased it by asking, "We see you've been doing investment banking. Tell us what was hard for you." That one stumped me. I was prepared to talk about the good things I did and knew I would sound like a jerk if I answered that I didn't find anything hard. I think I came up with something, but I don't remember it making much sense. Even though this firm was on the smaller side I got the sense they wanted someone with a bulge-bracket background and felt I was fighting an uphill battle. Because I lacked the bulge-bracket experience I felt I had to emphasize that my experience working on small deal teams and interfacing with senior executives made me just as good as and perhaps more versatile than someone who had spent all his time with his head in models and documents.

> *If you know a firm is hiring, send them an e-mail, or better yet call them. At a small firm you will get little to no direction and will need to show initiative.*

The next phase of the interviews was a modeling test. On a Friday I was given a redacted selling memo (names were changed, etc.) from a real company the firm had looked at. I was not given any financials and was told to come back after the weekend prepared to build a model on the spot. I felt this was my chance to do more. So instead of just reading the memo, I put together a 20-page pitch book complete with my analysis of the business, the industry, comparables of other companies in the same industry, and potential add-on acquisition targets. I printed five copies and presented them to each partner when I came back. They seemed to be quite impressed with this initiative and I knew I had done a lot to differentiate myself from other candidates. I also aced the modeling test.

Three days later I got another call. The partners said they really liked me, but there was one last stage. They wanted me to meet their deal team in another city. So I was flown to their offices. One partner asked me very quantitative questions and it didn't seem like he wanted to get to know me. It was more like he was giving me a proctology exam on my quantitative abilities. The junior guys there liked me.

All in all it was a very protracted process. Given my background, I may have had to jump through more hoops than someone from a bulge-bracket bank, but I got the offer and was the first non-bulge-bracket person my firm has hired. Unlike other firms, mine is not two and out. I've been told that if I demonstrate excellence in execution, polish, and fit, then I can stay.

My advice to anyone currently working in a regional banking program would be to take a targeted approach when applying to private equity firms where your experience can differentiate you, and that will likely be at smaller firms that need more versatile athletes—people with strong interpersonal skills who thrive in lean environments and have the ability to execute complex quantitative analysis. I'd also say don't give up, be aggressive, and don't worry that you won't be contacted by a headhunter. If you know a firm is hiring, send them an e-mail, or better yet call them. At a small firm you will get little to no direction and will need to show initiative. Making a call about a job is a good way to show you have initiative, that you are aggressive but thoughtful as well. In addition, I'd recommend targeting business development corporations (BDCs), which often accept a mix of people from bulge-bracket banks, smaller private equity shops, and even accounting firms.

I firmly believe there are opportunities in private equity for people who go to regional schools and/or work in regional banks. For these people it's all about differentiating yourself, highlighting your attributes with finesse, and going above and beyond the norm to land a position.

Case Study 6: Getting In from a Mid-Market Bank—Late Cycle

The experiences of this candidate are a good example of how an analyst at a mid-market bank can find a position. Although his interviews began later in the hiring cycle he didn't let that deter him.

■ ■ ■

I had four internships in college. I worked with a stock-broker, at a venture capital firm, at a fledgling private equity fund, and at a hedge fund. While I knew that I wanted to be in private equity after my internship experience, my mentor advised me that the best private equity players had investment banking experience, and that I should do the same before proceeding onwards. Thus, I began recruiting to get into investment banking with the full knowledge that I would be moving on after a few years.

When I applied for the bulge-bracket investment banking analyst training programs the firms didn't pay as much attention to my GPA or my internships. The banks clearly looked down on the school I attended and a perceived shortfall in formal business training. In addition, I wanted to stay close to home, which was not New York City, so there were limited options. Thus, without a bulge-bracket extending its hand my way, I wound up taking a job at a mid-market investment bank. I rose to the top of my analyst class. But in my experience, that is still a bit of an empty achievement in the eyes of the conservative private equity market, and you don't get the respect you would if you had worked at a bulge-bracket. It's a simple fact of life.

To move into private equity, I would have to work hard to dispel the thought that a bulge-bracket investment banker is more valuable than a mid-market banker.

I received a lot of flack for not coming out of the bulge-bracket program. I think the first question that came from most interviewers centered around, "With your board scores, GPA, and internship experience, why were you not at a bulge-bracket?" My response was the general "Because I wanted to focus on smaller deals, work with a smaller deal team, and get some hands-on experience, and not get lost at the bureaucracy of a bulge-bracket." As I interview people, I now realize what nonsense that is. Every kid who is in a mid-market shop either has not gotten an offer from a bulge-bracket, or took the mid-market job for other reasons.

What I had was experience at a private equity shop, deal experience, work ethic, and the knowledge of what I wanted. The realization that some of the industry's best bankers had moved on to become wildly successful in private equity, coupled with my affinity for the industry, decent pay, and more reasonable hours, helped solidify my resolve to enter the market. My only questions revolved around how to market myself in an industry that typically caters to analysts at bulge-bracket investment banks.

In my analyst program, I was able to work with smaller deal teams than those typically seen at the bureaucratic bulge-brackets, which is an advantage with a lot of private equity shops that don't necessarily have an established hierarchy. While in investment banking, I reported directly to a managing director or vice president. Today I report directly to a senior managing director. Having real deal experience on complex transactions, which many middle-market transactions certainly are, while still remaining relatively autonomous and resourceful is truly an asset and a great point to bring up to private equity shops.

> *All in all, I think that as a middle-market banker, you have much more to offer than you may realize; you just need to identify those traits that set you apart and capitalize upon them.*

Furthermore, I'd venture to say that a lot of the deals that will be lucrative for PE shops going forward will be proprietary or with companies that don't get widely auctioned. These companies are generally smaller and within the middle-market range. The more experience you have executing deals for these companies, the better a resource you will be for a private equity fund. All in all, I think that as a middle-market banker, you have much more to offer than you may realize; you just need to identify those traits that set you apart and capitalize upon them.

I had gotten headhunter calls, given that I was the top analyst, but never really followed up on them. Since I was closely tied to the financial sponsor coverage effort, I knew a bit about which firms I'd like to explore further. An ex–vice president at my firm helped secure a few interviews, and from there I used a recruiter and specifically defined the types of shops that I wanted to eventually join. Between these two resources, I'd gotten five interviews; I flopped the first two, and, once I got comfortable interviewing, secured final rounds at two shops. One ultimately turned out to be the right fit and the opportunity I was really looking for. I started my search in March 2005 and finished by mid-April 2005, to eventually join the fund at the beginning of June 2005. That was a bit early, but I wanted to get a sense of the market as I had heard horror stories from friends who had done 10 or more interviews and not secured an offer from a PE shop. Even though there is an unwritten code between the banks and PE funds under which the PE funds will not recruit analysts out of the banks before they complete the programs, that didn't prevent me from leaving early as I don't think a large PE fund would use my former middle-market firm as a banker, so there was no risk in harming a relationship that did not exist.

My program actually was supposed to end in another year or so; thus I was not exactly worried about getting a job somewhere. I think that in general, it is somewhat difficult for second-year bankers to get into PE, primarily because at the point when PE shops begin interviewing, second-year bankers would generally be only two to three months into their second year. At this point, second-year bankers generally don't have a firm grasp of investment banking and the complexities of deal making; thus I think the ideal time to leave an investment bank is really during the hiring cycle of the third year, provided, of course, that the analyst gets the opportunity to stay for the third year. If I were to do it over again, I might have waited a bit longer to see more opportunities and gain further leverage in terms of compensation or performance incentives, but I also left investment banking before my second year was completed, so, in a way, I got an early jump-start in private equity.

If I had waited for the typical hiring cycle, there would have been a lot more shops hiring, and candidates get a lot more opportunities to look at different shops. Getting into PE out of cycle is a bit difficult, just because there are fewer opportunities available and a lot of places have already filled their requirements. Also, during the hiring cycle, PE shops are forced to compete against each other to attract candidates, and thus compensation/incentive packages might be more attractive and lucrative.

I definitely did my homework and took a targeted approach and would recommend that others do the same.

The partners with whom I interviewed asked a few technical questions, but none were all that difficult to handle. I suppose there were a disproportionate number of questions surrounding the breadth and depth of my modeling expertise, but there was really nothing that I couldn't answer, given that I had intimate knowledge of the models that I presented on my resume. My difficulties arose when I was asked about tax structures and public equity deals, neither of which I had any experience in, given that my investment banking experience had not encountered either of these scenarios in detail. To these questions, I countered with the point that while I did not possess extensive knowledge about them at that moment, I could learn quickly. The hardest questions came from the firm I ended up with, and involved a full case study, with no advance warning, to assess my ability to think about corporate strategy and value creation on the fly.

I definitely did my homework and took a targeted approach and would recommend that others do the same. I first limited the geographic areas in which I would like to live—New York or Los Angeles. Then I focused on the kind of shops—primarily operations-oriented shops where I'd have more of a chance to work with management and look at strategy, versus being a pure financier and not having any involvement in the way that management runs the company. Finally, I wanted to find a bit of a smaller place that was less institutionalized, primarily because I wanted the opportunity to advance within the ranks should I be able to succeed. I knew most of the shops on the West Coast; getting to know the shops on the East Coast was a bit more challenging, but I had a few friends at various private equity shops and investment banks who provided some color on opportunities that I thought were interesting.

(See Resume 4 in Appendix B.)

Case Study 7: Mid-Market Bank to Mega-Buyout Fund

This person started out in a mid-market, regional bank. To reach his goal of working at a major buyout fund, he left the mid-market bank and spent a year working in a bulge-bracket firm.

■ ■ ■

I graduated in 2004 from a university in the Southeast with a dual engineering/math degree. By my junior year I realized that I was interested in finance (and not in engineering, where I feared I would be locked in a room by myself, measuring the stress and strain of beams on a bridge all day). Unfortunately, my school did not offer many finance or accounting courses. My initial interest in finance was piqued by two internships I had during school—one during the summer at a retail bank and another during my junior year at a local firm focusing on equity research.

I quickly concluded that getting into an investment banking program was the best way to learn finance and gain analytical expertise. Unfortunately, since my school lacked a finance major, it was not a place where bulge-bracket banks came to recruit for their programs. So I went to them. I also worked my network and grabbed whatever resources I could to learn the basics, such as what EBITDA was. I secured several interviews and always made a point of showing my eagerness and willingness to go above and beyond what was asked of me.

I found that once you have an offer at one bank it attracts the interest of others, and it's easy to use that as leverage to get other interviews. I ended up with an offer from a mid-market/regional bank as well as two offers from bulge-brackets in New York. I elected to accept the mid-market offer because it was with that firm's leveraged finance group, which I thought would give me the best experience (the ones in New York were general offers). I was also following the advice of one of my mentors, who told me that it was all about the group you're in, not the name of the bank, though now I'm not sure if I agree with that.

When I began the program I had no professional plan, but I did know that it would provide a foundational skill set while closing no doors in the future. Despite what my mentor friend had told me, I found out that it is not that easy to leave a regional bank and have a fairly good exit. I discovered that the reputation of a bank and how it is judged by the buy-side does go a long way in determining where you will work after your program, even if the role you had at the bank and the skills you have are the same as for people from the more reputable banks.

It didn't take me long to decide that private equity was what I wanted to pursue. I enjoyed leveraged finance and modeling and watching a deal go through the credit process, but I was ready to move on. I realized that I was viewing LBOs from a small window and that by the time I saw the deals they were nearly fully baked. I wanted to be on the principal side and learn more about these deals from an operations and investment side. I had watched my mentor join the private equity arm of our bank, but I wanted to move on to a larger firm in a larger city. I was one of 50 or more analysts in leveraged finance, had gotten top grades, and was one of two analysts who taught the LBO model to all incoming analysts and associates during my two years. Still, I felt that if I didn't take action I would be at a disadvantage in moving to a more reputable firm.

I knew that the hiring cycle meant that analysts at my bank wouldn't get a look from hiring firms until 10 months to one year into our first year in the program. I got the distinct feeling that those firms were looking at us as second-tier options. Even though I was asked if I were interested in staying on as an associate, I decided to leave my firm and began looking to join a bulge-bracket bank. I didn't want to go to a third- or fourth-tier shop. I wanted to be with a reputable name in a major city.

I wasn't elated about doing a third year in banking, but I knew it would help me get into a good private equity firm, so I pursued a banking position with a bulge-bracket bank. I had also decided that I wanted to live in San Francisco, so I narrowed my search to banks (or groups within banks) in that city. The stars were aligned for me because I ended up joining a well-known bank that was looking for a third-year analyst who could come in and hit the ground running from day one. I began in June 2006 (my third year in banking). I was honest with this firm and told them that I wouldn't enter the PE draft until the following year. One of the executive directors there sat me down on day one and said that if I gave him a year he would help me exit. That was just what I wanted to hear. My plan was to spend the first four to five months on building up my reputation and doing as good a job as possible. That worked well, because by December headhunters began calling. Unfortunately, there weren't a lot of opportunities that interested me.

My luck changed again when the precise firm that I had hoped to join contacted me, beginning a very drawn-out process. After an initial informal face-to-face meeting in December, I didn't hear back for two months. I later learned that the delay was because this firm was formulating its hiring plan. My next meeting was a phone interview, which I welcomed because it meant I didn't have to leave the office for an extended time, but that didn't mean it would be a simple conversation. The principal who interviewed me asked some very analytical questions. I'd term it a preliminary testing about models and deals. He asked me things such as how to calculate free cash flow and, if certain line items fluctuated in a model, what was affected by these changes.

The second meeting was on-site. The firm brought in 10 to 12 candidates, most of whom were third-year bankers (this was off-cycle), and the plan was to hire just two of them. We were there a majority of the day and met with all of the firm's partners, principals, and associates. To me, there are two types of interview questions—those designed to find out your personality and drive, and those that bring out your tangible financial and investing skills. The day began with much more of the latter. This was not the typical exercise of grabbing a laptop and creating a model. Among other things, I was asked to explain how to adjust for net operating losses (NOLs), what happens to cash flow when depreciation goes up, how to calculate internal rates of return (IRRs) in a multitude of scenarios, along with other general modeling questions. I was also asked a fair share of investing questions and the typical "Walk me through your deals." You have to know how to answer these questions from an investor's rationale (why is something a good investment), not from a banking one, and that is a very different way of thinking for most bankers.

> *My advice for anyone interested in private equity is that you have to be extremely focused. It's important that you are always preparing for the opportunity to impress in interviews.*

I used the personality questions as an opportunity to try and separate myself from the other candidates. When I was asked, "Why do you want to work here?" I spoke about the reputation of the firm and the types of deals it does. I pointed out that they would likely hear similar boilerplate responses from the other candidates, so I spoke about what I brought to the table. I made sure I was prepared for that facet of the interview. I knew that everyone coming to interview was well qualified and could model. I wanted to distinguish myself as someone who would fit in with the culture of the firm.

The next step was the background check, and this is one that should be taken very seriously. This is where your current or past employers can pull you across the finish line. In my case, my group came through with a great recommendation. A week went by—the longest week of my life—before I got my offer.

After going through this process and landing the job I wanted, my advice for anyone interested in private equity is that you have to be extremely focused. It's important that you are always preparing for the opportunity to impress in interviews. My actual face time with my interviewers amounted to a few hours, during which time I had to candidly present who I was, explain my past, and describe how my background prepared me to get where I was. There is no doubt that, above all, getting into private equity comes down to your understanding of the LBO model. Once you have that, you then have to be able to look at deals from the point of view of an investor.

I would also advise candidates to play up their personality. No matter who is hiring, they don't want to hire a robot. You want to pass the airport test: If you and someone from your firm are stranded at an airport, are you the type of person with whom he would want to hang out and have a beer?

In my opinion, an investment banking background provides the core skills to succeed in this profession. I wouldn't, however, be discouraged by your undergraduate major. At my current firm we have people with English, history, engineering, and finance majors, but they all come from investment banking, and I'd say 80 percent of them came from a bulge-bracket bank. I'd recommend people do what they can to get into a program at a bank with the best possible name—it just makes the exit so much easier.

Case Study 8: An Accountant Gets In—Later in the Cycle

Although this person came from an accounting background, he had significant exposure to private equity and LBOs and was considered a top performer at his firm.

■ ■ ■

I came out of Ivy League undergrad in pursuit of a job in either investment banking or management consulting. I had a strong GPA with a concentration in finance and entrepreneurial management. The process for getting an interview at a top-tier investment bank was extremely competitive. As a result, it was proving a bit challenging to find an opportunity in a top program. Also, I was leaning heavily toward Boston and there were limited banking opportunities there. Therefore, in addition to investment banking, I interviewed with a number of consulting firms and the corporate finance group of a major public accounting firm in New York. While it was my preference to work in Boston, I was attracted by the corporate finance opportunity and the firm's compensation model, and ultimately decided to take the job in New York. I was not thinking private equity at all. I simply wanted to work at a place where I would be compensated for hard work. I figured I would grind it out over the next several years and see where it led me.

I ended up in a group that provides corporate finance and transaction structuring support for the accounting firm's clients. It was highly technical financial accounting and my time was split evenly working with private equity firms, corporate clients, and investment banks. This was my first exposure to private equity and it definitely got my attention. After about a year or so, I was working directly for the head of the group and he wanted me to get my CPA. The job was already accounting intensive and my interests were in finance. I was much more interested in the investing aspects of what my clients were doing than the transaction structuring issues. As I had learned, structuring was only a small part of the deal process.

My stroke of luck came when I got an unsolicited call from a headhunter. This person represented a private equity firm that had just had a bad experience with an investment-banking analyst it had hired a few months earlier. Now they were looking for someone with a unique background, specifically someone outside of investment banking. They wanted someone who was hungry; someone who would keep their head down, work hard, and hold their ego in check. At this point I was well aware that I was not the ideal candidate for a PE firm and that I was off-cycle, but I was intrigued and took the interview.

The first few rounds of interviews were grueling. I had never built an LBO model from soup to nuts, but I believed that I understood how. After all, I had spent the preceding two years advising clients on purchase and leveraged buyout accounting.

My background gave me the ability to read financial models and follow the flow of funds through the income statement, balance sheet, and cash flow statement. During the interviews they drilled me hard on financial modeling. I was candid with them about what I knew and didn't know. I also told them that I was confident I could build a model, but I had to convince them of this. The entire process for me lasted about four weeks—it was clear the firm was in a rush to hire someone after their experience with the previous person. I think this firm saw in me someone who brought a different perspective, with no pretensions.

I knew the learning curve would be steep, but it was steeper than I thought it would be. There were a lot of late nights the first several months, and I spent a lot of time calling friends who helped me through some of the trickier parts of the models.

> *In my case, the biggest obstacle was that I did not have the customary requisite experience. The PE firms are so used to hiring I-bankers and consultants, they had a hard time understanding my background.*

In my case, the biggest obstacle was that I did not have the customary requisite experience. The PE firms are so used to hiring I-bankers and consultants, they had a hard time understanding my background. I also didn't fully understand the debt markets and other aspects of the deal process, but I knew I could learn that quickly. I would definitely say that the traditional route is still the absolute right track to get into private equity and will lead to the highest success rate.

I would also advise that people interested in private equity do their homework. A great shop doesn't mean great people. Speak with friends and colleagues who have worked at, or with, various firms to get their sense of the personalities in the organization. Go to their web sites, read the trade rags, and see what the funds invest in. When and if you get into a banking group, start to look at PE firms that invest in your area of expertise. Traditionally, it's hard to go from an industrial background to a media buyout shop. So if you happen to get stuck in a group that you don't like, you should try to change; otherwise you could greatly limit your opportunities.

(See Resume 5 in Appendix B.)

Case Study 9: Directly out of Undergrad—An Exception

Here is that exception to the rule—someone who was a star undergrad, did all the right things, and landed his dream job straight out of college.

■ ■ ■

I made it into a private equity shop directly out of undergrad largely because I was able to get differentiated experiences before I graduated that enabled me to talk intelligently about the industry. A lot of luck helped as well.

Although I graduated with a degree in history, I got great experience while I was in school by interning at a start-up tech company during my sophomore and junior years. It was a classic start-up and I got a view of all of the different pieces of the business.

The CEO there had worked in private equity, so I heard all about how great an industry it was. From then on, I wanted to work in private equity, and he helped me think about how to get into the business.

I spent the spring semester of my junior year studying in London. Following my studies I landed a summer internship with the London office of a consulting firm that has an affiliated buyout fund. I was happy to get the consulting experience, but really wanted to get exposure to the PE/LBO side, so I pushed a bit within the firm and ended up working on screening buyout deals all summer. I thought the finance experience would be a good complement to the tech background I got with the start-up, and I was willing to do anything—endless sets of comparables, blind competitor calls, you name it. At the end of the summer the firm offered me a full-time job after graduation. I wasn't ready to move to London, so I turned it down. Instead, I began fishing around in the United States.

I knew I didn't have the skill set of someone coming out of an investment bank, but I could talk the talk of the industry (or at least a bit of it), and I had a great story about why I wanted to work in private equity that was backed up by solid internships. I interviewed all over, and was offered a job by a firm that does hire sporadically directly out of undergrad.

Lots of talented candidates have a high GPA, good test scores, and a good banking internship, but no coherent story as to why they want to be in private equity. That will not set you apart. Be ready with your "I'm-dying-to-get-into-PE" story.

A few things stuck out in the interview process. First, the fact that I was able to speak the language of the industry was a huge advantage. The interviews quickly moved off of resume questions into discussions on private equity, recent deals, and the differentiation of the firm, which I think helped.

Second, preparation was essential. Before interviewing, I networked with alumni from the firm, who gave me a sense of what to expect. Most private equity firms have web sites where they give extensive information on their investments and the backgrounds of the people. I walked in with info on every person, thoughts on potential areas for investment, and opinions and questions on recent deals the firm had done. That gave me a lot to talk about in meetings and I think probably stuck out. Finally, having a clear, credible story on why I wanted to be in private equity was critical, and being able to back it up with experiences on my resume showed I was serious.

I spent the first two years doing nothing but cold-calling CEOs of privately held companies looking for possible deals. I knew that guys in PE hate to teach (or are too busy), so I plugged away, learned financial modeling on my own, and eventually moved into more of a deal role.

My advice to other undergrads (and even some MBAs) would be to step out of the campus recruiting mind-set of "I'm going to do the resume drop, and hope the job will come to me." If you want a job at a place that doesn't hire all the time, or even one that does but where your odds are low, you've got to create your own opportunity. Find a nontraditional way to get in front of people at the firm. Network and lean on friends and alumni. People will respect a cold call or letter if it is done in a high-quality way, and many folks will take that call and will appreciate you doing what you can to get into the organization. Often they will make introductions to people at other firms as well.

Next, I'd say you've got to have a unique story. Lots of talented candidates have a high GPA, good test scores, and a good banking internship, but no coherent story as to why they want to be in private equity. That will not set you apart. Be ready with your "I'm-dying-to-get-into-PE" story. Show them you have a burning desire to work in the industry and where on your resume they can see the evidence that you're developing skills that are required.

(See Resume 6 in Appendix B.)

Case Study 10: From Undergrad Directly to a Regional Fund

This person worked hard and successfully went from a regional university to a regional fund.

■ ■ ■

For me, a few factors helped me get into private equity without going into a banking program first. I had good investing experience, I could talk about what I looked for when making an investment, and I had solid coursework and practical experience. And luck was on my side.

I graduated in 2007 from a large university in the South with a degree in finance and IT. I would consider myself as much of an entrepreneur as a finance type—during the summer after my sophomore year I ran a painting business that taught me how to work 80-hour weeks and think on my feet. I had always been interested in public stocks and investing and had invested my own money. Following my junior year I interned at a 20-person quantitative hedge fund that also did some opportunistic investing. It was a highly analytical position that also helped me hone my Excel skills. I also took a class on venture capital and private equity that was quite useful at a high level to understanding the business.

When my senior year rolled around I interviewed with hedge funds, bulge-bracket investment banks, mid-market banks, and some management consulting firms. By late fall I was in second rounds at two hedge funds and two bulge-bracket banks, and second rounds were coming up at consulting companies, but I was pretty certain that I wanted to join a middle-market investment bank that would eventually lead to private equity. While I saw the benefits of a formal training program at a large bulge-bracket bank or management consulting firm, I preferred the environment of a smaller firm because of the breadth of skills that their employees must develop. I have always been interested in starting and running my own business and thought I would be dealing more closely with entrepreneurs at a mid-market firm. I had also sent my resume to some venture capital and private equity funds but they weren't open to undergrads.

This is when the luck came in. A regional mid-market buyout fund located in the same general area as my university posted a job listing on my school's job board. This firm had hired undergrads before and had two people from my school working there. I responded and had two phone interviews. During the first I was interviewed by two of the firm's associates (post-MBA positions). The questions were mostly cultural/fit in nature and less about my technical background. We talked about my college experience and so on. At the end I was instructed to take the Caliper Profile personality assessment test. I passed and had another phone interview before I was flown to the company's headquarters for an entire day (seven to eight hours) of interviews with about 75 percent of the firm. This was not an easy process!

I was very familiar with the 2-2-2 path that most people take to get into private equity and knew it was very rare that there would even be a fund that had an opening for an undergrad. Fortunately, by this time I had been through several interviews at banks, consulting firms, and hedge funds. I found the technical questions about finance similar to ones asked by investment banks—how do the three financial statements work together, explain working capital, and so on—and was also asked about the painting business experience. Obviously I couldn't be grilled about deals since I hadn't worked on any at this point.

I also had to defend why I should be in private equity out of undergrad, and I had to do it pretty rigorously. I found that I could naturally defend this. My past experience as a business owner/operator and my work at the hedge fund both buttressed my position by demonstrating my ability to develop a broad skill set on my own, which is a requirement at a middle-market private equity firm. Running my own business alone was instrumental in making me a more attractive candidate—not only could I demonstrate that I had a proven work ethic and abilities as a self-starter, but I had operating experience. Did I have a 3.9 GPA and meet the Goldman standards? No, but I had other things that made me stand out. I emphasized my leadership skills—I was president of my fraternity and ran the undergraduate mentoring program at my school. I also worked on the student-run long/short hedge fund. From the time I began investing on my own, to the summer hedge fund internship, to working on the student-run fund, I had always been able to answer the question, "Would you want to own this company?" and I knew that was integral to working at a PE fund.

In addition to answering all of the technical concerns the firm had, I was also told that I fit in with the culture, something I found to be equally important. I would recommend candidates read the bios of every person who works at a fund (if they are available on the fund's web site). If a candidate is not very similar to the rest of the fund, then it seems unlikely to me that he will be successful in his interviews, regardless of how good his resume is. One caveat here is that it can be very difficult to understand personality based on a four-sentence bio, but if you read all of bios and see a general theme, then that in of itself is a useful data point.

I'd love to say that I got the offer simply because I was polished and qualified, but I know luck played a role. This opportunity came late in the process and it was lucky

I was still in play. I had also consciously made good use of my senior year. While many students chose an easier course load, I enrolled in a high-level transaction accounting class. I made a point of telling this firm that if they made me an offer I would start preparing the next week so I would be ready.

Getting into PE without first going through a banking program doesn't happen all the time, but I'd still tell people it can be done. I would, however, caution candidates against taking a job that is primarily cold-calling. In talking with other PE analysts/associates, I would say my developing skill set, in terms of modeling, memo writing, portfolio monitoring, and business analytics, is comparable to others who have gone the more traditional routes. This is because I am challenged to apply these skills on a daily basis, and not treated like a well-paid administrative assistant. While you can learn a lot by rebuilding old models and rereading old memos, it will be hard to truly develop these skills if you do not get to put them to use during your normal work hours.

> *To improve your chances of getting into PE I'd recommend learning about investing any way you can.*

To improve your chances of getting into PE I'd recommend learning about investing any way you can. At least join the investment club at your school. Even though much of what happens in PE is outside of the public eye, following trends in the public market is important. I'd read any PE publications, free e-mails, and other documents you can. (I found investment memos written by the Pennsylvania State Pension fund, explaining why they invested in certain funds.)

Before I'd advise anyone to get into PE I'd ask them how they feel being on their own and learning on their own, because in firms like mine there is very little training and supervision. They should also know that by not going through a banking program they will be missing out on being a part of a large analyst class. It worked for me, but some may feel the need to be a part of that network. Ultimately, however, I have absolutely no regrets about taking an analyst position right out of college, and I believe that the challenges and growth opportunities here are truly unparalleled.

Case Study 11: From Industry into a Health Care Fund

> *This candidate did not have an investment banking or consulting background. He used his science background combined with his corporate experience to land a job with a firm that was launching a health care fund.*

■ ■ ■

I graduated from an Ivy League school in 2000 with a degree in biology. Up until my senior year I had planned to go to medical school and had never thought about finance or private equity. However, after spending several summers working in developing countries with relief agencies and volunteering at the university hospital, I realized that delivering health care went beyond medicine, and also involved finance, management, and operations. I graduated in 2000 and, like many of my peers, turned down an offer from a health care consulting firm and joined an early-stage software company. Once I found out that the company was to be acquired, I began looking for a new job.

I received an offer to run the national chapter of a health care nonprofit that I was involved with in college, but turned this down because I had made it to the final round of one PE firm that hired candidates right out of undergrad. Unfortunately, I didn't get the job. So now I was unemployed, with a degree in biology and one year with a software start-up under my belt. I knew banks and consulting firms had a hiring freeze, so I looked in the mirror and asked myself, how was I different from other people looking for a job? I decided to target biotech companies and probably contacted every one in the Bay Area. My new job was to find a job. I spent eight hours a day sending out resumes, cold-calling, and researching opportunities. Several months later, I landed a strategic planning role at a well-known biotech company launching new cancer products. I picked up basic financial modeling skills, giving me some hard skills to complement my operations experience.

I spent two and a half years at this biotech company. During this time, I became involved with a nonprofit venture philanthropy fund that linked business professionals (primarily VC/PE folks with nonprofits). Realizing that I didn't want to spend my career at a large biotech company, I started thinking about opportunities in PE again. I studied the PE industry, used the contacts from the nonprofit, and also called a recruiter. All the PE/LBO funds I contacted wanted people with either an MBA, two years of banking, or, on occasion, consulting experience. They didn't see the value of someone who only had two to three years of operating experience. The VCs that I contacted all wanted people with 15 years of operating experience. There was no clear path for someone like me. I even began to think that maybe I should go into a banking program or maybe business school. I was quickly advised against business school by friends who said I would have a hard time getting a summer job in PE, and without that I wouldn't be any better off with an MBA.

I wouldn't recommend that everyone who wants to go into private equity do it the way I did. But I would advise that when targeting PE funds, people should target a narrow subset of funds in which they fit. Taking a shotgun approach will not work.

I wasn't targeting many funds, but I did know that one that had posted a job opening with my recruiter was hiring because it had closed a new $650 million fund that would invest exclusively in health care companies. During one interview one of the partners asked me point blank, "We are meeting with someone from McKinsey and someone from Goldman Sachs. Why should we hire you?" I admitted to him that my weakness was that I didn't go through a two-year banking program and that I had no hard-core deal experience. However, I pointed out that I had been on the company side of deals and could bring a unique perspective from having actually worked on the inside of a biotech company. I also told him that he already had people with banking and consulting backgrounds. I had not done LBO/M&A models, but I did understand valuations. I guess he saw my point and I think he was willing to add someone with a different perspective for the new fund.

I wouldn't recommend that everyone who wants to go into private equity do it the way I did. But I would advise that when targeting PE funds, people should target a narrow subset of funds in which they fit. Taking a shotgun approach will not work. I would also say people should do as much background homework as possible to know the range of opportunities open to them. The 2-2-2 path may give you the highest probability of landing a job, but you will also be going against every Joe Banker. I believe there is a lot of value to getting operations experience early on, as it's hard to go back later in your career and get it. Bankers are often viewed as financiers, but not as people who understand businesses. If you have only operations experience it will be a tougher road, so you have to be persistent. You have to convince firms why they should hire you instead of a banker.

(See Resume 7 in Appendix B.)

Case Study 12: From Industry to Buyouts

This is what we would consider an A+ candidate with strong industry/corporate development experience. It is an example of a nontraditional candidate who was able to break into private equity.

■ ■ ■

I finished college in 2001 with a degree in computer science. I had an extensive tech background and was a summer intern in Microsoft's operating systems group, where I was a software design engineer. Outside of technology, I also did a lot of personal investing and financed my college education with proceeds from my own stock trades. After leaving college, I was looking into management consulting or a return to Microsoft. Except for my personal investing I had no finance background, so I didn't consider private equity or investment banking. I was basically a tech guy with an intuitive understanding of business.

I ended up going to Microsoft because they gave me a unique opportunity to do something different. They gave me a chance to play a key role in an internal start-up that had a high amount of executive exposure and potential impact within the company. After two years at Microsoft I thought venture capital was where I wanted to go, thinking it would employ a good combination of my business knowledge and technology skills. I called a few recruiters and ended up working with one who pushed me in the direction of private equity.

Upon interviewing with the individuals in my current firm, I was very impressed. They were an order of magnitude more intelligent and thoughtful than the people I had met at Microsoft or during my undergraduate experience. Despite my inclination for venture capital, private equity seemed to be a place where I would not only learn a great deal of core financial skills, but grow through being pushed by and surrounded with other excellent people.

Despite my telling the firm that I really had no financial modeling skills, they liked me enough to make me an offer and I took it. Unlike an investment bank, PE firms don't take the time to train you. The thinking is, "You're a smart and motivated guy; you will do what you have to do to get to the other side." I spent my first two months with my head in accounting and finance books, learning how to model for LBOs. My first year was really tough—I understood technology much better than my peers did, but really knew nothing about finance, M&A, or PE. I think the key thing that clinched the job for me was that they saw someone who was very technical, had done a lot of high-level business thinking, and had an intuitive sense for business and a passion for investing. I definitely played up those factors during my interviews.

When I interview investment banking analysts, the ones who come off as passionate investors do very well. It's critical that people come off as principals.

For a long time I thought I got the better end of the deal. Someone who comes from an investment bank might not have the business judgment that I had, but they will have the core finance and modeling skills, investment banking polish, and acclimation to intense workloads that I did not. I've learned an amazing amount and grown leaps and bounds in private equity, but the beginning was very tough and the two years I've been here have been a long and steep learning curve.

I would say that anyone looking to get into PE should at least get the core financial modeling skills before they interview. More importantly, I would also say to everyone, even those candidates who do have the modeling skills, they should follow the industry, know the numbers, and have opinions on deals in the market. They should read things like *The Daily Deal* and know what is happening.

When I interview investment banking analysts, the ones who come off as passionate investors do very well. It's critical that people come off as principals. My net advice if you really want to do private equity is this: Go to a good college, get a high GPA, and get into a top-tier banking program. It may sound trite, but that's really the only way to get a realistic and repeatable way of securing a job in PE.

(See Resume 8 in Appendix B.)

Case Study 13: Moving from Business Development to Growth Equity

Here's the story of someone who lacked the traditional banking or consulting background and landed a sourcing role at a growth equity fund.

■ ■ ■

I was one of the fortunate ones who landed a job in private equity (in my case, growth equity) without the typical banking or consulting background. I did graduate from an Ivy League school (class of 2004) with a degree in business economics and at one point was thinking of pursuing banking/consulting, as many of my classmates were, but I was not the typical finance-focused type. In fact, I had begun college with plans to major in computer science.

During the summer after my junior year I interned with a technology-focused VC firm. I spent my time performing market research for a specific portfolio company, which helped the fund evaluate a potential second round of funding. The experience gave me a glimpse into the world of venture capital and flagged it as a career that I might eventually follow. However, rather than pursue finance after graduation, I landed a business development job in professional sports, working with interactive media and emerging technologies. After about two years I was ready to move on to a more proactive position and looked into business development roles for major corporations focusing on technology. I knew the technologies inside and out and wanted to understand the business implications of those same technologies.

At the same time that I was looking into corporate positions I was also working with a few headhunters that specialized in private equity/venture capital. I was not dead set on PE, but thought that it would be a good way to learn about how a business is structured around a technology. I knew getting into PE was a long shot, but I gave it a try. I expected it to be tough, but I had a hard time even getting the attention of headhunters. They told me my background was not one that their clients looked for at the junior level. I should add that I had no idea how to build an LBO model. Fortunately for me, one headhunter took a chance and sent my resume to a few traditional venture capital firms. Still, I didn't get far. While I received positive feedback on my personality, that was overshadowed by the concerns about my lack of specific and applicable business knowledge.

My luck changed again when my resume was sent to a growth equity firm. I quickly discovered that growth equity is a unique subsector of private equity. Because growth equity is used to help mature companies grow, sourcing deals is a very different exercise than it is for venture capital and later-stage buyout funds. Indeed, I was interviewed for a sourcing role, which called for an outgoing person with sales skills. From the beginning of my interviews it was apparent that the firm was looking for more of a personality match than someone with deep technical skills. The first round was on the phone. Although I was asked how proficient I was with Excel, most of the questions were fit related. They wanted someone who could get on the phone and sell the firm's capabilities to well-respected CEOs. To that end, the final round of interviews included a mock phone call. One of the partners played the role of a CEO, and I had to role-play calling him up and asking him questions, talking to him about his business, and pitching our firm. They also wanted me to list the top three things I would look at in a potential investment. My sense was that this firm knew the things I lacked and didn't spend time grilling me on them.

My advice to anyone looking at private equity is that if they are dead set on buyouts they should take the traditional route because it definitely opens more doors, especially at the associate level. However, if you are open to taking a sourcing role and are not intent on working with Excel all day, then growth equity is a viable option for people with a nontraditional background. You will have to clearly demonstrate how your differentiated background helps you analyze a firm's target industries and also show that you understand the various aspects of what makes a good business.

I wouldn't have had a chance at a buyout shop, but as it turns out I was a good fit for growth equity.

Now that I'm here, I'd say my biggest surprise was how hard it is to get a deal done. No one can give you a sense for that when you are interviewing. I call 100 companies a month. I could do that for two to three years without closing a deal. Sometimes you lose out because of things that are not in your control—you may be competing against other firms or you may lose out on valuation. It's frustrating, but you can't let it distract you from your job and your number one goal, which is to close a deal. I'd say that in a pure sourcing role bankers don't have an advantage and that everyone comes in on an even playing field. Once the deal is in process, however, bankers have an easier time because they know how to sell it. They understand the process from day one. My learning curve was steep.

I wouldn't have had a chance at a buyout shop but as it turns out I was a good fit for growth equity. And there are many firms getting into this part of private equity—VC firms are moving up to growth equity, and buyout firms are dropping down—and that can open opportunities for people with less traditional backgrounds.

Chapter **IV**

OUT OF BUSINESS SCHOOL

As a current business school student, you're approaching a major crossroads in your professional career. This is when you hope that your years of hard work and schooling will pay off. You may be utilizing your MBA to solidify a career in private equity that began taking shape several years ago. Or perhaps you are hoping that the learning experience, coupled with the network and the degree, will be the elusive ticket you need to break into private equity. Either way, if you're passionate about private equity and are committed to working in the industry, now is the time to prove that you belong.

Whether you worked in private equity pre-MBA and are looking to continue your pursuit of a career in the industry, or are seeking to break into a principal investing role for the first time, the guidance in this chapter will help you understand what you are up against. Since the mix of professional and academic backgrounds across MBAs is so varied, it's difficult to give one-size-fits-all advice to current MBAs. At the same time, giving customized guidance to MBAs based on what they did pre-MBA (especially if it wasn't private equity) and where they go to school would be too exhaustive to be helpful. So instead, we focus somewhere in the middle and follow the general lead of the overall hiring market, which segments MBAs pursuing PE into two major groups: those with prior PE experience and those without.

The case studies at the end of this chapter are also divided into groups of MBAs with and without previous PE experience. Those in the first group illustrate the relatively smooth return to the industry, but also underscore that this return should not be taken for granted. The case studies of the MBAs in the second grouping confirm that although the process can be difficult and uncertain, getting a post-MBA position without prior PE experience is still achievable. If you are in the latter group we strongly recommend you read these stories carefully. Rather than accepting that there was a cookie-cutter approach to securing a position in PE, each of these candidates blazed his/her own path, made it through round after round of interviews, and eventually came out with a coveted offer.

Post-MBA positions, which are generally designed to be career track and require a bigger commitment from the hiring firm, naturally have a high hurdle to entry. This is why there is an overwhelming (in some cases almost absolute) preference to hire MBAs who have already worked and proven themselves in private equity. At least initially, most funds will try to hire traditional MBAs who excelled at a top PE firm before business school and are now at a first-rate business school. These are the obvious stars, the A+ candidates who have the highest expectations attached to them. Hiring firms see these MBAs as top performers who can step in and hit the ground running by adding value from day one as future leaders of the franchise.

And, just as when they hired at the pre-MBA level, PE firms know precisely where to find these candidates. At the pre-MBA level the leading investment banking programs are the major suppliers of talent. When it comes to finding the best pedigreed MBAs, many brand-name PE firms initially target the leading business schools for finance/investing (we list those later). Similarly, the PE firms know what they are getting—proven, experienced professionals from top schools and brand-name PE firms with high potential and little doubt that they will be immediate contributors.

Glocap Insight

Private equity is like any other exclusive club: Once you've been admitted, it's easier to return. MBA candidates with a background in PE have an obvious advantage to returning after they finish business school. We can't stress enough that if you lack that experience, just landing an *interview* with a PE fund will be a challenge. Getting an *offer* will be much more difficult.

THE HIRING CYCLE

As the private equity market has continued to grow and mature, a hiring cycle has developed at the MBA level similar in many respects to the pre-MBA hiring cycle we described in Chapter III. Just as at the pre-MBA level, there are also two waves of hiring.

Pedigree First

In general, the larger, preeminent, more institutionalized funds that have predictable hiring needs compete early and hard for the best talent. If you're at one of the top three to five feeder business schools (see accompanying list) and have previous PE experience at a brand-name fund, you may hear from select mega funds and recruiters as early as your first year. You will likely get multiple calls as the funds scramble to beat their competition to top talent, and your interviews could be compressed into a relatively short sprint.

The Second Wave of MBA Recruiting

More recently, there has been a shortage of top-pedigree candidates with prior PE experience in relation to the demand for these new hires. Therefore, some funds are coming up short in their quest for top talent and as a result have had to consider alternate pools of candidates. This predictable second wave of hiring is when some funds are willing to widen the scope of MBA programs from which they seek candidates while also beginning to consider some select candidates who haven't previously worked in PE. In fact, we have found that most top funds would admit that given the choice of a B grade candidate who has previous PE investing experience and an A+ candidate who has no prior PE experience, they would probably choose the latter (though the number of times this occurs each year is still small).

The interview process for MBAs with middle- and lower-middle-market PE experience and for those without previous PE experience may not get under way until later in the year (some begin as late as the second semester of the second year), and when it does, the interviews may be more episodic. The needs of some mid-sized funds are often not as predictable as the are for the larger funds.

Glocap
Insight

The business schools that are the most recognized national feeders into private equity are:

- Harvard Business School.
- Stanford Graduate School of Business.
- Wharton School of the University of Pennsylvania.

Schools that consistently place MBAs into PE funds each year include:

- Northwestern University's Kellogg School of Management.
- Columbia Business School.
- University of Chicago Graduate School of Business.
- Tuck School of Business at Dartmouth.

There are several additional programs that each year may also send some graduates into PE. These include (in no particular order):

- UCLA's Anderson School of Management.
- University of Virginia's Darden School of Business.
- MIT's Sloan School of Management.
- Fuqua School of Business at Duke University.
- New York University's Leonard N. Stern School of Business.
- McCombs School of Business at the University of Texas at Austin.
- University of Michigan's Ross School of Business.
- University of California at Berkeley Haas School of Business.

This list should not be viewed as comprehensive. Rather, these are the schools whose graduates we most often see securing positions in PE.

Unrelated to their size, there are also occasional funds that misjudge their hiring needs early on and are back in the market late in the second year. For example, they could be looking to replace someone who left unexpectedly, may need help for a new fund launch (we've seen firms that close $1 billion funds in January begin their MBA recruiting in February), or could even be starting late because they were too swamped to dedicate the time to recruit candidates earlier in the year (many funds are small and, lacking a dedicated human resources professional, often rely on a senior investment professional to oversee recruiting). Even though they may begin interviewing later, many can still be generally recognized, successful firms that are still going to be selective and will offer attractive opportunities.

In either of these cases, we recommend that all candidates start as early as possible so they are ready when their time comes. The author of Case Study 17 had the right attitude about early preparation when he said, "On day one, all I worried about was getting a job two years down the road."

THE MARKET AND THE COMPETITION

Although getting a post-MBA job in PE is still extremely competitive, the numbers indicate that, on a relative basis, over the past few years it might not be as competitive, especially when compared to the post-Internet bubble of 2002-2004 when securing a position was particularly difficult. Given the record capital raised by PE firms from 2005 through 2007, new positions have certainly been created in the industry. Couple that with a roughly steady supply of MBAs with previous PE experience (200 or so each year in the top business schools) and the lure of hedge funds competing for the same talent (this trend may slow, but will still be a factor), and the outlook continues to look positive for traditional MBAs. Significant increases in MBA compensation at PE funds is also an indicator that demand remains strong.

Nonetheless, the good news for funds, and bad news for MBAs, is that the tide is likely to shift over the next couple of years. There will likely be more quality talent applying to business school as a result of the recent market turmoil, and that may lead to more MBAs competing for PE jobs.

MBAs WITH PRIOR PRIVATE EQUITY EXPERIENCE

If you are part of the select group of MBAs who were top performers at a brand-name PE fund prior to business school and are at one of the top MBA programs, a position to return to PE should be waiting for you when you graduate. In fact, an increasing number of funds are now extending post-MBA offers to pre-MBA associates, either as they leave for their MBA programs or before they lock in their summer plans during business school. Very significant signing bonuses (sometimes to cover tuition) are being offered by some of the largest funds.

As someone with this sought-after experience, at some point you still have to identify what you believe is the best opportunity for you, and that includes deciding if you want to return to your pre-MBA firm or move to a different fund where the type of deals and/or culture could be different. Each of these options has trade-offs, so at this point if you are in this elite group you may want to skip to the case studies and then to Chapter IX, where we discuss the pros and cons of different opportunities.

For other MBAs with pre-MBA private equity experience who are coming out of a quality, but maybe a less brand-name fund, the odds are still in your favor to return to

> ### Glocap Insight
>
> Over the past few years we've found that about 75 percent of graduating MBAs who worked in private equity before business school return to private equity. We further estimated that 15 percent choose hedge fund positions over returning to PE (although this number may be decreasing). That leaves 10 percent who took corporate, consulting, or banking positions. We anticipate that the percentages of MBAs taking corporate, consulting, or banking jobs will increase as hiring patterns continue to fluctuate due to the less certain economic environment.

PE. However, a proactive effort to get in front of the right funds is still highly advised. Landing a position in private equity out of your banking or consulting program was a great first step, but it doesn't guarantee you a role after business school because the skill set that funds look for is different at the post-MBA level. If you haven't taken advantage of business school to further develop your professional skills, you could fall short in your quest to return to the industry.

Given that there are still more experienced candidates who want a PE role than there are positions available, your highest priority will be to maintain your edge and avoid getting crowded out when trying to return to PE. That includes developing additional attributes, including more maturity and insight, that can help to make you a great investor and convince a PE firm that you are partner material. Ideally, PE funds want professionals who can step in as a senior associate/vice president and hit the ground running with the ability to generate fresh investment ideas, put together a comprehensive investment thesis, and execute a deal from start to finish.

Larger funds with bigger deal teams that make complex, multibillion-dollar investments will also be focused on assessing whether you have the skills to support these deals and manage the investment process. By contrast, smaller funds (which may hire once every few years) may focus on different skills since the deals themselves may be more straightforward (with less complicated structures). Instead, these funds may prefer someone who understands companies and management, has similar signs of partner potential, and has specific interest in working on smaller deals.

While you are in business school it's imperative not only to maintain but continue to build your network of contacts. In addition to wanting people who understand the industries in which their fund invests, PE funds strongly prefer MBAs who have developed an up-to-date Rolodex that will hopefully include contacts who can be resources in originating deals and conducting deeper due diligence. You have to remember that at this level funds are assessing partner track skills, not only your ability to build and run a model.

Two common pitfalls that we've seen hold people back from returning to the industry are losing focus and becoming complacent. Regarding focus, we take the simple view that if you like the type of investing you did before business school and you were good at it, there is little need to make a significant change. Staying focused on a stage of investing and an industry should make your return to PE that much easier. If you lose focus by interviewing with too many funds, you may be burned out when you most need to be at your best. If you are seeking a change, just make sure that you are motivated by thoughtful reasoning and rationale as opposed to what is "hot."

In terms of complacency, now is not the time to sit back, relax, and assume you will have an automatic invite back into a top fund. You will be in for a surprise if you think you can simply go into an interview, brush off your pre-MBA interview script, and secure the offer. A lot of other people in business school have private equity experience and are going to fight for the available opportunities. Even in the best cycles there is no certainty that there will be enough positions for every person who wants to return.

The Summer

Hiring firms will definitely pay attention to your summer experience and will want to see that you made good use of the time. We view the summer as an acceptable time for traditional candidates to expand their knowledge by trying something different (see Case Studies 14 and 16). The most common summer experiences for MBAs with previous PE experience include working at a hedge fund (or other buy-side firm that invests in the public markets) or industry/operations roles. Doing something too safe—such as returning to the banking or consulting realm if you've already had that experience pre-MBA—could raise questions and work against you. An exception could be if you were previously a banker who wants to try consulting, or vice versa, but it is not often done.

Some people also spend the summer with their pre-MBA PE firm, especially if they have an offer to return. Others, however, who know they are not going to return to their pre-MBA firm may opt to intern at another fund, and it has helped that more PE funds are offering summer internships. Working for the summer at your pre-MBA firm may not expand your network and skills substantially, but it will be beneficial in providing some additional insurance for you to return. It's probably safe to say that if you do anything other than operations or some form of buy-side, you will probably be asked why you made that choice.

Glocap Insight For MBAs with previous PE experience, our recent data suggests that approximately 40 percent of those staying in PE return to their summer employers. Of those transitioning to hedge funds, almost 90 percent have summer hedge fund experience. About 60 percent of those who work in hedge funds over the summer accept offers from those employers.

MBAs WITHOUT PRIOR PRIVATE EQUITY EXPERIENCE

Not that it needs repeating, but as someone without private equity experience, you're in a more challenging position. You're at least missing the middle step of the traditional 2-2-2 path and you can't go back in time to make up for that. However, the good news is that each year we do see candidates securing PE roles who didn't work at a PE/LBO fund before business school.

As you will read in the case studies at the end of the chapter, those PE offers are usually secured with some good hustle, initiative, ingenuity, creativity, and an unrelenting drive to succeed. To join the PE world, you will have to possess at least the requisite finance/deal skills and be prepared to prove that to hiring firms, especially if you are to beat out those with previous PE experience. If you have those skills but lack that extra something special (which our clients sometimes refer to as the "winning factor" or "x factor"), and the raw ability to be successful and compete, you will face more of a challenge. Your objective is to have the hiring firm look beyond any deficiencies in your background to see the unique star qualities you offer that will make them want you on their team.

As someone without PE experience, it's helpful to know where you stand in relation to other MBAs. If you're at a top business school and participate in PE resume drops, some funds may select to interview you, but the chances of this increase later in the year when funds widen the candidate pools they consider (Case Study 18 does a good job of describing the interview cycle for a current MBA without prior PE experience). Although you may get some on-campus interviews, in general you'll mostly have to rely on your own efforts, since fewer PE/LBO firms will invite someone who lacks PE experience to be interviewed on campus.

Having said that, almost all of the candidates we know who secured PE positions without the benefit of pre-MBA experience did so by aggressively taking control of their search process. A good example is Case Study 21. Rather than sticking to a standard approach, this person set out on an ambitious search that eventually led to an offer. Interestingly, although he came from a top business school, he successfully fought through a bias against his school from the fund that eventually hired him. In many ways, this person, like the people in the other case studies, succeeded because he showed more initiative than his competition—mainly those with PE experience.

> Glocap Insight
>
> We look at MBAs without previous PE experience in the same way professional football teams would view a walk-on candidate who didn't excel enough in a Division I football program to make the draft. Just as NFL teams never *have* to look at walk-ons, PE firms do not usually need to look beyond the top business schools to find qualified candidates. In fact, they can afford to focus only on a small subset of candidates at those top schools—candidates who have previous PE experience. But both football teams and PE funds do look at walk-ons because they know there is the potential to find a hidden all-star.

We recommend that you start your search with a focus on those PE funds that have set a precedent for hiring MBAs without prior PE experience and, if you're not at a top feeder school, focus on those with alumni from your school. Some smaller, regional (and very successful) funds may even have a bias for a local school. If you visit the web sites of funds based outside of major financial centers and read the bios of the investment professionals, you will probably notice that a portion of them are not necessarily from the MBA programs listed earlier in this chapter. In general, firms like to hire what they know. If the funds are familiar with local schools or if the managers went to a particular MBA program and valued how they beat the odds and what they bring to the table, they will most likely be willing to consider someone whose background resembles their own.

The Summer

Given that you don't have PE experience, your summer will play a more crucial role in getting you a step closer to an offer. Although it may not put you on an automatic path to a post-MBA position in PE, getting a summer internship in PE does have its benefits: It will help you decide whether PE is for you and, if you perform well, you may even land an offer from your summer employer. Having that offer will be an asset as you pursue discussions with other firms, even if you don't intend to accept it. In a hiring market as competitive as PE, we believe that a summer associate position on your resume could be enough to get you on the short list of candidates who will get a look from PE firms (or perhaps recruiters as well), which is the first step to getting interviews.

If you're still in your first year, it's time to pull out all the stops to get the hands-on principal investing experience you need via a summer internship or by working during school. You may have some deal or project experience from the advisory side, but to really enhance your prospects you need to get PE/buy-side know-how while at business school. It may seem early, but the first week of school is the ideal time to start looking for that position. There are many methods to secure a summer internship in PE, and we recommend using any means available to you.

Two methods that we've seen work well are (1) networking with professors who could sometimes prompt a local fund to take a small risk (a three-month internship) on an excellent student, and (2) using geographic flexibility to your advantage. Funds in major financial centers (New York, Chicago, San Francisco, etc.) will be inundated with resumes, so try something in cities such as Atlanta, Cleveland, Dallas, Denver, Miami, Minneapolis, and so on. Relocating to work 10 weeks of the summer in one of these cities is a small price to pay if it increases your chances of getting a full-time position after you graduate.

Glocap Insight

From what we've seen, the MBAs without previous PE experience who fared best getting into the industry after graduation were those with two to four years of investment banking/consulting experience plus a summer PE internship. Another group who fare well (especially with venture capital funds) are those with deep industry experience in a sector such as health care or technology.

If you find yourself coming up short in your search for a summer PE internship, there are some alternatives. One is to work for one of the top investment banks or consulting firms. They generally have respected and influential alumni in PE who can help open some doors down the road. Getting into those firms will at least get you validated by a top institution. Next, we would say try to get any buy-side-type role (corporate M&A can have similar characteristics to private equity investing) with a company in an interesting industry. For example, someone who did M&A for a tech company and closed interesting, successful, and complicated deals could draw the attention of a tech fund. In the same vein, someone who worked at a major automotive company doing M&A in China could be interesting to a PE fund looking at opportunities involving exporting manufacturing to Asia, or a fund involved in a turnaround or distressed situation.

Insider Tip ▷

From a Principal at a PE Firm

If you want to get into private equity you have to focus on being an investor, an entrepreneur, an owner, and an operator. If you do that and realize that the rest of the skills are a commodity, you will show people that you bring value to the table. Financial modeling is important, but it's like a tool in your toolbox. Funds don't want someone who can simply put a model together. They are looking for people who can think about the results they get out of a model. That is how you can really add value.

Unfortunately, if you are a second-year MBA without previous full-time PE experience or a summer PE position, you have the steepest climb. You have few choices at this point other than to double your networking efforts with school alumni (we've found that alumni networks are particularly strong in smaller cities), both at the undergrad and business school levels and with your professors, as any strong recommendation could carry weight with a fund.

CASE STUDIES: MBAs WITH PE EXPERIENCE

The first three case studies are MBAs who followed the traditional 2-2-2 path, taking them from banking to private equity and then to business school. Although they all had previous investing experience before business school, they never assumed their return to PE was a certainty until they had an offer in hand. Each also enhanced the available options by trying other things during the summer.

We recommend all candidates read these stories, as these are the MBAs against whom you are competing. They had the turnkey investment experience PE firms want and were able to return to the industry relatively smoothly. After reading these, ask yourself two questions: Do you have what it takes secure a position ahead of someone with that background? And do you have the energy to devote to going after it, knowing that it will be difficult and uncertain?

The second set of case studies will show you the creative ways in which some people who lacked the traditional background landed a position in PE. The resumes that correspond to these case studies can be found in Appendix B.

Case Study 14: Returning to Your Pre-MBA Firm

Wouldn't it be nice to accept an offer from your pre-MBA firm early in your second year? This candidate did, and having that offer allowed her to experiment with other opportunities while at business school.

■ ■ ■

For me the traditional 2-2-2 path led me right into private equity. I've seen a lot of people move into PE, and doing it this way was definitely the easiest route. I finished my Ivy League undergrad in 2000 with a degree in economics. During the summer before my senior year, I interned at an investment bank in New York. Without that experience under my belt it would have been harder for me to get into a banking program after graduation, as I had no connections on Wall Street and was not a real finance type.

I ended up at a firm that specialized in M&A and did some work with the restructuring group. This particular firm was short on teaching but good on deal experience. I worked on several live deals but, unfortunately, not many closed deals. I did learn how to model, and the restructuring experience was pretty rare and gave me a bit of a competitive advantage at some PE firms.

I began interviewing at the end of the first year of my analyst program and I relied exclusively on headhunters. The people at my firm also helped out with contacts in the PE industry. I found the whole process demoralizing, but luckily I had a backup offer to stay on at my firm for a third year. I ended up taking an offer at a larger PE firm. I interviewed at about 15 to 20 firms in total. They all pretty much asked the same questions: How do you get to free cash flow? Walk me through an LBO that you worked on. How would you model it? They grilled me on my deals, asking if I thought they were good ones—basically anything on my resume was fair game. I think this is a weak point for people with banking backgrounds. They are used to burying themselves in the models. They have to learn to take a step back and judge the entire deal. Some gave me quantitative brain teasers, and all asked, "Why do you want to go into PE?" I would also add that since the PE firms don't train you, they will expect that you got your training from your analyst program, and they will test that during the interviews.

Being a woman, I also wondered if I was being treated differently since fitting in is so important. I felt this especially at the small firms. If they were only going to hire one person, it seemed that the attitude was that it would be more of a gamble on their part to hire a woman. Having one woman in a small group of men might raise the chance of a personality conflict.

Looking back, there is not much I would have done differently. Once you know you want PE and get into the traditional path, things pretty much go on autopilot.

I ended up accepting an offer in June, when my program was about to end. Even though this firm didn't require me to go to business school, after one year at the firm I decided to pursue my MBA. I was promoted at the end of my second year right before I went to business school, and I could have stayed on, but I felt I needed a break from working. The firm didn't think there was much value to me going, but they said they wanted me to come back after I graduated.

Having that offer in my back pocket allowed me to go to business school with a different mind-set than my classmates. I knew I had a job to come back to. I was always interested in operations, so during the summer I took a job with a leading computer company. It was a great opportunity, but in the end I knew it was not for me.

Looking back, there is not much I would have done differently. Once you know you want PE and get into the traditional path, things pretty much go on autopilot. I would recommend that undergrads be careful of the group they go into at the investment banks. Modeling-heavy groups such as M&A and financial sponsors will prepare you better for PE than will industry-specific ones.

I would also say that those interested in PE after business school should do anything they can to get even a little PE on their resume. Since there are so many people at business school with PE experience, most firms are not interested in hiring someone with no PE experience for full-time positions. Having even a little experience from the summer or other internship on your resume will give them something to grab on to.

(See Resume 9 in Appendix B.)

Case Study 15: Returning with Narrow Geographic Preferences

This person (MBA 2006) also had an invitation to return to his pre-MBA PE firm, but he chose to look around and ended up moving to another fund.

■ ■ ■

Given that I had PE experience prior to business school, I knew I was in a better position to get a job in PE upon graduating from business school. In fact, I ended up accepting an offer in November of my second year, which allowed me to relax a little bit the rest of the year.

My path into PE began at an independent middle-market investment bank in the Midwest. After graduating in 2000 from a university in the Midwest with a major in finance, I went straight into an investment banking analyst training program. At the time I knew I wanted to be in finance and knew that I-banking was what every high achiever was doing. It didn't take long for it to become clear to me that a great next step for me would be PE. I definitely wanted to work fewer hours than I-banking required, and I wanted something that was less advisory and more on the principal side. I also knew that I would need another job before business school.

All of my friends had done two to three years in an I-bank and then another two to three years in a PE shop or other place, so I thought that was the way to do things. I had an offer to stay at the bank for a third year, but I began interviewing for PE jobs in October of my second year. Basically, I wanted to work in Chicago, and I made a list of all the PE firms in that city. I contacted all of them, interviewed with eight, and got an offer in mid-January. Some of the bigger firms at which I interviewed had structured pre-MBA programs and a dedicated person doing the first-round interviews. Others used a recent business school grad.

At my firm, a traditional leveraged buyout shop, there were about 10 others in the pre-MBA group. About 75 percent of my time was spent doing modeling work, due diligence, and attending management meetings. During the rest of my time I did more proactive deal-sourcing work. We all knew this firm never really promoted people without an MBA and that we would be there for two years, three if we did well. I did get an offer to stay on at my PE firm for a third year, and because of that I applied to two of the top business schools, figuring that if I got in I would go and if not I would stay on for the third year and then apply to four or five schools.

When I got to business school, I was about 65 percent certain that I would go back to PE. I pretty much had a standing offer to go back to the firm where I worked before business school, but I didn't think I would go back, mostly because of two cultural things that bothered me: I didn't like the hypercompetitive nature of the senior partners and the large number of vice presidents, which would make moving up to partner difficult. I wanted to go somewhere where they saw me as a partner.

I spent the summer between my first and second years working at a hedge fund in New York, basically to see if I would like something outside of PE. I knew that if you have PE experience before business school there is basically nothing that can adversely affect you, unless you spend the summer on the beach. I didn't like the hedge fund business as much as PE. I prefer the deal process and more teamwork.

I jumped right into my job search in September of my second year. I targeted three cities where I wanted to work—Denver, Los Angeles, and San Francisco—and generated a list of firms. I treated the search much as I did my search for a PE job during my second year of analyst training. I methodically called each firm to see which ones were hiring. It took the entire month of September to get through the list and find out which ones were looking for associates. I only did one on-campus interview, as the firms that came to my school tended to be from New York.

> *I would also say that starting your job search early is critical, and that goes for people with or without PE experience. I thought by starting in September I was early, but I wasn't.*

One major advantage I had because of my prior PE experience was that the firms that did come to campus came to me instead of me having to go to them. All the PE firms would get hold of our resume book and sort candidates by those who had experience. I would get calls and e-mails from the funds, asking to interview me. Those same firms almost never posted jobs, so you would only get an interview if they contacted you after scanning the resume book. I found four firms that were hiring and even made one trip to the West Coast on my own dime. I accepted a position on November 10 and could relax until my September start.

Most of the interviews were pretty similar, and I would say that people should be prepared. Only one firm gave me a case to read and prepare notes. The rest had me walk through my background and asked about what deals I had worked on, why I wanted to work in PE, and why with that specific firm. The fact that I had worked at a hedge fund in the summer but was seeking a job in PE also came up at every interview. Some also asked questions like, "If you had money to invest, where would you put it?"

I would say that if you don't have PE experience, it is absolutely critical to do an internship, even at a small asset management shop or a hedge fund, to get some buy-side experience. Looking back, knowing that I really wanted to pursue PE after school, I probably should have been more honest with myself and looked for a PE job in the summer. I hadn't interviewed for a PE job in two years and, if nothing else, it would have been good practice. I would also say that starting your job search early is critical, and that goes for people with or without PE experience. I thought by starting in September I was early, but I wasn't.

(See Resume 10 in Appendix B.)

Case Study 16: A Pedigree Returns after Testing the Waters

This candidate tried venture investing and operations during the summer, but preferred PE. Even though he had an offer to come back to his pre-MBA firm he still interviewed around.

■ ■ ■

Having private equity experience before business school was a major advantage for me. I was pretty sure that I wanted to go back into PE and I had a standing offer to go back to the firm where I had worked before business school. That was a big deal. Some of my classmates who worked in PE before school didn't have a good experience at their firm, so they would be searching for a new firm. I could relax a bit and use my summer to try something new.

I wasn't too different from many others who took the traditional path into PE. After graduating in 1995 from an Ivy League college with a degree in economics, I went straight into an investment banking analyst program. At the time, I barely knew what PE was. Fortunately, I was placed into the leveraged finance group, which gave me exposure to the large LBO funds as I worked on senior debt and high-yield offerings for LBO sponsors. During my two years I got good experience in financial modeling, capital structures, cash flow generation, and leverage statistics. It was also at this time that I became familiar with the path to get into PE. I knew that having PE experience before business school would make it a lot easier to get back into the industry after getting my MBA.

I started looking for a job in PE halfway into my second year. Back then the process of getting into a PE shop did not begin as early as it does in today's market. Still, it was a rigorous process. The firms knew I had the finance capabilities; now they wanted to see my thought process on the deals I had worked on. They wanted to see if I could articulate and present deals to an investment committee.

During my second year of business school, having the prior PE experience made getting interviews much easier. At our school, all the buyout firms get the resume book and screen the candidates. Without PE experience on your resume, you most likely would not be picked for interviews.

The firm I ended up with did a wide range of deals including venture, growth equity, and buyout. I also liked the culture of the fund, and this is important because you want to feel good where you work and have a good fit. This firm had a strong mentorship culture and the investment philosophy meshed with my own. I had an offer to stay on for a third year and the firm offered to pay my way through business school if I stayed, but I was accepted into what I deemed was a top school and couldn't turn that down. Still, the firm made it clear that the door was open for me to come back.

As I entered business school, my thinking was that PE is a great career path and that I would probably go back, but I wanted to see what operations roles were like. I spent the first 10 weeks of the summer between my first and second years working in an operating capacity at a major Internet company and the next six weeks at a VC firm. The operations role was interesting, but I found that it didn't have the same breadth as PE.

During my second year of business school, having the prior PE experience made getting interviews much easier. At our school, all the buyout firms get the resume book and screen the candidates. Without PE experience on your resume, you most likely would not be picked for interviews. It's too bad. I think firms lose out by not looking at people with varied experiences, but that is the nature of the beast.

I had an open door to come back to my original firm, but I still interviewed with a few other firms. If you do this, be careful. You can bet that someone will give a reference call to your old firm and they will not like to hear that you are interviewing at other firms. To avoid this, I was selective where I interviewed and told them I had an outstanding offer. I also knew that no one would make a reference call until the later rounds of interviews, and I ultimately didn't take any final-round interviews. For me, it was better to go with a known firm than to try something different.

(See Resume 11 in Appendix B.)

CASE STUDIES: MBAs WITHOUT PE EXPERIENCE

The professionals in these case studies are the exceptions we've been talking about. They had the winning formula to beat out MBAs who had the sought-after pre-MBA experience. In general, they used an aggressive, multipronged strategy that involved a lot of tenacity and creativity. One person traveled extensively on his own dime to interview at PE firms that might not have invited him on their own. Why not do the same? You may have paid many tens of thousands of dollars in business school tuition, but you should be able to justify another couple thousand dollars if that helps get you in front of people and improves your chances. It may mean flying across the country without a scheduled meeting, or driving several hours to knock on the door of a fund in which you're interested, but it could be worth it if it bolsters your case.

Nearly all of these candidates probably utilized their entire roster of contacts, including professors, school alumni, and colleagues from previous jobs. Above all, they would most likely say that they worked tirelessly to achieve their goal and that you must be willing to take the same approach. To emphasize how challenging it is for most people, we also present the case of someone who tried to get into PE, but came up empty (Case Study 25). The resumes that correspond to Case Studies 21 and 22 in this section can be found in Appendix B.

Case Study 17: Relentless Approach, Early Start

Knowing that he lacked the requisite PE background, this person from the 2006 MBA class pulled out all the stops. First he secured an ideal summer internship. Then he used his extensive network to land an interview.

■ ■ ■

I graduated from an Ivy League school in 2000 with a degree in economics. While at school I did two summer internships—one at a bulge-bracket investment bank and another at a consulting firm. After graduating I took a two-year position with a leading consulting firm. Since I knew I would be done after two years I had time to plan my next stop, and I wanted that to be in private equity. I always thought I had a mind for investing and putting money to work, but I still liked business and being around companies. I knew econ majors were good for PE and wanted to work with private companies.

Unfortunately, my timing wasn't that great. I began interviewing with PE funds right after 9/11. I also only focused on PE funds in my hometown, which had a limited group of top-tier PE funds (fewer than 25), and ended up interviewing with six of them. None had the need for a pre-MBA analyst. So, I thought, why not work in industry?

I got a job with an Internet company doing M&A and corporate strategy. The job was very light on financial modeling and accounting, but I worked with our CFO to source acquisitions and develop the appropriate financial and strategic analysis. I also worked with lawyers, bankers, and accountants. When I left this company I could not build a model or do much accounting, but I still had a quasi buy-side experience.

I still knew that I wanted to work in PE, but I was well aware that I was look-ing more and more like a consultant/operator. I decided to go to business school and targeted one of the top schools that I knew had a great brand name, a strong alumni network, and a good track record of getting graduates into PE funds. Before I even got to business school I focused on getting a job in my hometown (not a major finan-cial center). I created a spreadsheet of all 25 firms in this city and loaded it with all my contacts (through my undergrad college, consulting firm, and business school) and every bit of information I could find about the firms, using my own research and other sources, such as Capital IQ.

I knew one of the first things I would have to do is get summer PE experience. By November 1, I was sending e-mails and making calls to all the people on my spread-sheet. I wasn't specifically asking for a job, but more introducing myself, telling them where I went to school, and asking if I could meet them for lunch. All of them said they don't do summer internships; they also thought my lack of PE experience was an issue and therefore I would be a risky hire.

It was now January, when most of my friends were securing investment banking and consulting interviews, and I was still coming up empty. But I continued to send e-mails, make calls, have lunches, and even offered to work for free over the summer just to get into the PE industry. Then a nice thing happened. I got a call in April from one of the PE firms that I had contacted back in November, offering me a summer position. It was nice to see the efforts of all my e-mails pay off. I ended up knowing only a few people in my class who got summer PE internships, but it was very aggra-vating to not know what I would be doing until April.

The internship turned out to be a great experience. Since it was a small PE fund ($50 million with only two MDs and me) I got to build buyout models, look at new investments, work with portfolio companies, and learn the business inside and out. I ended up working for this fund during the first semester of my second year while I was back at school. It was a real teaching type internship, and now when I went on interviews I was able to credibly talk about the deals I had worked on and the models I had built.

My search for a post-MBA job still focused only on my hometown city. Only two funds from that city came to campus to interview, so I hardly checked the job bank. I did have friends who also lacked PE experience, and I would say that for every 25 funds that came to campus they would get one to two interviews.

We learned very quickly that 2006 was a great year for recruiting. All of our classmates with PE experience pretty much got jobs with their old firms or new ones by the beginning of the year. My friends and I without experience wondered when the funds would find time to start looking at the riff-raff. Even though I didn't have experience, I got a few on-campus interviews because of the work I put in. Figuring that the same firms usually come back to campus, I looked at the list of those that had come to campus the year earlier and reached out to the ones that were appealing to me. It worked; I got a first-round interview at the firm where I ended up getting an offer.

I was still 100 percent focused on my one city. Fortunately, I got an offer from my summer firm, but I still looked at other opportunities. I interviewed at another firm that claimed they didn't care if you had PE experience. They asked me to talk about my deals, the merits of the companies, how I structured debt and equity on specific deals, and what types of companies I liked. They gave me a case study on the merits of buying a plumbing products company.

Then I interviewed at one more fund. This was the most intense interview I ever went through, but I was thankful for that. I figure if you don't have experience, but have gotten smart on your own, a rigorous interview will work to your advantage. It gives you an opportunity to prove yourself. I went through four rounds with this firm and there were about seven case studies mixed in. This firm brought in 50 people for first-round interviews, all of whom were from three of the top schools. Five people were brought back for second rounds and four for third rounds. My guess is I was the only one who lacked pre-MBA PE or hedge fund experience.

For the last phase of this interview process, I was given one week to prepare a major presentation on an investment opportunity. The firm gave me 1,500 pages of public filings on the company. I would guess I worked six to eight hours a day and put together an extensive model and a 20-page PowerPoint presentation for this firm's investment committee. This exercise was the best thing for me. It let me compete head-to-head with everyone else on a level playing field, and I was able to show them that I was the best out there.

I think I was able to beat out others who had experience by working harder on the final case study. I'm sure I spent two or three times more time on it than did those against whom I was competing. The firm even told me that my recommendations and analysis was very compelling. In addition to having strong references I was helped by some softer intangibles. This fund was in my hometown so they knew I would be there for the long term, and I had been talking to them for a year so they knew how committed I was.

My advice to other MBAs who lack previous PE experience is to be patient during your first year and the beginning of your second year, but to work hard networking and start early. You have to be willing to make phone calls and send e-mail, and have the attitude that all you need is one person to offer you something. On day one, all I worried about was getting a job two years down the road, and I didn't let rejections bother

You've got to expect that 99 percent of the people will say no to you, but all you need is one to say yes.

me. You've got to expect that 99 percent of the people will say no to you, but all you need is one to say yes.

I would also say not to expect to get too many on-campus interviews. Networking is the better way to go, and that includes talking to friends, reading the industry publications, and staying up-to-date with current events. You've got to be able to talk the talk of private equity. My summer experience ended up paying off for me. I'd say that anyone without PE experience should do what they can to get in the door. Why not offer to work for free during the summer? Volunteer to do a side project during business school, write a white paper, or do deal analysis. You need something to set you apart.

Case Study 18: Aggressiveness Leads to a Post-MBA Position

Note how this person did not back down despite knowing that it would be extremely tough to find a job without the typical experience. Instead, he got aggressive and his efforts were rewarded.

■ ■ ■

My Ivy League undergrad degree in economics led me into a tech banking job at a high-profile group in a bulge-bracket firm. After two years I was asked to stay on as an associate, and I ended up in banking for three and a half years before switching over to equity research for six months prior to business school. I did banking for four years, but I knew I didn't want to do that for the rest of my career. I had run hard for four years and decided to go to business school because I wanted to learn other parts of business that I hadn't been as exposed to, including operations, marketing, and leadership. At this time private equity was in the back of my mind, but I was more interested in venture capital, which I had more exposure to while I was in tech banking.

Once I decided to go after private equity job opportunities, I realized quickly how difficult it would be. I was at a top business school and many of my classmates had PE experience. So not only was I competing against top students, but they were top students with the experience that I did not have. I took courses on restructuring and investing, but many firms could not get around the fact that I had no PE experience. I tried for a summer internship, but there are very few available. So instead, I did a consulting internship and enjoyed that. Consulting gave me an understanding of businesses and organizations on a deeper level and confirmed my belief that working with companies to create financial and operational value was what I wanted to do.

I never got picked for interviews out of the resume book, but I started to understand what they wanted. I spent several months researching the industry so I could understand the business. I knew I had a lot of exposure to deals on the research side and was aware that deal skills are a commodity. With that in mind, I spun my leadership skills, showing that I was competitive and could manage people. I tried to explain how my experience as captain of my college sports team had taught me leadership and commitment. Through that example, I showed that I was not afraid of putting in time to achieve a goal. I got some interviews at PE funds during my second year, but I only made it past the first round on a few occasions. It always came back to the same thing: I had no PE experience.

I knew my options were limited, but I also knew I could get a job. I got aggressive and worked my network, setting up informational interviews with high-level people at PE funds and even at operating companies. I wanted to get on people's radar screens. I probably spent a few thousand dollars flying and driving myself around the country, meeting anyone in the industry. I saw the money as an investment in my future. And while I was going on informational interviews, I loaded my schedule with other interviews at VC firms and with friends of friends who are operators and had worked with VC firms. Those meetings helped me to refine my interviewing skills.

I also sold them hard on my consulting/equity research experience, which demonstrates how, while not making actual investments, I had to make investment recommendations based on my analysis and research.

An opportunity came in February when a fund posted a job listing at my business school. The fund asked for a case study, which I did. I spent quite a bit of time on it, feeling that I had to prove something and needed some kind of an edge. The interviews lasted through March and I got the offer in late April. I think I benefited because the firm wasn't on the East Coast, which is a more popular destination for my classmates. In addition, I think this fund was more open-minded about non-PE backgrounds. I worked hard to convey my desire to be in that city and that I was not a flight risk. I also sold them hard on my consulting/equity research experience, which demonstrates how, while not making actual investments, I had to make investment recommendations based on my analysis and research.

The whole process was tough. April was very late in the semester to get a job offer and I knew I was going against 20 to 25 business school classmates, at least half of whom had PE experience.

I would say that the sooner you know you want to get into PE, the better. Looking back, I probably would have tried to get into PE after my banking program. That path is the easiest way to do it. If you don't take that route, you should definitely work your network (meaning you have to *have* a network) and try to convince people to take a chance on you. You must also educate yourself about what the firms do and understand the nuances of their investment strategies. Finally, you have to understand how to market yourself in your resume as it pertains to the industry. Put simply, you have to sell yourself and your skills.

Case Study 19: The Benefits of Networking

This person made good use of his summer to make up for his lack of PE experience.

■ ■ ■

Upon arriving at college, I was planning on pursuing a career in medicine and studied science at school. During my senior year, I decided that medicine was not the career for me and wanted to focus on business. Because I had a pre-med background and hadn't taken a business class, I thought the best entry into the finance world where I could learn the most and still maintain a health care interest would be an analyst position on Wall Street. The investment banks had vigorous training programs and an intense work environment where I could learn the needed business and analytical tools. Fortunately, I was able to secure an analyst position in the health care group at a top-tier investment banking firm.

As an analyst, I had great deal of exposure, including direct interaction with the venture industry through private placement issuances I had worked on. In my third year, I was able to join the financial sponsors group, which gave me exposure to the LBO world through client interactions and transactions. Honestly, I didn't even know the VC and buyout world existed before I went into banking. I was offered a direct promotion to associate, but I had decided that my goal was to move to the buy-side at either a buyout or venture firm. I decided to go to business school, mostly because I had never taken any finance classes and thought this would be a great way to round out my business education. I also thought it would make me more attractive to the PE industry.

I enrolled in several VC/PE classes in business school and participated in the VC club. I also took advantage of my school's internship program, which allowed students to work with a local company during the semester for credit. I completed one internship with a VC firm and another with a small start-up biotech company. The internships gave me direct VC and small company exposure. For my career, I decided to focus on VC because I thought my scientific educational background and health care financial experience would make me a more attractive candidate to a VC firm than a buyout firm. I felt that the buyout shops were looking for someone with more M&A experience, which unfortunately I didn't have.

I went back to Wall Street during the summer between my first and second years of business school—it was 2001 and VC firms were not hiring, not even if you offered to work for free. My job search began in October of my second year and took about nine months. I networked and contacted everyone I knew from my past work experience, internships, and my own personal contacts. The networking definitely paid dividends. I think finding a job without networking will probably be based more on luck, simply being in the right place at the right time.

The 2-2-2 path into PE is absolutely the best way to get into buyouts, but not necessarily true for VC. One obstacle I faced that pertains specifically to health care VC was not having a PhD or MD. However, as one moves from early-stage investing to later-stage and into the LBO world, the advanced science degree becomes less and less important.

Strategy-wise, I believe it's important to target the right funds given your background. You shouldn't waste your time or the funds' time looking at places where there will not be a good fit. Knowing what I know now, if I had to repeat the process all over again, I would probably have done my two years at a VC or buyout fund before going to business school. In my case I had an opportunity to go straight from my banking program to a VC fund, but I wanted to get business school out of the way. Having the two-year experience at a private equity fund before business school makes it much easier to pursue a career on the buy-side after school. And based on the number of firms that have these two-year programs in place, it seems that it's now almost becoming a necessity.

> *Strategy-wise, I believe it's important to target the right funds given your background. You shouldn't waste your time or the funds' time looking at places where there will not be a good fit.*

Case Study 20: Taking a Targeted Approach

This person may not have made it if he hadn't identified the fund that was best for what he brought to the table.

■ ■ ■

After graduating from college, I spent two years teaching high school. I then earned my joint degree in business and education. I decided to pursue private equity while I was in business school—I had taken some private equity classes and thought that it was an excellent field to hone one's understanding of business fundamentals. I was hoping to move to New York after graduating, and heard of a private equity firm that invests in education and training companies from one of my professors. I thought it would be a good way of combining interests in education and business and getting a different experience than I had as a teacher.

I do not think I was in a very good position to get a private equity job with minimal business experience. I received some good advice from a counselor at my graduate school: Do a research project for the private equity firm as an independent project for credit. The firm suggested that I do a project on financial aid options outside of federal aid, and it worked out well. Still, they said they weren't hiring anyone. Eventually, we worked out a deal where I would work there for the summer. After that, they appreciated my work and offered me a permanent job in the fall. At first, my role was largely market and legislative research, but since then I have become a true investment professional—building models, working on transaction details, etc.

If I had been intent on a private equity career earlier on, I would have gone the I-banking route from the beginning. In my case, though, I would not have done anything different to set myself up for the job. I do not think my firm will seriously consider a younger candidate from a nontraditional background. I think the only way to get a job at this firm if you have not been in PE or banking (or had officer-level experience at an education company) would be to do something that gave them solid proof that you were bringing something to the table: conducting a substantial research project, bringing in a deal, coming to them with a specific, well thought out investment idea.

Case Study 21: Going after the Opportunity in Person

The efforts of this candidate are a prime example of going the extra mile to get what you want.

■   ■   ■

I finished undergrad in 1998 and went straight into a two-year analyst training program in the M&A group of a major New York–based Wall Street firm. After the two years I was promoted to associate, but instead got into a top business school and decided to go, making me one of the younger people in my class. From day one, I began thinking about how I could get into private equity. I knew that private equity is a challenging, dynamic industry and I wanted to be an investor rather than an adviser.

Unfortunately, my timing for securing a private equity job was as bad as it could be. Just before I entered business school the Internet bubble burst and the economy fell into a recession, so most Wall Street I-banking firms and many PE firms were simply not hiring. With only a banking background, I knew I had to get PE experience somehow. I lined up a summer internship at a small private equity firm, but it was rescinded two weeks before I was to start because of the downturn, leaving me with nothing to do for the summer. I called a former MD from the M&A group with my former employer. He had moved to Tokyo to strengthen the firm's M&A practice and asked me to come out for the summer. I didn't want to go back into investment banking but I wanted something to do for the summer, so I joined him.

When I returned for my last year at business school it seemed that everything was stacked against me and my goal of working in private equity: I had no private equity deal experience, I was young, and people were asking me why I went back to investment banking for the summer if I really wanted to be in private equity! I was set to graduate in 2002, again the lowest point in the economic downturn with many of the top-tier Wall Street firms instituting hiring freezes—many for the first time that anyone can remember!

In February of my final year I received an offer from an investment bank to work in their M&A group in London. I didn't necessarily want it, but it gave me something in the back of my pocket while I searched out my dream private equity job. I was able to put the firm off until April (which was no small task) while I did what I could to get a job in private equity.

I decided to take the same approach to my job search that I knew I would use when and if I got a job in private equity. I wouldn't wait for the job (or investment opportunity) to come to me. Rather, I began contacting firms myself. I targeted the entire country. I was open to most any city because the market was so bad. Finally, I made a cold call to a middle-market investment banker in the city where I went to college and he said I should call the CFO at a local PE fund. I did. The fund wasn't looking for anyone, but I knew they were raising a new $450 million fund. So I made a point of visiting my college buddies, calling the fund professionals in advance and asking if I could stop in. I probably repeated this trip four or five times beginning in November. It wasn't so bad since I liked visiting my friends and there were several world class ski resorts within close proximity.

> *I decided to take the same approach to my job search that I knew I would use when and if I got a job in private equity. I wouldn't wait for the job (or investment opportunity) to come to me.*

Ultimately, they said yes, they wanted to hire someone, but asked me, "Why should we hire you?" They were adamant that they didn't like my business school and that, even though I had gone to school in this city, I wasn't from there. It took a lot of convincing, but they finally said, "We like this guy," and brought me on. I was very honest with them from the beginning and admitted my major weakness: I told them that if they had come to my business school to interview MBA candidates, they would have found many more experienced people than me. However, they should look at me as a longer-term investment and recognize that I had proven in my past experiences to be a quick learner.

My advice to others would be to treat your job search as if you are an investor looking for an investment opportunity. As an investor, you are looking for companies that are under the radar screen. When I targeted funds I looked for ones that others hadn't discovered yet. I thought if a mid-market fund could raise $450 million in a small market then it must be good. On top of that, it had first class investors, solid investments in interesting industries and a good, but very limited, reputation. I didn't let my lack of private equity deal experience deter me and I think my attitude, willingness to work, general fit, and likeability eventually got me the job.

Needless to say, my decision turned out to be a terrific one. The economy began to turn and there was, and continues to be, a robust environment for buying and selling companies. It took roughly two and a half years for the firm to invest most of the new fund, which provided me with a firehouse of activity, on both the buy- and sell-side. Off the back of this heightened level of activity and broad experiences I was fortunate to land a principal level position with a very successful middle-market PE firm in New York City.

(See Resume 12 in Appendix B.)

Case Study 22: Taking a Pre-MBA Role as an MBA

Knowing full well what he was up against, this candidate took the unusual step of accepting a pre-MBA job after business school.

■ ■ ■

I had a somewhat atypical background going into my search for a private equity job. After graduating from undergrad in 1999 (bachelor of science in physics with distinction and a minor in economics), I worked for two years in the technology group in the San Francisco office of a mid-tier M&A boutique turned semi-bulge-bracket via acquisition. I got little actual deal experience given the market timing of this position.

I went straight to business school after two years at the bank. Once I was in business school, I started thinking about getting into private equity and was focused on doing something in the San Francisco Bay Area. There were no summer positions available at private equity firms, so I decided to try for a summer job at a top investment bank, which I got. I made an effort to round out my skill set a bit by trying to focus on transactions involving leverage. I received an offer to join full-time after graduation.

When I began my private equity job search in the fall of 2003 (which consisted of setting up informational meetings by leveraging the network I had from business school), I was told "No," outright. I had half a dozen or so informational interviews, and people just said, "You seem like a good guy, but there is no way we would hire you." They all had too many candidates who had private equity experience. Why take a risk on somebody who didn't? I decided to pursue a pre-MBA job, arguing that I had similar work experience to other candidates they were talking to. Some of the more institutional firms did not accept this idea, but a few of the firms did. At the end of the day, I got one offer, but that's all it takes. I think this firm brought me on for a couple of reasons: (1) it is relatively younger and less institutionalized, and (2) despite my lack of experience, everything else on my resume was strong—3.98 undergrad GPA, promotion to associate at my banking program, 770 GMAT, first-year honors at business school, and an offer for a full-time position at Goldman. All of that made them more inclined to take a chance on me.

> *One key to getting the job was recognizing early that I was passionate about PE. Even though my nontraditional strategy worked for me, I would suggest that others follow a more traditional path before business school.*

Even though I looked good on paper, I had to know my LBO stuff cold. I had to be sincere about wanting the work, explaining that my alternative was to return to Goldman and that comparing those two scenarios I would learn more in private equity, get paid about the same, and be much better positioned after the two years. I also had to give them the sense that I was mature about the decision and not expecting any special treatment because I was an MBA. Finally, I had to be open about not expecting any full-time positions at the end of the two years. I didn't worry that I was taking a step back by accepting the pre-MBA position, and it was easy for me to convince them of that because I truly believed that I would get good experience. I was basically reversing the order of the MBA and the pre-MBA private equity experience. After one year at the firm and having performed well, I was told that I was expected to stay on after the second year as a post-MBA. My strategy worked!

One key to getting the job was recognizing early that I was passionate about PE. Even though my nontraditional strategy worked for me, I would suggest that others follow a more traditional path before business school. That said, a lot of people find themselves already in business school and then wanting to go into PE. In that case, recognizing this as early as possible will increase chances of getting a job. Other keys were making the decision to go for the pre-MBA job (and demonstrating in an interview maturity and sincerity in taking this position) and having an extremely strong academic background (good schools and high GPAs and GMAT). Having an offer in hand from a top investment bank also helped.

(See Resume 13 in Appendix B.)

Case Study 23: Using Industry Expertise to Your Advantage

This person had never worked in private equity before business school. However, he did have specific industry experience and landed an internship during school that led to a full-time position.

■ ■ ■

My path into private equity was anything but typical. I started out as a pre-med student at a major West Coast university and had every intention to go on to medical school after graduation (in 2002). While in school I spent three years doing neuroscience research and even took the MCATs. The prospect of 7 to 10 more years of school and residency, however, deterred me from pursuing a career practicing medicine. I knew I wanted my career to revolve around science, but I also knew I didn't want to be stuck in a lab all day. With that in mind I turned to pharmaceutical sales.

I ended up spending about four years in two different pharmaceutical companies (six months in one and three and a half years in the second), getting sales experience, learning how to manage a territory, and working with doctors in the field. I helped the second company launch two new dermatology products and was promoted to a senior sales position. Although I was excelling at this company, I concluded that being in sales was not what I wanted to do long-term.

Rather than remain somewhere I didn't want to be, I applied to business school with the thought that it would help me explore my options. Fortunately, I got into a top school with a strong and involved alumni network. I began grad school in 2006 and knew that science would be a part of whatever I did post–business school, but had little idea where that would take me. When I arrived at school I didn't even know how to do Excel, let alone construct a DCF model. The school did offer a math camp in the summer, but I didn't attend that (in hindsight it would have been a good idea, but I wasn't invited to attend because my experience and abilities in math were seen as sufficient).

A lot of my classmates had consulting and banking backgrounds, but I knew I wanted a better work/life balance and didn't think those were for me. I considered pursuing professions in investment management and private equity/venture capital even though I didn't completely understand what the careers entailed. After talking to people who had done private equity and researching it myself, I decided to pursue a summer internship in that field. I was intrigued by the entrepreneurial nature of private equity/venture capital and saw it as a way to combine my knowledge of science and interest in finance without having to be at a desk all the time. I also saw it as a way to be involved with cutting-edge scientific discoveries.

It's amazing how quickly you have to start looking for a summer internship. With the summer position so critical, what you do during the first few months of school ends up being very important (interviews for summer jobs start as early as January). Given my background (no previous private equity or venture capital), most people told me that a life science–focused fund would be the only type of VC/PE fund that would be open to me, and even that would require that I had worked in operations in a biotech company for 8 to 10 years. Nearly everyone made it sound impossible. I had met someone two years ahead of me who had three years of VC experience, and even he couldn't find a job. But I knew that getting a summer internship would help and that it could possibly turn into an offer for full-time work post graduation. Needless to say, it was pretty intimidating. Making things harder, a practitioner and alumnus in the industry told me that many PE/VC firms don't even know until February or March if they need someone for the summer, and I knew that was late in the game. He advised me to construct my story about my pursuit of a career in PE/VC and do whatever extracurricular activities I could to show I was passionate about PE/VC.

I worked on a consulting project and an academic project with two VC-funded start-up technology companies. I also volunteered to work with our school's private equity center on a project contacting alumni. I taught myself Excel and how to model, took the appropriate corporate finance courses at school, and worked on the student-run investment club.

If you can't get what you think is an ideal summer internship, then focus on a position that will help make getting a full-time position easier.

As with everyone else, my goal was a paid internship, though I was prepared to take an unpaid one if it was with the right firm. If all fell through, my back-up plan was to try for a business development role at a biotech company, preferably one backed by a VC fund, something I knew could help me get into PE/VC later on. It wasn't easy. I made lots of calls and sent loads of e-mails and did get several interviews, but it was getting later in the year and I was nervous. By April and May I was hardly sleeping, knowing I hadn't secured an internship yet.

My luck changed when I answered a job posting from an alumnus. This alumnus said I lacked the finance skills for his fund, but told me his firm had an affiliated company that might be attracted to my pharmaceutical and science background. After a few phone interviews I went to New York for an on-site interview. Although the partners made sure I understood the investment strategy and what the key drivers were, most of the interviews were fit related. It's a small firm ($250 million) and they wanted to know they could work with me. Still, I did my homework and made sure I could talk about the pharmaceutical industry. I even researched the market and selected a few products that I felt would fit their investment strategy in case they asked for ideas. I was surprised that I was not asked many technical questions, though they did want to know that I could model since I had nothing in my background that showed I could. I got an offer the first week of May.

This was a paid internship and gave me tons of experience. There was also the understanding that if I did well I would be asked to return full-time after graduation. I worked my tail off while I was there, making sure I was the first one in the office before the partners arrived and the last one to leave after they had left. At the beginning I was asked how long I could stay, and ended up working for 14 weeks, nearly until the day before classes began—well more than the usual 10-week internship. Toward the end of the internship I was offered a full-time position and was told I would be there as long as I'm happy and the fund is happy. Needless to say, that has made my second year of business school very enjoyable.

Looking back, knowing that my strengths were my science and pharmaceutical backgrounds, I knew I had to play those up as this would be the main way I could differentiate myself from my classmates. I made a point of only pursuing life sciences VC funds and health care–focused private equity. The fact that I had a pre-med degree, had done scientific research, and had pharmaceutical industry experience often got me in the door with funds. From there, it was up to me to show I was passionate and convince them that I had worked on my weak spot—modeling. I ended up busting my butt for a lot of opportunities that didn't come to fruition, but that's what you have to do.

My advice to others interested in this field who also lack the private equity, venture capital, or operations experience would be to emphasize the skills they do have, specifically if those are technology, telecom, or life sciences. If you can't get what you think is an ideal summer internship, then focus on a position that will help make getting a full-time position easier. Typically, that could be business development or something that gives you operating experience if you want to get into VC, and banking experience if you want to get into later-stage private equity. Looking back, if I had known earlier that I wanted private equity, I would have gotten more involved in operations. But for me, business school proved the best avenue to get in—both my classmates and the alumni opened my eyes to opportunities I never knew existed.

Case Study 24: From a Foreign Government to a Buyout Fund

This person parlayed his governmental background and on-the-ground contacts into a position with a fund that was expanding outside of the United States.

■ ■ ■

My personal story of breaking into private equity is far from typical. As an Asian I went to university in my home country (I was ranked first among 35,000 students in a nationwide college entrance exam) and was then recruited by the government to work in its Ministry of Commerce. I spent 11 years working for the Ministry, with 6 of those years being spent in two separate foreign assignments. During my time in government I was exposed to many aspects of international finance. I also received a master's in Finance from a local university. I met two friends who went to business school in the United States and felt that would be a wise choice for me as well.

Initially I thought business school would lead me into an investment banking or corporate position, possibly with a firm that was interested in expanding its Asian operations. Unfortunately, I didn't get an investment banking summer internship. In fact, although I began looking for a summer internship soon after I arrived on campus, I didn't secure any position. I even went on a school trip to Asia to speak with alums but that didn't lead to anything. It was very demoralizing. I had classmates with banking and accounting backgrounds who were getting all the attention. How could I compare with them? Most of the hiring firms saw my governmental background and felt I was not a fit for what they wanted, and maybe I was too old. It was a very painful process and I eventually ended up doing research for a professor over the summer. Also, thanks to a friend I knew, I did spend a month back home working for one of the Big Four accounting firms (he ended up offering me a full-time position after graduation, but the position and compensation were not adequate).

As my second year began I was more prepared to search for a full-time position. I focused my search on companies with offices in my home country—either MBA leadership or rotational programs that would eventually send me back. I went to second rounds with a few corporations, but by December I still had nothing and was again receiving the same feedback about my background not being a fit. I didn't think about private equity because I felt it was for the star students who had the proper backgrounds, and that was not me.

They were drawn to me because of my government contacts and my local network that would help source deals.

In February I expanded my search to include private equity and venture capital firms that would be looking for a native person. I sent e-mails and resumes to 100 alums from my business school no matter when they graduated. I told them that I would like to work for an investment firm with business in my country. If their firm didn't do this, I asked if they knew any that did. I had many conversations with PE and VC professionals and learned a lot from this process, but I didn't get any interviews. Still, I was getting more and more confident that something would come through, and in March I interviewed with a small venture capital fund in New York and also with a commodities trading company that was expanding into Asia. I still had no offers, and I was getting worried about paying back my loans, not to mention that my wife was pregnant with our second child.

My luck finally turned in late March/early April when I got an interview at a late-stage private equity fund. They were interested in having me open an office for them in my home country. During the first interviews I told them about the country and the industries that are attractive there. They were drawn to me because of my government contacts and my local network that would help source deals. I was asked very few technical questions. The partners seemed to know that I could learn what I needed to know. My second round of interviews was easier. I got the sense that the managing partner decides almost everything, and if he believes something the others tend to agree. I got a conditional offer the next day. I was told if things went well for the first four months that I would be offered a full-time position.

In my case I think I was very lucky. In many ways I was not as good as my classmates, and the partners who interviewed me had some concerns about my lack of technical skills and experience. But I came from a country that was a hot spot for private equity investing, and I had a lot of invaluable contacts and a strong network, which works all the time. I'm also very persuasive and I realized that a successful investment person is not always a finance person—it can also be a person with excellent interpersonal skills who can persuade clients and influence other people.

Case Study 25: One Who Tried But Didn't Make It

This is the plight of one MBA grad without previous PE experience who couldn't break into the industry. It paints a good picture of what you are up against.

■ ■ ■

My work background includes about four years at a major consulting firm (not PE-specific) followed by two years as an associate on the private equity team of a major corporation's pension group. After business school (class of 2003), I tried to find a job at a buyout firm. After talking to many partners at LBO firms, as well as a few headhunters who specialized in these positions, I was told that it wasn't worth my time because I had none of the following: an investment banking/M&A background, strong industry experience, nor any direct deal experience. I was told numerous times that there was such a large supply of candidates looking for LBO jobs who had those skills and experiences, and so few positions, that I pretty much had no chance. I even tried to get a pre-MBA position, but was also told that they preferred people coming out of an investment banking program.

My advice would be don't even think of working at a private equity/LBO firm unless you have a good contact with someone at the firm or someone who knows the firm well. Blind resume submittals almost never work.

Chapter V

POSTGRADUATE SCHOOL: EXPERIENCED DEAL/ADVISORY PROFESSIONALS

At this point you are probably set on a nice career trajectory. In all likelihood, you are on a growth track toward perhaps becoming a managing director at an investment bank or consulting firm, or perhaps the equivalent transaction role at a well-known accounting firm, and heading toward the pinnacle of your profession. However, you have concluded that private equity is where you feel you belong, and you're worried that hiring firms may think you are too expensive, too advanced in your career, or, most likely, that you don't have what it takes. As someone with little or no direct private equity–related experience, you are aware that the window to get into PE was open wider when you were more junior, but you also know that you can't go back in time. There is really no reason to make the switch to private equity, other than the fact that you want to.

You've chosen one of the most difficult times in your career to attempt to get into private equity. At this point PE funds are looking for the next generation of leaders and are resistant to training someone more senior who is less proven as an investor. Maybe you've seen your peers transition into PE at a similar stage, or perhaps you've gotten close enough to people already in PE to become familiar with what they do. Either way, you believe you have similar skills and therefore think there is little to disqualify you from making a move to the principal side and being successful. Basically, you've been watching the industry from the sidelines and are itching to get on the field and play.

From our experience, we feel the select people who land positions at this stage of their careers are usually the high achievers who always had the appropriate investment skills, but had yet to apply them in a principal setting. Most likely they didn't realize the allure of private equity until they got to business school or were deep into their careers. We refer to these individuals as *late bloomers* and have included some successful examples in the case studies at the end of this chapter. These professionals certainly didn't *need* to switch careers since they were on the fast track to success in their professions. However, they were motivated to pursue what they thought was their true calling.

To move off the sidelines you will need more than just skills and desire. At this stage of your career there is no definitive hiring cycle and no one best path to get into private equity. Just as a 30-year-old athlete who still dreams of playing in the majors has to show extraordinary skills to even get a tryout, so too will you have to demonstrate that you have superior talent to get a look by a PE fund. And even if you have that ability, you will probably need some help to get that tryout.

From what we have seen, that help can come in different forms, including from your clients, senior people at your firm, people in your own network, and, in some cases, the help will come from a recruiter. Historically, a recruiter's hands are tied. If we get mandates for 10 post-MBA searches and all require five years of previous LBO experience, we have little room to introduce a banker or consultant who lacks that tightly defined specification. It's not that we don't want to help people in your situation or that we think you're not going to make it. It's just that we are limited to introducing only the candidates who closely fit the specifications we are given by the clients who retain us.

As you will read in Case Studies 26, 27, and 28, most people say that if they had known there was an easier path to get into private equity that they could have followed earlier in their careers, they probably would have taken it. While the stories of how they made it are unique, these authors have some things in common: They were all top performers at top firms, showed an unrelenting determination to succeed, and also had fortunate timing. In their cases, since they were too late to take advantage of the traditional path that worked for others, they had to find creative ways to get in front of PE funds while at the same time being star performers. These examples include one person who had CEOs at his client companies make calls on his behalf, another who joined a PE client who knew him, and a third who got in by writing a cold letter to someone who was forming a new fund.

POSITIONING YOURSELF

If you are truly serious and dedicated to moving to the principal side, you should first make sure you have the answers to several inevitable questions—both for your own self-assessment and for the PE funds with which you hope to interview. If you are interviewed for a position, you will be asked why you want to get into PE (in fact, that is one of the most commonly asked questions of all candidates which we address more in Chapter XI). However, in your case, the question could take on more meaning since you never worked at a PE fund before and are more advanced in your career. You will most likely also be asked: Why do you want to get into PE *now*? Did you think about working in private equity before? If so, did you try to get in at an earlier time in your career? If not, why didn't you try before? What happened? Why do you think the timing is right for you now?

Those who did get in at this stage in their careers would probably have answered these questions by saying part of their plan was to work hard to excel and get the most robust deal/project experience so they could move up through the ranks of their firm. Most likely they weren't thinking about how that experience could have helped them move into PE. They would probably be able to honestly say that they didn't know there was a traditional path that they could have followed to get into PE earlier in their career.

If a private equity firm is considering making an exception to bring you on, the partners will grill you until they are satisfied they are making a good choice. Since you haven't cut your teeth in PE, your investment judgment, financial knowledge, and deal skills will be scrutinized. In addition, since you would most likely join in a more senior role, PE firms will want to see that you have all the signs of a potential leader. Be ready to be convincing that while you never did principal investing, you do bring something of extra value to the table that more than makes up for what you lack.

If you thought you were good enough to have gotten into PE earlier in your career, they will want to know why you didn't. Perhaps you didn't know the path. Perhaps you went to a regional school or were at a smaller bank or consulting firm where the knowledge of the path was not as pervasive. It's possible that you took your career in another direction and only found your stride in finance after your first few jobs.

As you embark on your PE job hunt, there are some specific strategies that can help you put your best foot forward. Before you initiate the process, it should be a given that you are a top performer and are most likely at a well-respected investment bank, consulting firm, or perhaps accounting firm as a transaction professional (Chapter VI focuses on strategies for more traditional accountants). If you aren't, it will be incrementally more difficult for you to break in.

At this point, getting exposure will be a key to your success, and our first recommendation is to do what you can to make yourself visible to PE/LBO funds if you're not already. The best way to do that is to get into a PE-related group if that is still possible. Being in a group such as financial sponsors, leveraged finance, or even M&A (or a comparable one in a consulting or accounting firm that works on the other side of LBO/PE deals) will allow you to be viewed as more deal-ready by some PE firms.

Our second suggestion is to make every effort to get close enough to your clients so that they become more willing to be advocates for you. We've noticed that most of the investment bankers who make the transition into PE come from groups that have worked in some way with PE funds, and in many cases those bankers ended up joining one of their clients (see Case Study 27). This is especially important to those bankers, consultants, and accounting transaction professionals who are not in groups that work with PE funds. Many top CEOs seem to be networked into PE funds, but they will more likely only proactively recommend pure all-stars who they believe truly outperformed for them. Maybe the CEO saw the value you created for his business and can suggest that you can step in and do the same for the partners of a PE fund. Either way, in our experience, finance professionals who get into PE without having been in a group that gave them exposure to PE funds are at least fluent in PE deals and therefore able to keep up in interviews.

The third part of your plan should be getting a senior member of your firm to champion your cause. Many professionals we see securing positions at this point in their careers had managing directors at their firm support them, often by placing a call to a PE fund on their behalf (or at least they were willing to call once a candidate had traction with a particular fund to which they had some connection). Give a thorough read to Case Study 26 to see how helpful a senior person's contacts can be.

CASE STUDIES

As we indicated before, these are all examples of people who broke into private equity a little later in their careers. For all of them, the combination of being a late bloomer, a high achiever, extremely tenacious, and visible to PE firms created opportunities for them.

Case Study 26: An All-Star Banker Makes It

This person didn't go to a top-five business school, but he was a star performer at a top-tier investment bank. Note how he had CEOs and clients make calls on his behalf.

■ ■ ■

My undergraduate degree in accounting led me to a job with a major accounting firm in the audit department. At the time I had heard of a few major LBO firms but was generally unfamiliar with the private equity industry. The accounting job seemed like a reasonable first step to take out of undergrad. I spent four years at the firm and then decided to go to business school. I had become interested in private equity through friends and thought that a post-MBA position in investment banking was the best route to get there. I also knew that an MBA was a great long-term career move regardless of the moves I made immediately following graduate school.

During my second year of business school I made some attempts to learn more about the PE industry, but quickly realized that without prior PE experience it was a long shot. I also learned that banking was not a sure route into PE—banking provides good deal experience, which is a requirement for PE, but there were tons of MBA students out there with prior PE experience and they would get the few available jobs over people without any PE experience. At the time I knew that my two biggest hurdles were no PE experience and no real deal experience. This process also confirmed that the best way to get into PE would be to work at one of the premier investment banks, but this route would still be a challenge.

I decided to accept an offer from a premier investment bank during the fall of my second year after spending a summer at the firm. I felt that working for this firm would be a great resume builder and was a better option than toiling for months in the post-MBA PE job market. Given my background, I assumed that if I was lucky enough to get a PE job it would be with a no-name firm that didn't necessarily have a stellar track record—so working for a top-tier I-bank made a lot of sense. Before accepting, I made some calls to PE folks and friends in the industry. Everyone told me that, for me, getting into PE would be an uphill battle. They all told me to go work for the bank for a few years, so I did.

As an associate I was in a generalist group doing deal execution, M&A, and various financings. I had a long-term interest in PE but was firmly committed to succeeding in banking in the short term. At the time, my thoughts were "I'm doing this now and I'll see what it's like. If I like it, I'll stay. If not, I'll look around." I put the PE search on the back burner.

This was 2001 and there was a recession. A lot of my banking colleagues had been laid off so I was happy to have a job. My first year and a half was rough—the markets were bad and deal activity came to a halt. The following 18 months were much better as deal activity picked up significantly and the firm was quite lean thanks to numerous rounds of layoffs. Anyone who survived got good deal experience. We had small teams and I worked on M&A, debt financings, and a few PE deals. I got to know people at PE firms and worked with their portfolio companies.

Unfortunately, there is no published list of firms that will hire people without prior PE experience, so it was a bit of a buck-shot approach to the market.

At the end of 2003 I began making calls to assess the possibility of a move into PE. Once January 2004 rolled around I launched a broad PE search. I made lots of calls—to clients, to headhunters and to friends in the industry. Some CEOs/clients made calls on my behalf and through that process I lined up a few interviews. My understanding was still that to get a post MBA job in PE one would need prior principal investing experience. When I launched my search process people confirmed that my lack of PE experience would be a significant impediment. I also quickly learned that once you are out of business school there is no fluid hiring market—it's more like a spot market where people get hired once in a while. As such you need to be in front of as many firms as possible so that when they are hiring you will likely be on their radar screens. Casting a broad net was important. I eventually found a PE fund that was open to my background. Unfortunately, there is no published list of firms that will hire people without prior PE experience so it was a bit of a buckshot approach to the market.

For me, being at one of the top investment banks was crucial. It made me (and my resume) stand out, especially because I was a generalist. I'd say if you are a specialist banker, the group you are in is important. There is no doubt that the brand name of the firm that you join is crucial. If you are using the bank as a stepping-stone and have choices, I would say always go with the best brand-name firm even if you do not like the group/people as much. For me, it was an easy decision because I liked the people and the firm a lot.

If I could dial back the clock to when I was 22, I would have gone into banking after undergrad. Taking that path would have saved me a few years. The path I chose eventually led to a position in PE but it was a long process. I would say that building a network is crucial. It's important that you develop a personal rapport with your professional contacts. In my case, my contacts opened doors for me that would have been closed otherwise. In the end, it's a combination of being good at what you do, being very opportunistic and very aggressive, and, of course, catching some breaks along the way.

Case Study 27: A Top Banker Joins a Client

This person was a top performer in undergrad and in banking and had an MBA from a top school. He was also able to prove himself over time to his client. He helped his own cause by leveraging his personal and business network.

■ ■ ■

My path into PE was definitely circuitous and difficult to manage. I went to a military academy, where I pursued a major in the social sciences. At the end of my five-year service commitment as an armor officer, I decided it was time to go to business school for a variety of reasons. Based on my limited exposure to the private sector at that time, I thought I would follow many of my nonmilitary friends into consulting post business school. It seemed to offer the best training for someone with my background.

Many of my business school classmates had come from PE and, to a person, all of them wanted to return to the industry. Their descriptions of their experiences and responsibilities sounded exciting, so I continued to learn more. In contrast, those who had come out of banking and consulting didn't seem to have as much enthusiasm about going back.

I soon realized that there was no way I would be able to join a PE firm with my background. Everyone I spoke to encouraged me to do something else in a related field and try to get into PE later. If I was determined to become a PE professional, they encouraged me to work in an M&A group at a leading investment bank first. But even with that addition to my background, my chances of transferring into PE post-MBA with no pre-MBA PE experience were slim.

I ended up taking an associate position at a top bank, where I was fortunate to work on portfolio company transactions for my current PE firm. Along the way, I asked many folks for general PE career advice. Time and time again, I was told how difficult it would be to make the transition from banking. "The PE skill set is just too different and your timing is too atypical," they said.

When I entered my third year at the bank, I figured it was the last year I could leave without wasting time. An extra year in banking wouldn't make me any more marketable to a PE firm. It was time to focus either on leaving banking or on staying and becoming a managing director. I made the choice to move on. I wanted to work at a late-stage, large-scale technology-focused fund on the West Coast. I thought the leadership and management skills I learned in the military, coupled with the deal experience I gained in banking, could be conducive to leading teams of consultants, bankers, lawyers, and accountants on complex PE deals. When I met with PE folks during the recruiting process, I asked them to set aside the bias against my banking background and focus on the skills required for success in PE—quantitative skills, analytical rigor, and highly developed process management experience. It took a lot of selling, but it worked out and I joined a West Coast PE firm as a principal.

The hardest thing was convincing people to interview me. I called 10 to 20 business school classmates before beginning my search process and I didn't get many words of encouragement. No one thought I could make the transition. When I did see job listings the specs certainly didn't include my background. Even headhunters told me I would have to do it on my own.

I set a uniquely high bar for what I wanted to do in PE, knowing that I also would have been thrilled to stay in banking for the rest of my career if things didn't work out in PE.

If I could go back in time, the only thing I would do differently is stay in even closer contact with more people in the PE industry throughout my banking career. Individual relationships are critical. Building and maintaining those relationships over time—and staying patient and flexible—allowed my search to be successful. It requires a bit of work, to be sure.

In my case, the stars aligned for my current firm to hire at the same time I was looking. It would be hard to count on that happening again. Most important, I wanted to ensure that I was happy with my alternatives. I set a uniquely high bar for what I wanted to do in PE, knowing that I also would have been thrilled to stay in banking for the rest of my career if things didn't work out in PE. While my road to PE may have been eased by doing something in PE before business school, that path perhaps would have been even more challenging. Making the transition from a tank into PE overnight, without any financial background, would have been tough.

Case Study 28: The Bold Approach: Direct Outreach to a Firm

Take note of the especially creative way this person got his foot in the door of a major PE fund. The strategy may not work for everyone, but the determination should be emulated.

■ ■ ■

I graduated with a degree in English literature and religion—not the traditional course of study that someone would pursue to go into finance. I tried to get a job in publishing, but came up empty. I had interned at an investment bank one summer during college and ended up returning to the same bank, working on the mortgage-backed securities trading desk. I had never taken an accounting or finance class and had little understanding of what the traders were doing, but the buzz excited me and I wanted to be a part of it.

I stayed at the bank for two years. I could have stayed longer, but I had applied to business school and got in. My plan was to go into I-banking. In business school I majored in decision sciences (statistics), accounting, and finance. I interned during the summer at a different bank and had an offer to come back full-time after graduation. Somewhat fortuitously, I met a partner from one of the leading banks at a high school reunion. He advised me that if I wanted to move ahead in the industry I should work at either his bank or one other, but not the one at which I had an offer. He ended up getting me an interview and offered me an associate position. I did a wide range of corporate finance work on industrial, real estate, lodging, and gaming companies.

I've had more luck with nontraditional routes than traditional routes. I know that most people get into the business the traditional 2-2-2 way, but I suspect that is because it's the path of least resistance.

My thoughts quickly turned to PE. I didn't like the large institutional feel of a big bank and wanted to get closer to the action. I figured that swapping banking for a principal investing role would put me even closer to the action and away from being just an adviser. No one really told me it would be hard to get into PE.

My fortunes took a turn for the better when I wrote a letter to a leading figure in the world of private equity. I had read that this person was leaving his firm to start a new one. It was a gutsy move, but I wrote him and said it would be great to get to know him. At the time there was no money going into the industrial economy; it was all earmarked for tech and telecom. This person had a view similar to mine on the importance of industrial companies. I wrote that I thought what he was saying made a lot of sense. After sending the letter I harassed his secretary for weeks and finally met with him and his partners. I put it on the line and said I wanted to be an associate at his firm. It took a lot of coaxing, but I got in.

I've had more luck with nontraditional routes than traditional routes. I know that most people get into the business the traditional 2-2-2 way, but I suspect that is because it's the path of least resistance. The fact is the skills that you use in PE are not only those you learned in the banking and consulting programs. Now that I'm working in the industry, from my point of view if we're hiring someone who worked at PepsiCo for two years in corporate development and knows modeling, that person may be more valuable than a pure banker.

Over the next 5 to 10 years I suspect that the hiring focus will change and the nontraditional will become traditional. Candidates should realize that the world has changed. There are a lot more funds. People should do their homework and find out: What are the senior guys in it for? Do they have one fund, or more? Are they good investors? How do they make decisions? And will you be a part of those decisions?

Chapter VI

POSTGRADUATE SCHOOL: EXPERIENCED NON–DEAL/ ADVISORY PROFESSIONALS

Perhaps you are a lawyer, doctor, accountant, or maybe you work in industry. Although you have yet to reach the pinnacle of your current profession, you're definitely on that track. Nevertheless, you feel like you have a true sense for business and have decided that you are interested in becoming an investor. You want to know if it's possible to transition into private equity and, if so, how this can best be accomplished.

Even though you have probably established yourself in your profession, you may be intrigued about becoming an investor or owner. It's not that you're unhappy in your current profession, but you believe private equity may be more appealing and could be your road to long-term career satisfaction. We should point out that those who secure a PE position at this juncture (the non-partner, non-CEO level) are more the exceptions as they most likely lack any kind of proven investment track record and most requisite finance/deal skills. At this point there is no set pattern, no hiring cycle, and no getting around the fact that you're off the typical path followed by most.

Nevertheless, if this is something you're passionate about, we encourage you to pursue your goal. Whether your background is purely legal, medical, accounting (this does not refer to the transaction role described in the previous chapter), or if you are an industry professional, you may be able to make the case that you have an important skill set that pure finance candidates don't and which can add value to a PE fund. Examples of these skills could be deep science/industry knowledge (that could come with a good network as well), business building/turnaround skills, legal skills associated with structuring complex transactions (especially bankruptcies), and forensic accounting expertise that allows for more penetrating financial analysis.

Although there have been some very prominent CEOs who have moved directly into a private equity fund (such as Jack Welch of GE joining Clayton, Dubilier & Rice, and Louis Gerstner joining The Carlyle Group), that is not the level we discuss in this chapter. This class of industry professionals would be able to walk into several PE funds and a position would probably be created for them. This chapter is more about offering ideas on how to transition into PE for professionals who are advanced in their career but have not reached that apex.

BREAKING IN

Based on our experience, many of the non–deal/advisory professionals who enter private equity or venture capital funds benefit from a direct proposal from someone they know and are not necessarily actively pursuing a move into PE. Those who don't have such good fortune have to map out a longer-term strategy to break into PE by taking an intermediate step. In those instances, we found that most lawyers, doctors, accountants, and industry professionals secured positions via a couple of common strategies, one which we'll call a back-door method and a second that we describe as a two-step process.

 **Glocap Insight** — If and when you do interview for a PE job at this stage, make sure you arrive armed with specific investment ideas (or, better yet, maybe even existing deal flow).

We define the back-door method as using your profession to get a foot in the door at a PE fund (for example, a lawyer becoming an in-house counsel at a fund) and parlaying that over time into an investment role at the same fund. The two-step path, by contrast, entails taking an intermediate step into a more direct feeder industry, such as consulting or investment banking, and then using that as a launchpad into PE. If you are committed to getting into private equity, either path would offer an opportunity.

However, in our opinion you also have to be ready for it to *not* work, or at least be prepared for the process to take time. You will likely have the most success if you have the mind-set that you would be happy staying long-term in whatever intermediate step you take. And, most importantly, you could jeopardize any chances of making the switch if you don't allow yourself enough time to excel in your new role.

The Back-Door Method

The back-door method works well for lawyers and senior accountants who can fill similar roles at private equity funds. For example, as mentioned earlier, a lawyer could join a PE firm as in-house general counsel. This type of entry can also work for industry professionals with strong operating backgrounds, as increasingly more funds have developed in-house roles that work primarily with portfolio companies. These roles, which may focus on assisting portfolio companies with sales force optimization, cost reduction, and so on, can be suited for someone with similar operations experience. These roles have opened the door for industry professionals to join a fund and possibly eventually take on more prominent roles in new deals. Industry professionals specifically from tech-related fields or entrepreneurs with tech experience can also use the back-door method to get into a venture fund by becoming an *entrepreneur in residence* (see Chapter VII for a more detailed discussion of that role). Note: Most of the industry professionals whom we have observed securing a role at a PE fund did have some type of formal business training, either before or after their industry experience.

While in either case you will not be entering as a dedicated deal professional, you will at least be in the mix of working in transactions and could possibly, over time, develop into such a role (this is by no means a guarantee). Although there is little use for an in-house doctor, an MD could also follow this path by becoming a special adviser to a health care fund and then perhaps a board member of a portfolio company in his field of expertise before being invited to join the fund in an investment capacity. A senior accountant at a prominent institution could parlay his skills into a role as a CFO at a PE fund and could eventually move into a senior investment position.

No matter your profession, if you get into a PE fund through this method you should make the most of the opportunity while you are there, and try to avoid rushing things. It would be a mistake to go to the partners of the fund during your first few months as an in-house general counsel or special adviser and ask to move to the investment side. They should not be given cause to believe that you have your eyes on another job in their firm. Most importantly, you must be willing and mentally prepared to buckle down, work hard, perform well, and make the most of your given position.

We know of an accountant who got in via the back-door method. After working at a major accounting firm for five years, this person joined a client—a start-up PE fund—as a controller and then switched to a larger fund that needed a CFO. This fund allowed him to work a little on deals (he was a liaison to CFOs at portfolio companies after deals closed and got some operations experience from those contacts), but his main role was CFO. He eventually received an offer to join another large, well-known fund—also as a CFO. However, he had obviously proven his potential to his current fund and was offered a full-time associate position on the investment side if he would stay. Needless to say, he took it—and hired his own replacement CFO.

The Two-Step Process

Another way in which people make the move into PE at this stage of their careers is what we call the two-step process. This can work for lawyers and accountants, but it is often effective for doctors or industry professionals as well. In this process someone would first move into an investment bank or consulting firm or other deal/advisory role to learn some of the necessary transaction skills and then attempt to transition into a PE fund. We have seen this path be helpful to doctors and scientists because the finance or consulting skills obtained in an intermediate step, in combination with their medical/science knowledge and training, could potentially make them better positioned to get into a health care or biotech fund than would an average career banker or consultant without that additional accreditation. (Most commonly, the MDs who get in at this stage of their careers were the ones who may not have practiced medicine for a long period.) Once you get into an appropriate banking or consulting group, your move into PE will be similar to the route followed by the professionals we described in Chapter V.

One MD we know who secured a role in PE by taking this path joined a major consulting firm after his medical training. At the consulting firm, he specialized in pharmaceuticals and medical products and worked closely with the senior management of large and specialty pharmaceutical companies. He also focused on alliances in the industry and product launches and then joined a PE firm to work on its biopharmaceutical investments. Scientists and MDs may also go through a two-step process by first moving to an industry role and then potentially making the jump directly from there. As people who can often be on the forefront of groundbreaking discoveries, they may be able to join a biotech or medical devices company right after medical school or getting their PhD. In that way they could get involved in developing breakthrough products and lay the early groundwork to pursue a position at a health care VC firm (we go into that in more detail in the next chapter).

WHAT ABOUT THOSE FROM INDUSTRY?

In our experience, a mid-level industry candidate (below the CEO, CFO, COO, etc. level) with non-tech operations experience will have a more difficult time making the move into a more traditional private equity role, especially if that person has *only* operations and not much deal/finance experience. (In this chapter we don't talk much about technology industry professionals as they are usually targeted by venture capital funds, which are discussed in Chapter VII.)

The non-tech candidates who historically have had what it takes to make it into PE are usually those who have excelled in many different categories, having substantial success managing divisions and products and helping grow and/or turn around companies. Take the case of a senior manager at a corporation such as General Electric who may have helped launch several products and grown two divisions while having direct management of a few hundred people. This person wakes up one day and thinks, "I'm an operator. I've successfully built companies just like the PE/LBO pros, and I'd like a share of that upside." He/she may have the skills to move into a PE/LBO fund, but will have to convince the fund that they can create similar substantial value in a less structured environment and that they are generally worth the risk over other PE finance pros whom funds can always take first.

Examples of Some Who Made it Directly

Here are some brief examples of professionals who made it directly into PE. Given that many of those who made it this way benefited from good fortune, it's hard to give identical advice on how to pursue this means of entry, but the stories still have value. Something worth emphasizing is that all these individuals were top performers and had direct exposure to the PE industry.

- Person A was the leading science officer at a major research institute. In addition to having an MD degree, he also had a PhD and an MBA. He was an accomplished author and won awards for his biomedical and technology research. His scientific and research background allowed him to join a PE fund where he focused on biotechnology and medical device companies.
- Person B had a varied background as he worked at a major accounting firm prior to law school. After graduating he spent four years as a mergers and acquisitions associate at a leading law firm. His legal work gave him exposure to PE and he was invited to join a family office structuring and negotiating public and private investments.
- Person C was an M&A lawyer who had significant private equity experience at his firm. While practicing law he got to know one of his LBO clients, and they asked him to join the firm with the understanding that they would train him in exchange for some help with legal housekeeping.

CASE STUDY

Following is a case study of an attorney who transitioned into a role at a buyout fund.

Case Study 29: An Attorney Moves into a Distressed Shop

This lawyer secured a position at an LBO fund directly after being exposed to private equity for many years.

■ ■ ■

Before entering private equity, I spent 14 years working as a bankruptcy and finance lawyer. I became intrigued with working as a principal in a distressed-debt private equity investment firm after working with, and sometimes against, a number of distressed-debt investors. I thought my legal background in leveraged finance and insolvency would suit me well as a principal with a firm that invests in distressed debt, since a major part of the investment analysis requires an understanding of creditors' rights and the bankruptcy process.

Fortunately, my law firm was the general fund counsel for just such a fund. And, even more fortunately, the fund was looking for someone with legal bankruptcy experience. This firm was launching a new multi-strategy fund that had a significant target allocation for distressed debt. One of my colleagues at the law firm told me about the opportunity and I approached the PE firm and got an interview. I went through the same interview process that the candidates from traditional business backgrounds went through, which included the preparation of an investment analysis of a company selected by the PE firm. That took a lot of work and required me to come up a steep learning curve. Aside from the relative unfamiliarity of the project, I was handicapped by the lack of access to the financial resources that someone at a bulge-bracket investment bank would have. Fortunately, I did well enough on the project for the firm to hire me as a director. As the firm grew from $800 million in assets under management to $2 billion, I added general counsel duties to my responsibilities. Now about 60 percent of my time is spent doing deal work and 40 percent is general counsel work.

You really have to become known by people in the business who can verify that you know what you're doing.

The bottom line is it's not easy to transition from law into PE unless you start on it very early or late in your career. And when and if you do make it, you should know that PE is harder than it looks. Business analysis is different from legal analysis and is not something that most lawyers have experience doing. If you make a mistake, you, and not your client, have to live with the results. Moreover, there is no shortage of lawyers who would like to be doing anything other than practicing law.

If you want to shift to the business side, you have to make yourself visible. Your best entry will be through connections, not by throwing your resume around. This is a very clubby world and it is very hard to get in. You really have to become known by people in the business who can verify that you know what you're doing.

Chapter VII

BREAKING INTO VENTURE CAPITAL

Although early-stage venture capital is a subsector of private equity, the career path and the entry points have many unique characteristics. For the most part, breaking into the world of early-stage venture capital has enough of its own nuances that we felt it deserved its own chapter.

Do you closely follow companies that start as a couple of people with an idea and become industry leaders? If you do, you can probably not only name the founders of those companies, but also the venture capitalists who provided the start-up funding. Perhaps you are attracted to revolutionary technologies and want to be a venture capitalist who helps discover, fund, and build the companies that will comprise the next generation of technology or life science leaders. Maybe you are even considering working at one of those companies or starting your own. Either way, you may think working at a VC fund will get you that much closer to being an insider at one of these success stories. You know what? You're right—but not necessarily in the way you may envision. While the career path to partner is not as defined as it is in later-stage private equity, simply working in venture capital can provide a great springboard to other attractive opportunities.

To set the tone for this chapter, we offer a description of what you can expect from your first role in venture capital. Following that, we provide an overview of what is involved in breaking into the VC world. We also outline what it entails to evolve into a partner, but since that process is so unique we address it more specifically later in this chapter. We also offer four case studies of candidates who broke into venture capital in different ways. To emphasize even more clearly what VC funds look for when hiring, we thought it would be especially useful to present some job specifications

103

from actual searches that we were mandated to fill; you will find these at the end of the chapter.

For nearly everyone who is just beginning their initial pursuit of a position in venture capital, we advise focusing less on the career track and, instead, more on merely breaking into venture capital. If it seems that this chapter goes out of the way to emphasize that your first role in VC is less likely to set you on the path to becoming a partner, it's because that is one of the things that makes venture capital so different from other careers in finance, and it's something that will affect your future in the industry as well.

The career path in venture capital can have key differences from that of later-stage private equity. For example, one of the main pieces of advice we give people looking to build a career in later-stage PE is to get in as early as possible. In venture capital, however, getting in early is not necessarily the most relevant requirement. In fact, getting on the partner track has less to do with having an advanced degree (MBA, PhD, etc.) or a few years of banking, consulting, or operating experience. In the venture world, one of the biggest challenges—and one of the themes of this chapter—is that getting in is one thing, but staying in and becoming a partner is a separate challenge altogether.

YOUR FIRST ROLE

We purposefully don't call the first role in venture capital *entry-level*, as doing so would be misleading, even though this is typically a support role. Although it represents the first entrance into the world of venture capital, the position should not necessarily be viewed as a junior role or the first stop on an automatic path to a career in VC. For simplicity's sake we refer to these positions as *non-partner* roles.

Regardless of the point in your career at which you join a VC fund, the actual role is usually very similar—you will support the partners by helping source, screen, qualify, and structure new deals while at the same time supporting some of the portfolio company activity. However, the level of responsibilities can vary depending on your prior experiences, and even if you take on some very senior responsibilities you should not necessarily infer that you are close to becoming a partner. Traditionally, in most cases, your initial foray will be a limited one in terms of duration—it could be two years, maybe three or four, but frequently not much more.

As you will see in Job Searches 1 through 3, when VC funds hire at the pre-MBA level they generally require that candidates have a few years of work experience with a background in banking, consulting, and/or operations as well as a good knowledge of technology or biotech/health care/medical devices (also with a preference toward those having engineering/science degrees). The funds that hire at the post-MBA level more frequently implement what we call an *apprentice model*. This is also not usually expected to be a promotional role, but given the increased requirements—most funds ask for several years of senior operations experience, a deep knowledge of a specific industry, strong finance and market knowledge, and at least a bachelor's or master's

> ### Glocap Insight
>
> In early-stage venture capital the *pre-MBA* and *post-MBA* designations are even less literal than they are in later-stage private equity. Rather than categorizing them as pre- and post-MBA, it could be more logical to classify the non-partner opportunities in venture capital as *junior non-partner* and *senior non-partner* roles.
>
> We define pre-MBAs as professionals who have generally been out of college for five years or less and have spent the majority of that time as the most junior professionals in their organization or team. Post-MBAs are those who have been in the workforce for at *least* five years (sometimes with as much as 10, 15, or more years of experience). They may or may not have gone to business school but, more importantly, have probably moved up the ranks at least once and are starting to take on more mid- to senior-level responsibilities.

degree in engineering/science—it's expected that post-MBAs bring more to the table on day one than pre-MBAs.

Part of the reason it's so hard to climb through the ranks of a VC fund is the common belief that to be a successful venture capitalist you will have to demonstrate consistent value creation over the long term. As you would expect, it's unlikely you will be able to do that while at a VC fund for only a few years, and VC firms are probably less inclined to keep non-partners around for 10 years while they try to develop the skill set needed to build successful companies. In fact, the logical conclusion is that you will have to do that outside of your venture investing role.

From what we've seen, possessing about 10 years of successful operating experience *pre-venture* significantly increases the chances that you will be invited to stay on at your VC fund, because at that point you may have acquired advanced business building skills—but of course there is no guarantee. A good example of someone who entered venture capital with significant previous operational experience can be found in Case Study 33. As of mid-2006 this person had been out of undergrad for 16 years. He has a bachelor's and a master's in electrical engineering and spent nine years steadily progressing in various industry positions in both product design and marketing roles. Six years after joining the fund his long-term status was still uncertain. As you would expect, the reverse is also true: The less operating experience you have pre-venture, the stricter the two- to three-year commitment will be.

AN INSIDER'S VIEW OF THE VC MIND-SET

In his essay, "Mastering the Fundamentals of Venture Capital" in *Inside The Minds: The Ways of the VC* (Aspatore Books, 2003), Terry McGuire, co-founder of Polaris Venture Partners, points out that venture is an intuitive business, which makes an apprenticeship appropriate. He writes that:

Developing an intuition for what is going to work requires exposure to many great entrepreneurs (and many unsuccessful entrepreneurs), many great deals (and many mediocre ones), many promising new technologies (and many that fail to deliver). This takes time; it can't happen overnight. Even when a venture capitalist has done his homework and studies all the objective data carefully, investment decisions boil down to gut reactions.

McGuire goes on to point out that his mentor, Stan Golder of Golder Thoma Cressey, once told him that "venture capitalists use four parts of their bodies—their minds, hearts, guts, and the seat of their pants. The last three have nothing to do with quantitative analysis. You have to develop a sense for the deal."

BREAKING IN: THE PROCESS

If we had written this guide in the early 1990s, there probably would have been little advice we could have given about breaking into venture capital. Most would agree that, back then, the VC industry was mostly comprised of an exclusive group of funds in which each had not much more than a mere handful of partners. The small majority that did employ non-partner professionals rarely promoted them through the ranks to partner roles.

The industry, however, has evolved in many ways. Today's market is more global; there are more deals to pursue, more companies to research, more conferences to attend, and overall more competition to identify and invest in the highest quality deals. Table 7.1 presents some data on how the VC market has evolved. The nature of today's entrepreneurs has also changed the dynamics of the industry, as many are not necessarily aggressively seeking start-up financing for their ideas (especially given that many of these are Internet businesses, which do not need as much initial capital).

Table 7.1   Evolution of the Venture Capital Market

	1994	2007
Number of VC firms in existence	391	798
Number of VC funds in existence	660	1,343
Number of professionals	4,210	9,257
Number of first-time VC funds raised	16	33
Number of VC funds raising money	128	206
VC capital under management ($ billions)	35.2	277.2
Average VC capital under management per firm ($ millions)	89.9	235.8
Average VC fund size to date ($ millions)	40.7	295.5
Average VC fund size raised ($ millions)	71.7	175.6

Source: Thomson Financial/Venture Capital

Therefore, to secure these types of deals, venture capital firms are increasingly looking for non-partner resources who are networked into this community of entrepreneurs, in order to gain better access. The scope of technology has also expanded dramatically, seemingly making it harder for partners to maintain by themselves the level of expertise and global network needed to find and make the best investments. Although the industry remains very clubby, VC firms are willing to hire non-partners to provide the necessary leverage to stay competitive and successful.

Insider Tip ▷

From a Partner at a Venture Capital Fund

I would say someone shouldn't even think of working in venture unless they like to compete, keep score, and win. For me, the three most important attributes/skills of a venture capital analyst are (1) good instincts–knowing how to judge people, smelling the money, and getting to the core of an issue quickly; (2) skill at building, maintaining, and leveraging networks; and (3) the ability to make objective decisions–sometimes the hard decisions, and not falling in love with a deal.

We don't only target business school grads. We once hired a summer intern from Stanford Business School who had a law degree and no technology operating experience into an early-stage technology venture fund. We liked him because he was enthusiastic, bright, and hungry.

For an early-stage venture fund, the best way to prepare is to have operating experience so you can realistically judge business plans and be helpful to entrepreneurs.

We estimate that 60 to 80 well-known VC firms hire at the pre-MBA and post-MBA levels each year. Pre-MBA hiring in venture capital can follow a cycle similar to the buyout world (outlined in Chapter IV) as certain VC funds compete for some of the same candidates—mainly tech bankers and consultants, and especially those with an engineering background. At the post-MBA level, VC funds typically hire with less frequency, and when they do it's generally with less urgency. In fact, from what we've seen, VC funds rarely need someone at the post-MBA level, but at the same time they can always make room for an all-star. We've had venture clients who were not looking to add personnel specifically tell us, "If a great candidate comes along, we'd be happy to take a look at them."

There are few defined entry points at which professionals generally break into venture capital. Instead, there is more of a continuous spectrum of instances throughout your career when you can break in—including pre-MBA, right out of business school, and even several years out of graduate school (as in private equity, it's rare that someone enters venture capital straight out of undergrad). The key to getting a VC role is being patient and disciplined. If now is not the right time to get in, you should continue to build your skill set to be better prepared for the next window of opportunity.

BREAKING IN: THE SKILL SET

To understand the skills required by VC funds, it might be worth revisiting the differences between early-stage venture capital and later-stage PE/LBO investing. To refresh your memory, PE/LBO funds invest mostly in later-stage, mature, cash-flow-producing companies that are usually profitable and therefore more straightforward to evaluate. By contrast, early-stage venture capital funds target companies with little or no cash flow and rarely utilize debt in their investments; therefore they put less of a premium on the pure financial modeling and deal skills valued by PE/LBO funds.

Venture capital investment analysis frequently focuses on product risk (will a specific product even work?), market risk (if it does work, will customers buy it?), and ultimately on getting a company to profitability and positioning it for a possible sale or IPO. Venture capital investing combines deep technology and business-building expertise with good financial know-how, so not surprisingly, VC funds target candidates with operations exposure, solid business skills and investment instincts, and an extensive knowledge of the industry in which a specific fund invests.

Given the importance of hands-on experience, VC funds tend to prefer professionals with direct product management backgrounds—seeing products from the conceptual stage through to sales. Consultants, by the nature of their project or assignment work, arguably develop a good, balanced understanding of finance, strategy, and operations, and are thus also frequently sought after. Candidates with pure investment banking backgrounds are generally less emphasized because their strength is in the numbers and deal complexity, whereas venture investing is less about evaluating cash flow and more about analyzing companies and products that may still be in their infancy.

Venture capital funds favor those professionals with technical undergraduate degrees, mainly in electrical engineering (EE) or computer science (CS) (most job specifications list EE/CS degrees as a strong preference if not a requirement) but also in mathematics, physics, and biology, and so on. A master's, a medical degree, and/or sometimes a PhD (usually in the case of health care–focused VCs) are also common requirements (see Job Search 7). We have seen candidates break in and excel without these degrees, but they were able to make up for it by developing a deep expertise in a specific technology as well as having a combination of strategy, product management, and business development skills (a good example is Case Study 30).

Over the past few years, some select early-/mid-stage venture capital funds have expanded their traditional investing activities to include more later-stage venture/growth equity investments, venture buyouts, and even some leveraged investing (Table 7.2 lists the largest VC funds ever raised). Some mid-size firms have also adopted multistage platforms. This movement toward more multistage investing has

Table 7.2   Largest Global Venture Capital Funds Ever Raised (as of December 2007)

Rank	Fund Name	Firm Name	Location	Year	Amount ($Billion)
1	TCV VII LP	Technology Crossover Ventures	Palo Alto, CA	2007	$3.00
2	Oak Investment Partners XII LP	Oak Investment Partners	Westport, CT	2006	$2.56
3	New Enterprise Associates XII LP	New Enterprise Associates	Baltimore	2006	$2.50
4	New Enterprise Associates X LP	New Enterprise Associates	Baltimore	2000	$2.30
5	Spectrum Equity Investors IV LP	Spectrum Equity Investors	Boston	2001	$2.00
6	Technology Crossover Ventures IV LP	Technology Crossover Ventures	Palo Alto, CA	2000	$1.70
7	VantagePoint Venture Partners IV LP	VantagePoint Venture Partners	San Bruno, CA	2000	$1.61
8	Oak Investment Partners X LP	Oak Investment Partners	Westport, CT	2001	$1.60
9	Menlo Ventures IX LP	Menlo Ventures	Menlo Park, CA	2000	$1.50
	Oak Investment Partners XI LP	Oak Investment Partners	Westport, CT	2004	$1.50
	Softbank Capital Partners LP	Softbank Capital	Newton Center, MA	1999	$1.50
12	Technology Crossover Ventures VI LP	Technology Crossover Ventures	Palo Alto, CA	2005	$1.40
13	Weston Presidio Capital IV LP	Weston Presidio Capital	Boston	2000	$1.37
14	Insight Venture Partners VI LP	Insight Venture Partners	New York	2007	$1.25
	Mobius Technology Ventures VI LP	Mobius Venture Capital Inc.	Boulder, CO	2000	$1.25

Source: *Private Equity Analyst*

led many of those funds to increasingly prefer junior-level (associates) and mid-level (senior associates/vice presidents) candidates who possess strong domain expertise (technology/health care knowledge) and financial/deal skills as well.

From a Managing Director at a VC Fund

In 1997 I made an investment in optical technologies for communication applications. I was considering making another four or five investments in the space. I had a reasonable grasp of the markets and applications but wanted to be able to evaluate the alternative approaches (i.e., different technologies) in depth. So I hired a recent PhD in his late twenties who had worked in the business for a couple of years. He had the specific technology depth as well as a taste for the competitive environment. We scoped it out together. Together, he and I scouted out some of the more interesting and promising opportunities. More importantly, we avoided the major dogs in the space.

BREAKING IN: HELPING YOUR CAUSE

Even if you have the academic degrees and the skills previously listed, breaking into venture capital will still be tough. One of the first ways to help your cause is to find a way to get in front of VC funds, because they may not necessarily know where to find you. Venture capital funds know that the next generation of top associates and principals can come from many different places (consulting, operations, banking, research, etc.) and be in numerous roles (business development, marketing, sales, etc.). So even if you are an ideal match for a venture fund, it may be difficult for anyone, including recruiters, to track you down.

One of the best ways to get the necessary exposure is to network with as many people in the venture community as you can. Every employment guide probably lists networking among its recommendations, but in the case of venture this holds true even more and should be an essential part of your strategy. As we said, venture is a clubby industry. Venture capital firms do deals together, work near each other, and are often in the same social circles. There are numerous conferences and industry-specific social gatherings that are good opportunities to meet people, especially in major tech hot spots such as Silicon Valley and the Boston area. If you get into that network, there will be a better chance of someone making an introduction for you.

Glocap Insight

Some venture capitalists will post openings on the alumni boards at their undergraduate and business schools or directly on the intranets of the larger pre-MBA investment banking or consulting programs. So if you went to a leading school or worked at a bulge-bracket firm, don't forget to check the job boards.

Another unique aspect of venture capital is that if the partners of a VC fund think you're good but have no position for you in the near term, they may still want to put in the effort to build goodwill with you. (Remember, club deals are still common in venture, so a fund may see you as a potential deal partner down the road.) In that case, don't be surprised if you speak with a VC fund and they tell you, "We're not looking, but I might have someone else I can introduce you to." The VC introductions can also extend to other channels—even recruiters. We frequently get candidate referrals from people we know in the industry and we give priority to those recommendations.

One additional way you can help your cause is by being on top of the VC industry basics, including how funds are structured and how they invest. If you are fortunate enough to land an interview, you will probably inhibit your progress if you are not familiar with commonly used terms such as *preferred equity, Series A and B financings, Angel funding, pre-money, post-money, up-round, down-round,* and so on. If you don't quite know these terms and their context, we recommend you learn them. (See Appendix A for a list of industry resources.)

Glocap Insight

VC firms, like their PE counterparts, still put a lot of weight on intangibles and the star quality of candidates. We've had one VC tell us flat out: "At the end of the day we're looking for someone with a high 'winner-factor.'" Another put it this way: "I want a future moneymaker to whom I would feel confident giving my own money."

THE ENTREPRENEUR IN RESIDENCE

Some funds have *entrepreneur in residence* (EIR) programs that allow professionals with a strong operational and/or entrepreneurial track record in a specific sector to break into venture capital. Above all, EIRs are encouraged to apply their sector-specific knowledge to pursue new business opportunities. By having an office at the VC firm, EIRs have the support of the firm's infrastructure and its network while utilizing the investment professionals as a sounding board. In addition to benefiting from having someone with sector expertise in the office, the venture fund also generally has right of first refusal to invest in the start-ups sourced or created by the EIR. Entrepreneurs in residence generally stay with a fund for an agreed upon length of time, but there is always the chance that they could be kept on in a more permanent role, and there is precedence as some have stayed on and become fully integrated into the partnership.

The EIR role can take on different forms at different funds. In a 2003 *Seattle Post-Intelligencer* article, "Venture Capital: VCs call on heavy hitters for help," Dan Rosen, a venture capitalist with Seattle's Frazier Technology Ventures (and now retired general partner), described the entrepreneur in residence as "one of those terms of ours that covers all sorts of things. In some cases, it is a holding place for somebody who you want to have in one of your portfolio companies. In other cases, it is somebody who helps define your strategy. And in other cases it really is somebody who has some specific skills that can help your companies in a lot of ways and does short stints with those companies."

THE KAUFFMAN FELLOWS PROGRAM

It's worth pointing out the existence of a unique program that offers an opportunity to level the playing field and help a handful of professionals enter VC each year. The Kauffman Fellows Program is a formal 24-month apprenticeship program designed to educate and train the next generation of leaders in venture capital and high-growth companies. The Fellowship, which began in 1994, combines an intense educational program with individual mentoring from professionals at major firms in the venture capital community. Kauffman Fellows work at leading VC firms that sponsor them.

The only two unconditional requirements to apply for the Fellowship are that you have a graduate degree in business, science, or technology and five years of full-time professional experience. (On average, Kauffman Fellows have 10 years of successful operating experience, deep domain expertise in a specific field, and a history of proven leadership, according to the program's web site, www.kauffmanfellows.org.) Candidates go through a series of interviews in person and then a matching process to pair them up with a VC fund.

Although this program offers an alternative entry option into venture capital, the Kauffman fellow frequently still has the same promotional uncertainty as individuals who landed non-partner roles in other ways.

ARE A FEW YEARS AS A NON-PARTNER WORTH IT?

At first glance, it may seem that the VC funds are getting more out of the non-partner role than you are, especially if working those initial few years doesn't necessarily set the stage for promotion or an eventual return in a more senior role. However, we don't see it that way and we don't think you should either. We believe there is a favorable quid pro quo in that you would also gain a lot from working at a VC fund.

At the least, a few years at a VC fund could open doors to some great opportunities, such as other roles in non-venture investing as well as roles in start-ups. There is a high likelihood that you will emerge from a few years in venture capital as an experienced technology or life sciences investor, and you could leverage that knowledge to do a host of other different things. For example, many professionals consider venture investing a great way to learn how to run their own company. As a junior professional, you will learn many best practices of early-stage businesses from accomplished business builders and investors. You will examine countless business plans, help construct term sheets, and get exposure to many different portfolio companies. All of this will give you a bird's-eye view of how funds are invested, how start-ups raise capital, how CEOs are hired, how deals are structured, etc. At the same time you will

> **Glocap Insight**
>
> In venture capital you can see a company go from 5 to 350 people, and you could see it happen multiple times. You will also read hundreds of business plans, which will hopefully help you avoid any pitfalls if you start your own company.

be privy to the inner workings of management strategy and product development and will see start-up companies go through several stages of growth.

It's possible that you may identify one of the start-ups that you work with as the next industry leader and end up joining it. Or, if the venture fund partners consider you an absolute top performer and a value creator, they may specifically ask you to take an operational role at one of their portfolio companies, thus keeping you close so they can continue to evaluate your development. We estimate that about half of the people who complete their term at a VC fund after a few years end up in operations to continue learning how to grow and manage businesses and products. Those who were in operations before they entered venture capital will most likely return in a more senior role, with a new set of managerial skills and a better understanding of cutting-edge technologies.

Of those who don't land a role in operations and instead return to the financial side of technology or life sciences, some have moved into public market investing with a hedge fund or equity research at an investment bank. (Note: They would most likely not have gained the modeling and deal skills required to join a later-stage PE fund or the M&A group of an investment bank.) Some junior professionals who are starting their careers as pre-MBAs may use their time in venture as a stepping-stone toward business school. Even if they end up leaving venture capital altogether, they too should be better off from the experience for the reasons we mentioned. We have seen a smaller percentage make a lateral move to another venture fund that values the training of those who have completed apprenticeships at other high-end funds, and with a lateral transition there's a good chance these professionals will be on the partner track at their new fund (see Job Search 9).

At the very least, you may find that getting into venture capital early will give you an idea about whether the industry is for you, which is a useful perspective to have since in most cases you would have little problem returning to doing what you did before you got in. In addition to the skills that you will acquire, you will also develop an all-important network in what we have said is a very tight-knit industry, and that alone will benefit you no matter what you do moving forward. There is no doubt that your time in venture capital will be a great learning experience and, of course, there is still the possibility that you can stay on at your fund and possibly get on a partner track.

BECOMING A PARTNER

Despite all of the challenges we have presented, you might still want to know how you can best position yourself to reach the pinnacle of a VC fund. Some professionals do join VC funds as partners, but they are usually those who have had considerable success in business/operations—maybe they launched a few successful companies and took them public or sold them—or are very successful in other areas (Al Gore joining Kleiner Perkins is one example). If you're in one of those categories of people, this guide is not for you. For the others (and that should be most of you) there are few shortcuts you can take to become a partner.

In a perfect world, VC funds would prefer to hire partners (or future partners) who have been involved in full product cycles—conception to commercialization—as well as full company cycles, from start-up to maturity. They would bring on professionals who have been at companies that have grown exponentially and preferably been sold or taken public for a significant profit. Not surprisingly, historically many partners at venture capital funds enter the industry as a second career after having been part of creating successful, profitable companies or profitable divisions of larger companies. Hence the catch-22: Generally, to become a partner at a VC firm, you have to have been very successful beforehand in your career, but if you were successful in building a company and reaped the financial rewards of that, you may not need or want a position at a VC fund.

Having said that, a more recent trend we have noticed is VC funds beginning to loosen the requirement that candidates have "substantial" success in industry to be on partner track. We see this as a result of the evolution of the market over the past decade. In our experience, VC funds that previously looked to hire non-partners to mostly manage their deal pipeline are now placing an increased premium on a new generation of professionals who have strong access to deals, especially in emerging technologies. This, in turn, has opened the door for more professionals to be on the partner track in spite of the fact that they may have limited operations experience. Similarly, we have also seen some returning to venture capital after having left to get more seasoning in operations (especially if their first turn in venture was earlier in their career). This further validates the idea that the non-partner role can be a prelude to an eventual career in venture.

CASE STUDIES

Following are the stories of four individuals who secured roles in venture capital. Although each took a different route—graduating from business school with an entrepreneurial background (Case Study 30), leveraging consulting and engineering experience before business school (Case Study 31), the uncommon course of breaking in with a law degree (Case Study 32), and going through many years of operating experience (Case Study 33)—they all had backgrounds that closely tracked the requirements listed in the job specifications later in this chapter. In fact, the author of Case Study 31 ended up obtaining the position described in Search 6. At the same time, you will see that the first three don't necessarily see themselves in their current positions in venture long-term. The resumes that correspond to Case Studies 31 and 32 in this section can be found in Appendix B.

Case Study 30: The Advantage of Successful Entrepreneurial Experience

This person had an undergrad degree in economics, but got his technology experience at a start-up company. That experience led him to launch his own company, which he grew and eventually sold. He then went to business school before joining a VC fund. He knows that his stay in venture capital depends on how he performs and that even if he shines there are no guarantees he will be promoted.

■ ■ ■

Getting into VC is tough. Most people recommend allocating 6 to 12 months to look for a job in venture. I got lucky and it took only a few months, but that is definitely not the norm. I had the things that people check off: I work hard, have a good academic background, some banking, consulting, operations, and entrepreneurial experience, and good references. But there are tons of other guys who have that as well. It's unfortunate, but it's a crapshoot.

After my summer experience in California, I knew I wanted to return and thought that VC would provide a great avenue to build a network, gain breadth of knowledge in multiple sectors, and keep me close to start-ups.

I wasn't even thinking about venture when I finished undergrad in the mid- to late 1990s with a degree in economics. I did two summer internships while I was in school—one at a private equity firm in Asia and another at a Wall Street firm doing equity research. Econ grads from my Ivy League school pretty much went into finance, consulting, or to law school, so I followed suit and began an investment banking analyst program at a major Street firm. I was in the M&A department focusing on tech and telecom.

Like many others, I realized pretty quickly that I didn't want to be an investment banker forever, and I left the program after my first year. I saw a lot of friends and classmates doing entrepreneurial things and wanted to do the same. I joined a start-up Internet services firm that did consulting and development work. I saw it as a great segue into the start-up environment. I was one of the first guys hired into a burgeoning strategy group.

I stayed at the start-up for a little while and then some friends and I decided to start our own company. It was 1999–2000 and the Internet world was in full force. In just a few years we raised equity funding, acquired another company, and then sold both pieces of the company. While building a company was exhilarating, I was not sure that I wanted to tackle another one right away. Given where the market was and at this stage in my career, I made the decision to attend business school.

In business school my plan was to start another company. I even thought about taking a leave of absence or leaving school to do it, but for a number of reasons the timing was not perfect. I had been an East Coast person most of my life and wanted to try California, so I worked for the summer at a consulting firm's tech group. After my summer experience in California, I knew I wanted to return and thought that VC would provide a great avenue to build a network, gain breadth of knowledge in multiple sectors, and keep me close to start-ups.

Getting into VC is a lot different than PE and the process varies from firm to firm. I know some people with one or two years of experience at an I-bank or a tech company, some of whom are younger than me, and they are on the partner track (after having proven themselves). I know others who are older than me with more experience but are not on the path to becoming a partner. I've learned that the earlier-stage firms want more operating/entrepreneurial experience, while the later-stage firms are more willing to take guys with banking and consulting experience. Of course, all venture firms would love to get guys who started billion-dollar companies, so the single best way to get into VC is to start a really, really successful company.

Market timing also has a lot to do with hiring. At any one time there may only be a few venture firms actively looking to hire. If a good guy comes along, most firms will at least bring him in to take a look. I was told by many firms, "We're not necessarily looking to hire, but why don't you come in and chat?" When I got the offer for my current position I was actively interviewing with a number of other firms.

Venture is very binary—either you make money for the firm, or you don't. I'm here now, and if I show the aptitude to discover good deals and make the firm money, then I can probably stay on. If I show an inability to make money, why would they ask me to stick around, and why would I want to stay in VC?

Case Study 31: A Traditional Pre-MBA VC Hire

This person leveraged his consulting experience and electrical engineering degree to land a pre-MBA position.

■ ■ ■

I graduated from a school in the Midwest with a degree in electrical engineering. While in school I did two internships—one at IBM and the other at an investment bank where I worked on the tech side supporting the quantitative research group. I decided I didn't want to go into engineering full-time. I liked technology, but I wanted to understand the bigger picture, so I decided to go into consulting.

Although my school was not preferred for recruiting, I was able to land an associate consultant position at a major firm. I gained wide exposure to companies in the consumer products, automotive, and industrial sectors. I ended up getting very little exposure to tech companies. This was a two-year program with an option to stay a third year. Instead of pursuing a third year I decided to target private equity and venture funds. I looked at tech-focused buyout funds and smaller, mid-size buyout funds. Unfortunately, the initial feedback I got from both PE and VC firms was not encouraging. Private equity firms told me I didn't have the finance background or deal experience they wanted. The VCs liked my electrical engineering background, but worried that I hadn't been on a consulting engagement with a tech client. I ended up getting dinged by three VC funds and four buyout funds. I did get one offer with a buyout fund, but it was in a city in which I wasn't interested in living.

I eventually clicked with one venture fund that looked past my lack of tech experience. This firm appreciated the fact that I had kept my electrical engineering knowledge up to date. Since the analysis done by a venture fund is more qualitative compared to that done by PE funds, this fund appreciated my consulting background. I was also able to show that the skills I developed in my consulting program would be relevant to the type of venture diligence done at VC funds. I found a venture fund that has less of a desire for associates to have deep technology experience in the area in which the fund focuses. They looked more for generalists.

You should understand your motivations. If you want to be a partner in venture, you should be aware that very few partners came through the associate program. There may still be time for you to get into VC later on.

Even though I succeeded in securing a VC job, my search was anything but easy. I started with a long list of VC firms and at the end of the day had one offer. I would definitely advise those looking to do their homework. I ended up applying to some firms to which, in retrospect, I would not have applied or at which I would not have wanted to work.

I would also tell people to prepare well for interviews. There was a stark difference between the interviews at buyout and VC funds. The buyout partners grilled me on financial matters, asking me the different ways that I might structure a deal, what different sources of funding I might use, and when I would use one over the other. Venture capital firms asked more goal-type questions than skill-testing questions. I was asked why I wanted to be an investor. What stage of investing do you like? What types of companies do you like? I know one venture fund that gave candidates an assignment to evaluate a company by coming back with a PowerPoint presentation and model. That seemed a little cumbersome and excessive for an interview process.

Looking back, I should have done more due diligence on firms. I still can't believe that I didn't do more primary research on the funds to which I applied. The venture community is a small one, so there is a lot to be learned about a fund by talking to people in the industry and with people at venture-backed companies even if they didn't get funding from the firm. You should understand your motivations. If you want to be a partner in venture, you should be aware that very few partners came through the associate program. There may still be time for you to get into VC later on. If you really want to do operational stuff early on in your career, then you can do that and not hurt your chances of getting into VC. You must also be comfortable with the partners at your firm, as you will likely be spending a lot of working time with them.

(See Resume 14 in Appendix B.)

Case Study 32: A Consultant with a Law Degree Gets In

This candidate went to a top Ivy League school, got a law degree, went into consulting, and then made the improbable jump into a health care/biotech venture capital fund.

■ ■ ■

I came out of undergrad with a double major in philosophy and economics and went straight to an Ivy League law school. I didn't have any grand plans. I just wanted to do something intellectually stimulating. While at law school I cross-registered and took some courses at the business school. I passed the New York Bar exam, but went into consulting instead of practicing law. My full-time associate position at a major consulting shop gave me my first real exposure to business. Although I started as a generalist, I gravitated to pharmaceuticals and biotech and found it more appealing to work with entrepreneurs than with big business.

I began to look at venture after two years of consulting and it was definitely not an easy jump to make. I used a recruiter who made no promises to me, given my background. I knew it would be hard to do, so I didn't get my hopes up. I could think of 100 reasons why I should not try to get in, but my thought was, you have to throw your hat in the ring because if you don't you will never get in.

Luckily for me I clicked instantly with the fund at which I am now working. They were open-minded about me and took the approach that they would look for talented people whom they could train. Since there are so many skill sets needed to do well in venture, firms don't have to take a cookie-cutter approach when hiring. I am now the only person at my firm with a JD. I think I brought a different way of thinking to the firm that they liked. So in my case, I was a good fit and the diversity was a plus. Would it have been better if I had operational experience? Sure!

Getting a job in venture is dependent on a person's opportunities and, unfortunately, the opportunities don't come around very often. My advice to others would therefore be that they should be proactive and opportunistic. You can't set a plan and say you will follow a certain path and have a job in VC in three years. It doesn't work that way. You must find experiences that will help you reach your goal. Operations experience is, of course, very helpful. Looking back, I may have taken more finance and science classes, but they are not essential. If you are quick and sharp you can learn the ropes.

I am now the only person at my firm with a JD. I think I brought a different way of thinking to the firm that they liked. So in my case, I was a good fit and the diversity was a plus. Would it have been better if I had operational experience? Sure!

The most important thing is to be passionate about venture investing. You should not be in it for the money and should definitely not come off as if you are. If you are passionate, curious, and excited then you will want to learn the science and finance. And the passion should not just be for venture—it should be for venture, biotech (in my case), and being an entrepreneur.

(See Resume 15 in Appendix B.)

Case Study 33: Extensive Operating Experience

This person got into venture capital investing with three years of product marketing and six years of engineering experience. He has deep industry knowledge and was at a start-up that successfully went public. At the time he had been at his current VC fund for five years, was promoted twice, but still had no guarantees he would stay on.

■ ■ ■

I knew in my mind I was on a technical track and wanted to stay on it when I got my undergrad degree in electrical engineering and followed that with a master's. I was in no way thinking about venture capital. I can honestly say I didn't even know what venture capital was at that time. Rather, I took a technical position as a design engineer at a technology company. I left that after one year and joined another company, also as a design engineer. I later joined a third company, a start-up communications company, in a similar capacity. It was at this company that I had my first introduction to venture capital.

A couple of weeks after I joined (I was one of the first 15 people at the company), the CEO called everyone into the main conference room and passed around an $8 million check from a VC fund that was our Series B financing. I remember thinking at the time, "Hey, what's this role of a venture capitalist and how does one become a VC? How do they decide what is a promising opportunity and what isn't?" Sometime after that meeting I began to look into the backgrounds of the people at some of the major VC funds and saw a lot of people with Stanford and Harvard MBAs, and was intrigued by the fact that there were people solving interesting problems on the business side of the world like I had solved on the technical side. So I thought, if I ever wanted to do venture, I would need to balance my technical knowledge with some business acumen.

As I was looking into getting an MBA, I also switched over to the business side at my company in product marketing. During my time at this company I saw it go from fewer than 15 people to 600 employees. I saw it get additional funding and was there when it went public. My thoughts were to get into business school and then try and get into venture. If I didn't get into a VC fund I thought I could at least get a senior executive position at a venture-backed start-up.

I applied to business school, but didn't get into Stanford or Harvard. In parallel, I contacted a recruiter who was looking to place associates at VC firms and who said he knew of a VC fund that was looking for someone with my background. The interview process took about six months and the firm seemed in no hurry to bring someone on. I met with everyone on the investment team and was asked things like what did you learn while at the start-up? What areas do you think are promising to invest in? How would you evaluate investment opportunities? There were no tests or case studies.

I started working at the fund in 2001 and am still there. When I joined, the length of my stay was left open. I was told something like, "You could just not work out," "You could stay a couple of years and leave," or it was left open that I could stay longer. There were definitely no promises one way or another. I was certainly hoping that I would be on the partner track. I was told to work hard and prove myself, but there are no guarantees. Nevertheless, I thought that joining the fund would create more options for me even if I were to leave after a few years. I clearly thought that, if nothing else, I would be exposed to and evaluate numerous business opportunities and enhance my network by meeting the crème-de-la-crème of management teams. I also knew that I would be better equipped to start my own company after the VC experience, and it has certainly worked out that way.

> *There were definitely no promises one way or another. I was certainly hoping that I would be on the partner track. I was told to work hard and prove myself, but there are no guarantees. Nevertheless, I thought that joining the fund would create more options for me even if I were to leave after a few years.*

I've been promoted twice, first to VP and then to managing director. The indications I've gotten are that I'm doing a great job, but I also know that I have to continually perform to stay around—that means sourcing, building, and exiting opportunities that create value for our limited partners.

In my case I think the nine years of operating experience I had prior to joining the firm helped and are a significant reason why I am not being told to get more operating experience. If I had to give advice to someone who wanted to get into venture investing, I would first tell them that there is no single path. Every firm is different; some are run by ex-entrepreneurs, some by ex-investment bankers, and others by ex-consultants. An MBA from a top school definitely helps, but I think operating experience at a successful start-up is really the critical ingredient. Relevant industry expertise is also important. If you have sector-specific knowledge in a hot industry, when the VC industry stumbles upon it you will be in good shape—just like people who knew optics or telecom in 1999–2000. Basically, I wouldn't worry about whether you will be on the partner track or not. If you can join for even a few years and see how people build companies, why not do it?

SAMPLE JOB SEARCHES

To get a better understanding of what venture capital funds look for when they hire, we suggest you take a good look at the job specifications for the following nine positions. Pay careful attention to the description of the roles, the amount of experience sought, and the academic and professional training required. Job Searches 1 through 4 are for pre-MBA positions while Searches 5 through 9 are for post-MBA roles. You will see that there are usually consistent themes in the requirements for both positions. Both usually require an engineering background, technology expertise, strong academic and professional background, and solid research and communications skills, among others. The VC funds are also very clear about whether a job is potentially partner track (most are not, but some, such as Searches 5 and 9, leave the door open).

Pre-MBA Job Searches

Search 1: Pre-MBA Associate

This is a search for people with two to five years experience only (people with more than five years experience were discouraged from expressing interest).

Responsibilities
- Prequalify investment opportunities.
- Proactively source new investment opportunities.
- Create competitive landscapes in the firm's areas of interest.
- Perform research to determine emerging markets within the firm's areas of investment focus.
- Work with the partners to perform due diligence on potential investment opportunities.
- Work with portfolio companies in all aspects of the company building process.

Requirements
- Minimum of two to four years experience at a top-tier management consulting firm, investment bank, or equivalent operating positions.
- Passion and understanding for media, entertainment, and technology industries.
- Understanding of capitalization structures, cap tables, financial analysis, and term sheets.
- Mature personality who can interact with C-level executives.
- Personable, self-motivated, and analytical individual who enjoys operating in an entrepreneurial environment.

Search 2: Pre-MBA Associate

Note the distinct requirement for technology expertise and preference for an engineering degree. This firm specifically defines the time horizon of the role.

Description
The associate candidate will have two to three years of experience coming from a top-tier background in strategy consulting, technology operations (technology business, business development, or corporate development), or investment banking.

Requirements
- Must have strong general technology understanding, having worked on several projects in the tech sector; engineering degree is preferred but not required.
- Must be ranked at the top of your class with regards to problem solving and quantitative skills.

- Must have an extremely high level of maturity and ability to multitask with little supervision (will not be part of a large group of associates).
- Must have excellent communication skills, both written and oral.
- Must have a top academic pedigree (both undergraduate school and GPA).

Responsibilities

The associate role has a broad range of responsibilities, which include:

- Due diligence and investment execution.
- Portfolio analysis and fund management.
- Consultative projects for existing portfolio companies.
- Research into new investment areas.

This is a two- to three-year associate program.

Search 3: Pre-MBA Associate

This search is from a venture capital firm focused on health care and technology industries which was beginning to focus on venture growth equity investments in the technology and life sciences sectors.

Responsibilities

The firm is seeking an associate. Associates will work in small teams with senior professionals on all phases of the investment process, in a generalist capacity. Specific responsibilities include:

- Working with partners to build sector investment plans.
- Developing relationships with leading companies.
- Executing due diligence (including business analysis, industry thesis, competitive landscape, business/pricing model, financial modeling, and deal structuring).
- Working in a strategic capacity with the firm's portfolio companies.

Requirements

- Two to four years of full-time experience in a top-tier investment bank, consulting, operational, and/or private equity/venture capital investing roles (or any combination thereof).
- Candidates will be highly motivated, self-confident, with good interpersonal skills. They will have strong strategic and commercial skills and the ability to present complex ideas and information clearly. They will have the passion and energy required to participate in an entrepreneurial setting.
- Computer science and/or electrical engineering degree a plus.

Career Path
This position is for a two-year minimum commitment, with an opportunity for retention and promotion based on candidate's performance.

Search 4: Pre-MBA Analyst

This fund clearly explains the research and deal support nature of this role, the need to understand the markets in which the fund invests, and the importance of working with its portfolio companies.

Description and Responsibilities
The analyst will work alongside senior investment professionals to support all aspects of investment evaluation and execution, including:

- Original research on market sectors, companies, products, and technologies.
- Analysis, including technical analysis of software architectures and suitability of products for markets.
- Financial modeling (valuations, company analysis).
- Participating in firm deal flow sourcing and evaluation.
- General due diligence (customer, management checks).
- Assisting in transaction processes, deal structuring, and deal documentation.
- Working with portfolio companies as needed.

The ideal candidate will demonstrate the ability to conduct original research and assess technology market opportunities, and will have mature thinking and instinctive good business judgment. The candidate should also have knowledge of at least some market sectors within infrastructure software, applications software, and media and information businesses. The analyst will be assigned to deal teams and will have the opportunity to take on increasing responsibility within the deal team as he or she demonstrates capability.

Requirements
Candidates for the analyst role will have demonstrated the ability to rapidly understand and evaluate markets, companies and technologies.
Specific requirements include:

- One to three years of experience in a top-tier management or strategy consulting firm with experience in strategic market analysis; similar strategic analysis experience in a comparable position such as venture or private equity will be considered.
- BA/BS from top-tier undergraduate program with superior academic record.

In addition to:

- Demonstrated knowledge of or strong interest in at least some of the markets where the fund invests: software and information services.
- Demonstrated quantitative and qualitative analysis skills and talent for understanding the evolution of new market segments.
- Strong communication and presentation skills, both oral and written.
- Self-starter and a leader with the drive and creativity to find information from multiple sources and the ability to motivate others within a small, rapidly growing firm.
- Ability to build good personal relationships and work closely and credibly with the firm's partners and portfolio companies.

Post-MBA/Grad School Job Searches

Search 5: Post-MBA Associate

This job search is for an information technology venture capital fund.

Description

This information technology venture capital fund is looking for a post-MBA level associate to add to its team. This fund leads investments in early-stage start-up companies and in established business services companies where technology can be applied to increase productivity and profitability.

This associate will work closely with GPs to source information-intensive business service businesses with $50–$200 million in revenue and positive operating margins. The associate will also be involved in the due diligence process of target investment companies. This fund has significant capital to deploy and offers a dynamic learning experience in a busy deal environment.

The ideal candidate will have three to six or more years of experience; an MBA from a top-tier school is preferred.

Responsibilities

The post MBA associate is expected to:

- Proactively develop and pursue investment hypotheses, with guidance from GPs.
- Systematically plan and execute deal-sourcing efforts on an industry-by-industry basis with emphasis in the business services sector.
- Be comfortable in engaging CEOs and business owners in a dialogue about potential investment opportunities.
- Have comprehensive understanding of generally available enterprise information technologies.
- Coordinate the due diligence processes, including market diligence, industry/customer diligence, and the preparation of internal investment memorandums and presentations.

Qualifications and Skills

The ideal candidate will have:

- Strategy consulting experience, particularly in the business services sector.
- IT consulting/integration experience, especially with middle-market clients.
- Extensive ability to develop and analyze financial models.
- A consistent track record of success and achievement.
- Genuine interest in technology and venture capital investing.

Candidates Who Are Eligible

- Recent/soon to be MBAs from top-tier business schools (preferred).
- Those with experience in corporate development/business development roles at large technology companies.
- Individuals from strategy and IT consultancies—large firms and boutiques.

It is expected that GPs will work with the associate to develop his skills as an investment professional over a two- to three-year period. At that point, a discussion will take place regarding a continued career path with the firm.

Search 6: Venture Associate Position (Post-MBA/Grad School Level)

Note the additional (and more detailed) experience required, even though this is still considered a two-year position.

Company

This established, highly successful venture capital firm has a deep history of identifying and investing in disruptive technologies and has performed in the top tier in its peer group over their past several funds. The postgraduate level associate will have four to eight years of technology-related work experience. The associate will focus primarily on investments in the consumer wireless space. The firm is very lean and therefore the associate will spend the majority of his or her time working directly with the senior partners. The expectation is for the position to be a two-year apprenticeship in venture capital.

Candidate Requirements

- Must have a deep understanding of technology, preferably in one of the domain areas listed above.
- Computer science or electrical engineering degree strongly preferred, but technical acumen/background an acceptable substitute.
- Must have a strong complementary business skill set. Experience at top professional services firm, preferably consulting (even if just for summer, though two years preferable).

- Should have experience at a high-technology company, preferably in a nontechnology/developer role. Preference for candidates with backgrounds in product management, sales, marketing, and/or business development.
- Must be a self-starter, have a high-level of maturity, and have superior communication skills. Hardworking, outgoing, and other strong personal attributes. Part of the role will be to identify and source new business for the firm—a sales background would be a plus.
- Undergrad degree from top school (Ivy or equivalent) with strong academic performance. Advanced degree, preferably an MBA, from a top school.

Search 7: Postgraduate Level Associate Position

This is a health care fund; note the specific requirements for a science degree and consulting background with a preference for health care experience.

Candidate Background
- Must have consulting experience. The ideal candidate for this position should have two to four years (postgraduate) experience in the health care (particularly biopharma) industry at a top-tier strategy/management consulting firm (McKinsey, Bain, and BCG).
- Must have a postgraduate degree (MBA, PhD, MD preferred).

Roles/Requirements
- Member of the VC's BioPharma team.
- Focus on all aspects of due diligence on health care opportunities:
  - Locate and interview key physicians.
  - Perform primary and secondary market research.
  - Work closely with all members of the BioPharma team.
  - Be good at working out ways to answer difficult questions.
  - Be highly comfortable with building complex Excel spreadsheets.
- Ability to interact effectively with senior management/board members at portfolio companies and potential investments.
- Excellent communication and problem-solving skills.
- Sound judgment, based on real-world experience, regarding issues faced as the firm does due diligence on companies (e.g., physician adoption; technical development issues/intellectual property; market size; go-to market strategies; regulatory/reimbursement risks; management team evaluation).
- Highly self-directed and hardworking.

Career Track
This opportunity is for a minimum of a two-year commitment with an opportunity for career retention based on associate performance and the firm's needs.

Search 8: Post-MBA Associate

This VC firm seeks someone with operations experience for a two-year minimum position that very clearly is not partner track.

The senior associate position is *not* intended to be a partner track position. Candidates are expected to have a high level of maturity, strong presentation skills, and a deep network of high-end entrepreneurs and venture capitalists in the area in which the fund is based.

The ideal candidate will have the following:

- Four to seven years of total work experience in technology and network infrastructure/enterprise technology domain experience, primarily with an operating company.
- Sales and/or marketing background as a product line manager or equivalent position at a technology operating company. We are also open to seeing candidates with previous VC (early- and/or late-stage) or financial deal experience with technology companies from an investment bank or consulting firm.
- Solid understanding of technology at the macro and micro levels.
- Exceptional communication skills and a high level of maturity.
- Technology due diligence and strong research skills (top priority).
- A proactive attitude with good business judgment.
- Exceptional modeling skills. Must be quantitative and analytical.
- MBA from top school is (preferred).

Search 9: Vice President

This is a partner-track position and therefore requires many more years of work experience and, preferably, previous venture experience. Candidates are expected to have been significant value creators and have ideally seen a company go through several stages of growth.

Seeking vice president for software/services/communications services or hardware team who would be cultivated throughout the next fund in hopes of achieving a partner-level promotion within the next five-plus years.

General Preferences/Requirements for VP Candidates

To be considered, the VP candidate must have an extensive record of high achievement in previous endeavors which should span a range of 10 to 15 years of relevant operating and/or investing experience in software/services/communications services or hardware-focused industries, and preferably at least three of those years should be in a venture capital firm or venture-backed company. Ideal candidates will have been significant ring leaders in their organizations, having been integral contributors to the growth and prosperity of their product groups and/or companies/portfolio companies over an extended period of time.

Relevant candidates are expected to be able to cite distinct examples of longer-term value creation for which they were responsible and most likely would have been promoted aggressively as a result (through significant contributions related to product management, marketing, sales, engineering, etc.). Preferred candidates would have also been involved with a company throughout several stages of its growth cycle, starting from a pre-profit/pre-IPO level, progressing towards an IPO/or other liquidity event, and having run larger teams in a multifaceted, multiproduct organization.

Desired candidates for this role will most likely have spent a significant portion of their career in varying operating roles across a few very successful companies, augmented with a few years of quality VC investing (where a more intense level of scrutiny will be applied in relation to individual track records and expectations).

For a hardware candidate, an engineering background is required, with a strong preference for advanced degrees in engineering and/or business (MA, MBA, PhD, etc.).

For a software/services/communications services candidate, an undergraduate engineering background is preferred (but not required) along with an advanced degree (including an MBA).

The VP candidates will within a few years be expected to lead their own investments and grow into significant board-level contributors. Therefore, on top of strong analytical skills, candidates must be strong communicators, have a high level of maturity, and have exceptional investment judgment.

Chapter VIII

WORKING AT FUND OF FUNDS, HYBRID FUNDS, AND SECONDARY FUNDS

Fund of funds, hybrid funds, and secondary funds are a subsector within private equity. While these are similar in many ways to traditional PE funds, there are also key differences. Despite, the differences, securing a position at one of these funds is still a quality route to take and can set you on a path to a unique and fulfilling career in private equity.

FUND OF FUNDS

Unlike traditional PE funds, pure private equity fund of funds, which are also called multi-manager funds, do not invest directly into operating companies, but rather, they are pooled vehicles that invest in a selection of other PE funds (at times called single-manager funds). In simpler terms, these plain vanilla fund of funds raise money from Limited Partners (LPs), and invest the pooled capital as an LP in other PE funds, which in turn invest that money directly in companies.

Fund of funds usually offer two main benefits to LPs. First, they provide advice on sophisticated asset allocation strategies (how much an LP should have in venture capital funds versus buyout, real estate, international, etc.) and which are the best funds in which to invest. Second, they offer diversification by providing access to funds that LPs could not invest in directly by themselves (either because a fund is closed to new investors or because an LP couldn't meet a fund's minimum investment requirements).

Within the asset class, there are fund of funds that focus their investments in specific types of PE funds. For example, there are buyout fund of funds, venture fund of funds, distressed debt fund of funds, international fund of funds, and so on. There are also diversified fund of funds that invest in a combination of these sectors. Fund of funds and hybrid funds (we define those in the next section) are a sizable force in the overall PE universe. In fact, U.S.-based firms (these include secondary funds) raised $26.3 billion in 2007, according to *Private Equity Analyst*. When that amount is combined with European figures (*PE Analyst* noted that funds of funds typically invest across the globe) the total figure climbs to $37.9 billion, a 12.4 percent increase from 2006.

EXPANDING INTO HYBRID STRATEGIES

Over the past few years, larger fund of funds have been increasingly expanding beyond plain vanilla partnership/LP investing into strategies such as co-investing (making direct investments into companies alongside PE funds) and secondary investing (buying other LPs' interests in funds), both of which more closely mirror the traditional private equity investing we describe in previous chapters. We classify these funds that have expanded their activities as *hybrid funds*.

A fund that co-invests typically piggybacks off the due diligence conducted by a PE fund of which it is an LP. Co-investing allows the fund of funds to enhance its returns, as it typically does not pay a performance fee (carry) to the PE fund alongside which it is investing. Many of the major investment banks, including Goldman Sachs, JPMorgan, Credit Suisse, and Merrill Lynch, operate hybrid funds; some are listed in Table 8.1. There are also many independent firms that do hybrid investing, such as HarbourVest Partners, Pomona Capital, and Auda Advisor Associates.

> **Insider Tip ▷**
>
> ## From an Investment Professional at a Hybrid Fund
>
> In co-investing, we work with the sponsor to understand the investment opportunity. I review several opportunities a week and am able to touch all industries and interact with a wide variety of PE funds, from the mega funds to middle-market players. Unlike direct investing, in which a lot of the work involves portfolio companies, once we accept a co-investment, we monitor it but do not take an active role in managing it. Co-investing has the advantage of taking a fresh look at an investment on which a sponsor has spent months doing primary diligence work.

Secondary investing entails purchasing part or all of an LP's interest in an existing fund. As such, secondary funds (or hybrid funds that make secondary investments) analyze portfolios of investments already made by a PE fund. While most secondary funds are embedded in hybrid funds, there are also firms that have funds which focus almost exclusively on this type of investing; examples of these are Lexington Partners, Landmark Partners, and Coller Capital.

Table 8.1   Top Fund of Funds Managers (by Amount of Capital Managed for Third-Party Funds)

RANK	NAME	LOCATION	ASSETS ($ BILLION)[1]
1	Goldman Sachs Private Equity Group	New York	$18.00
2	Pantheon Ventures Inc.	San Francisco	$16.90
3	HarbourVest Partners	Boston	$15.70
4	AIG Global Investment Corp.	New York	$12.00
5	Adams Street Partners LLC	Chicago	$11.10
6	JPMorgan Investment Management Inc.	New York	$10.80
7	Credit Suisse Customized Fund Investment Group	New York	$8.00
8	SVG Advisers Ltd.	London	$7.40
9	LGT Capital Partners Ltd.[2]	Switzerland	$7.40
10	Horsley Bridge Partners Inc.	San Francisco	$7.10
11	Pathway Capital Management LLC	Irvine, CA	$6.30
12	Commonfund Capital Inc.	Wilton, CT	$5.50
	Landmark Partners	Simsbury, CT	$5.50
14	Pomona Capital	New York	$4.10
15	Standard Life Investments Private Equity Ltd.	Edinburgh, Scotland	$3.90
16	Unigestion	Geneva	$3.50
17	FLAG Capital Management LLC	Stamford, CT	$3.30
18	Private Advisors LLC	Richmond, VA	$3.20
19	Auda Advisor Associates LLC	New York	$3.20
20	Morgan Stanley Alternative Investment Partners	West Conshohocken, PA	$2.70
21	Abbott Capital Management	New York	$2.60
22	Adveq	Zurich	$2.60
23	Wilshire Associates	Santa Monica, CA	$2.40
24	Capital Z Investment Partners	New York	$2.30
25	Danske Private Equity	Copenhagen	$2.20

Source: *2007 Directory of Alternative Investment Programs*

[1]May also include separate account mandates and other types of discretionary assets.
[2]Includes private equity and hedge fund of funds assets.

SKILLS

Although most of the investing done by pure fund of funds, hybrid funds, and secondary funds takes on a different form from traditional private equity investing, many of the skills required of the investment professionals are similar. However, the emphasis on those skills will vary by fund type. At pure fund of funds (those that primarily invest in other funds), solid quantitative skills are important, but qualitative skills (such as written, interpersonal, and communications skills) may be more emphasized since a significant amount of time is spent interacting with and assessing fund managers and presenting reports to an internal investment committee. Not surprisingly, funds that focus more on co-investing and secondary investing emphasize quantitative skills, since the type of analysis these funds conduct more closely resembles that done by traditional PE funds that invest directly in operating companies.

ROLES

Beyond the skills, the roles can also be different. In the following section, we discuss the roles at pure fund of funds and the roles at hybrid and secondary funds.

Pure Fund of Funds

At pure fund of funds the role of an investment professional includes some company-level valuation but is more focused on market and portfolio analysis. These professionals monitor the underlying funds in which their fund has already committed capital, while also researching potential new funds in which to invest. They look into what drives fund performance. For example, they seek to answer questions such as: In what sector are the fund's investments? Are the investments concentrated in a specific industry or geography that was hot but may not be anymore? Did most of the returns come from one deal? What professionals led the top deals? Are they still at the fund? Is there a succession plan in place? And so forth. Ultimately the fund of funds wants to know if the same manager can produce an above-market return for the firm's next fund.

A senior investment professional at a fund of funds notes that pre-MBA analysts at his firm spend most of their time analyzing data used to evaluate fund manager performance, drafting investment memos, analyzing industry trends, and reporting to the fund of funds' investors. More senior professionals would focus on the same activities but would be involved less in the details. Rather than creating the actual Excel spreadsheets or memos used to construct reports, senior professionals would instead supervise the analysis done by the junior professionals and inject their higher-level ideas and thoughts that are needed to round out the report.

Hybrid and Secondary Funds

Investment professionals at hybrid funds (specifically those that co-invest) and secondary funds concentrate more on company-level valuation than would professionals at pure fund of funds. However, the analysis is still not as detailed as that done by traditional private equity funds. By their nature, funds that co-invest are making direct investments; however, since they don't *lead* the investments, they are not constructing as in-depth LBO models and interacting as frequently with company management.

Instead, investment professionals at these funds utilize the due diligence conducted by PE funds to formulate their own investment decision: Does the investment meet the objectives of the fund's co-investment portfolio? Does it satisfy the firm's risk/return profile? And ultimately, do they want to participate in the deal? By contrast, secondary funds analyze the interests of other LPs, of which a significant part may have already been committed (or already invested by the fund). Thus a portion of the role is company-by-company analysis to determine the value of the portfolio as a whole.

Insider Tip ▷

From an Analyst at a Fund of Funds
Analysts at fund of funds need by nature to be meticulous and organized. The role involves a lot of reporting and diligence and you are scrutinizing a lot of documents. It's a lot different than looking at a few pitch books. For example, if we have invested in 20 managers and each of them has made 10 investments, we have to look at each of those individual investments at the company level. That's a potential universe of 200 investments we have to know. It's a lot to cover, compared to an associate at a buyout fund who may be following two deals.

CAREER PATH/HIRING

The career path at a fund of funds is very similar to that of more traditional private equity funds, with most candidates following the 2-2-2 path described in Chapter I. In the case of a fund of funds, that would mean working two years in investment banking, consulting, accounting, or a comparable industry, followed by two years at a fund of funds or hybrid fund, and then spending two years in business school before potentially returning to the industry in a career-track position. Unfortunately, there is still no guarantee that you will be hired back when you leave after your initial two years, either for business school or to try something different. However, just as with traditional PE funds, there can be exceptions in which some funds may be open to promoting top performers without them having to go to business school.

Fund of funds (and for that matter hybrid funds) tend to begin their annual junior, or-pre-MBA, level hiring in late fall to early winter (well into the second year of a banking or consulting program), a bit later than the more traditional buyout funds. When hiring at this level, most pure fund of funds target candidates from banking programs, but many also consider consultants, especially if they have worked on private equity due diligence projects. Pure fund of funds may also be open to professionals at accounting firms who have relevant experience (i.e., transaction services) and candidates who have worked in equity research. Not surprisingly, hybrid funds with their greater emphasis on quantitative skills tend to predominantly hire bankers (with less preference to specific groups within the banks), though some may consider consultants with knowledge of the private equity sector.

As in traditional PE, there are fewer cases where candidates are hired out of undergrad. One hiring manager noted that for a senior in college to even be *considered*, that candidate would have to exhibit "truly exceptional academics, leadership on campus, some experience with modeling/spreadsheets, and a strong reference from professor(s)."

Glocap Insight

Perhaps the most notable similarity to traditional PE funds is how difficult it is to secure a position at a fund of funds. Don't get us wrong—despite the differences in how they invest and the less stressful lifestyle, landing a position at a fund of funds will still require initiative and hard work. Indeed, the requirements can be just as rigorous, and therefore our advice for those interested is the same—do the right work and get on track early.

In addition to the more traditional backgrounds, there are other industries that can be a stepping-stone into a fund of funds. For example, working at an institution that allocates large pools of investment capital, specifically a university endowment, a state pension fund, an insurance company, and so on, can provide skills that could translate into a manager selection role at a fund of funds. We've also seen some funds of funds open to professionals who have worked at placement agents or in the fund placement groups of investment banks, where a significant portion of time is spent analyzing managers of funds for which they are raising money. Thus, our advice to more senior professionals who are interested in fund of funds but lack buy-side experience would be to consider pursuing these additional roles as an intermediate step.

INTERVIEWS

Similar to interviews at PE funds, fund of funds interviews tend to focus on both technical and nontechnical skills (see the qualifications listed in Job Search 3). One senior professional who oversees the recruiting said his firm first wants to know that a candidate has basic finance knowledge and skills: Are they proficient at working with spreadsheets? Do they know what mezzanine debt is? Do they know the difference between senior and junior debt? Are they familiar with the mechanics of an IPO? In addition, the candidate must have a solid GPA and test scores. After these criteria are met, he focuses attention on the individual's character and maturity, as junior professionals will often conduct face-to-face meetings with fund managers and CEOs at portfolio companies.

In later rounds of interviews, his firm presents candidates with a private placement memorandum or a quarterly report. The candidate is given about 90 minutes to answer some basic questions and present an Excel spreadsheet with the information in a clear format.

From a Hiring Manager

We want to see that candidates are smart, motivated, and can learn fast. Above all, we want to know that working at a fund of funds is truly what they want to do. If you approach fund of funds like they are your second choice, we will read right through you and it will be difficult to convince us that you are sincere.

TRENDS

Given the increased growth in hybrid funds, there has been an escalating demand for junior professionals with deal/investment skills, and hybrid funds have thus found themselves having to compete more with traditional PE and venture capital funds for the same talent. As part of their need to adapt to these new competitive pressures, hybrid funds have had to raise compensation more aggressively to stay in sync with the traditional PE funds. In contrast, compensation at pure funds of funds has increased more modestly, but they have been able to emphasize their virtues, such a balanced lifestyle, to continue to win over top talent. One pre-MBA who joined a fund of funds from a banking program noted:

> The lifestyle compared to banking is amazing and it is good compared to a buyout fund. I come in at 9 A.M., and 9 P.M. is a late night for me. During the weeks before quarterly reports are sent to our LPs the nights can be later, but I know those deadlines are coming and they are balanced by other times when I can leave earlier. By and large I can control my own schedule. I've even joined a band and get to play music. I don't think that would happen if I was working at a mega buyout fund.

SAMPLE JOB SEARCHES

The following are job specifications from actual searches that we've conducted, which we thought would give you a better grasp of the skills sought by fund of funds and hybrid funds and the expectations of the roles.

Search 1: Pre-MBA Associate

This is a two- to three-year pre-MBA associate position with a premier multibillion-dollar fund of funds that has four strategies.

Responsibilities

The associate role includes performing a wide variety of tasks and analysis in direct support of the firm's investment partners, with specific responsibilities including:

- Analyzing and monitoring the performance of the firm's existing fund managers and underlying portfolio companies, preparing for and participating in meetings with assigned managers, and conducting on-going diligence.
- Screening new investment opportunities, including reviewing offering memoranda, preparing for and participating in meetings with prospective fund managers, and conducting detailed due diligence.
- Completing analytical projects pertaining to portfolio construction, industry trends, or organizational strategy, and writing research-based papers as requested.

Associates are called upon to set priorities, assess sensitivities, and exercise judgment in effectively carrying out their duties. Strong analytical, research, and writing skills, an innate curiosity, as well as meticulous attention to detail are required for success. The firm's culture is team oriented and client focused. The successful candidate will enjoy working with others towards a common goal and fostering positive internal and external relations. This position offers the opportunity to work directly with senior management in a flat organizational environment.

Requirements

- BA/BS degree from a leading undergraduate institution with a strong GPA.
- Two to three years of investment and/or analytical experience, preferably with an investment bank, consulting firm (with modeling/quant skills), asset management firm, or related company.
- Strong quantitative/modeling skills.

This is a two- to three-year pre-MBA position, and there is no commitment made by the firm beyond that.

Search 2: Pre-MBA Analyst

This multibillion-dollar fund also makes direct investments in private equity transactions through its co-investment program and acquires limited partner interests in the secondary market.

Responsibilities

- Due diligence of private equity partnerships and direct co-investment opportunities.
- Quantitative and qualitative analyses (e.g., strategy assessment, market analysis, financial modeling, company valuation).
- Preparation of and active participation in on-site due diligence meetings.
- Private equity market research (industry analysis, competitive analysis, strategic analysis).
- Preparation of investment proposals and presentations.

Qualifications

- One to two years of experience in private equity, investment banking (corporate finance/M&A), or relevant consulting experience.
- Strong quantitative skills, particularly comfortable with company valuation.
- Strong Microsoft Excel skills and proficiency in other Microsoft Office programs.
- Experience with financial databases (Bloomberg, Capital IQ, etc.).
- Outstanding communication skills, verbal and written.
- Ability to work effectively and independently in a boutique, international company.
- Team player who possesses intellectual curiosity, sound judgment, thoughtfulness, and attention to detail.

Search 3: Senior Associate (Post-MBA)

This search is for a post-MBA position.

Responsibilities

- Due diligence of private equity partnerships.
- Active participation in on-site due diligence meetings.
- Private equity market research.
- Preparation of investment proposals and presentations.
- Managing workload and development of analysts.

Qualifications

- MBA preferred.
- Four to six years of experience in private equity, investment banking, or relevant consulting experience.
- Outstanding communication skills, verbal and written, in English (additional language is a plus).

- Ability to work effectively and independently in a boutique, international company.
- Team player who possesses intellectual curiosity, sound judgment, thoughtfulness, and attention to detail.

CASE STUDIES

The following three cases studies show some of the backgrounds sought by fund of funds and hybrid funds. The first two candidates were hired into pure fund of funds, and the third focuses more on co-investments at a hybrid fund.

Case Study 34: A Typical Fund of Funds Hire

This person had a banking background and was also able to demonstrate an understanding of the effects of the bigger market on the private equity industry.

■ ■ ■

Although I graduated with a degree in finance (from a small school in New England in 2005), I was not one of those types gung ho on a career in finance. Up until my senior year I was thinking more business than hard-core finance. During the summer after my junior year I did an internship with a private bank, which convinced me that I didn't want to go that route. Instead, I did apply for and was accepted into a typical bulge-bracket banking program where I chose to work on the coverage side (industrials).

Even though I knew I would have to plan my exit from the banking program, I didn't begin looking for my next position until December of my second year (something I admit was a mistake and put me behind the curve). I considered myself more of a public markets person and was not as interested in turning around businesses; thus, I gravitated more toward hedge funds than private equity. When I finally began interviewing I found myself torn because (1) I didn't want later-stage private equity, which typically hires the summer before your expected start date; and (2) although I wanted hedge funds, I was reluctant to leave my program early. I also limited my options by being overly selective about my geographic preference. By the time March 2007 rolled around, I was open to interviewing with both private equity firms and hedge funds, since both would be open to a summer 2007 start.

Fortunately, a headhunter contacted me about a position with a fund of funds. I hadn't been pursuing fund of funds—it was more that the opportunity came my way and I had to listen. Also, at that point, the rosy scenario of being wooed and interviewed by five different places just wasn't happening. I went through three rounds of interviews with this firm. The first was with four people—the VP who eventually became my mentor, the portfolio manager, the CFO, and the head of legal. I met with them for about two hours in their offices, with most of the questions focusing on my experience at the bank. They asked me to tell them about a deal I had worked on and to walk through my involvement in it at each stage.

After that, most of the questions were more of the personality/fit variety. They wanted me to talk about myself and why I wanted to work at a fund of funds, and to see how I would make a good fit within their firm (remember, many of these firms are much smaller in nature). I was honest with them at all times and told them I was looking into buyout funds, hedge funds, and fund of funds, and was open to opportunities at all of them. As someone who follows the public markets, my theory was that buyout funds would have a tough time, and I expressed my concerns during my interviews. By chance, this fund felt the same way and they were building their strategy around it. I think it was important to show them that I was able to step back from the modeling I was doing and look at the bigger picture that was happening in the markets.

> *I quickly found that working at a fund of funds entails more reporting and diligence than valuation type work.*

During the second round of interviews I met with the firm's two partners and again with the VP. There were no technical aspects to the questions. Rather, they wanted to know why I had chosen my bank, what I liked about it, and what my long-term goals were. (I later learned that the position was not a standard two and out one and that they wanted someone who saw the role as more than just a stopping-off point before business school.) I stressed that, for me, business school was not a priority, and I would recommend other candidates be similarly up front with their interviewers.

The third round of interviews was a type of test, but it was not like buyout shops that give you a company and ask you to build a model. For this fund, I was given the name of a fund manager, told what its returns have been, and asked to write a report on the manager, with emphasis on what I thought about the manager and its investments. This is the precise work that is done by funds of funds, and they wanted to see that I could do the work. I got my offer soon thereafter.

I quickly found that working at a fund of funds entails more reporting and diligence than valuation type work. There is also a lot of writing and editing involved as composing reports, especially leading up to the end of each quarter, is a big part of the position. I became sold on this particular fund of funds because of the people and the growth opportunity. Although I was interviewed for the main fund of funds business, the firm did have some other direct investing activities that I was told I could also work on. Now that I'm working, I realize this is where I belong. The work is challenging and suits my personality.

While I'm very happy where I am, looking back, if I could do anything differently I would have been more proactive about starting my job search earlier and been more open to leaving my program immediately upon receiving an offer (I was paranoid about leaving early and possibly burning bridges). I would also have cast my net as wide as possible. I would stress that those seeking jobs now should make sure they are joining a firm with a growth platform. I don't think people spend enough time thinking about the strategy of the places at which they are interviewing, and they are sold on a name basis alone.

Case Study 35: From Retail Banking to a Fund of Funds

This person had a less traditional background. He was able to secure an opportunity at a fund of funds with a background that was mostly with a small retail broker-dealer.

■ ■ ■

When I began college at a small liberal arts school in Connecticut, my intention was to become a high school physics teacher, and I modeled my academic structure as such. After two years of mathematics and physics, I elected to branch out and try something more applicable to real life: a macroeconomics class. Sitting through this class, I began to gain interest in basic financial topics including economies, markets, and institutions.

Building on my newfound interests, the following summer I secured an internship with a local broker-dealer. There I worked on basic financial models, studying correlations between specific indexes and macroeconomic trends, all along trying to make sense of how this could apply to specific debt and equity instruments.

When I returned to school that fall I felt I was fully equipped to run a portfolio, and with much gusto I turned to the alumni community and attempted to raise a mini-endowment fund. After two years of being turned down many times by both alumni and the school's annual fund, I got lucky and convinced one alum to donate $50,000 to my cause. With this newly raised money I founded a student-run fund and hired my friends to help me run it. Together, we invested the money across a portfolio of equities and debt and returned over 35 percent over the last six months of my senior year.

While coordinating my efforts on raising and investing the student fund, I also interned with another local retail broker during the summer after my junior year. This internship included far more investment research and stretched across my senior year. During this time, I worked approximately 30 to 35 hours per week helping a small team of investment professionals manage their practice.

As college began to wind down, I focused my efforts on finding a full-time job in an interesting field within finance. During this process, I tried to leverage my dual majors in physics and economics to help get interviews; however, getting in the door seemed to be the most difficult part of the process. Despite my lack of specific experience, I did manage to get interviews in investment banking, consulting, and with a private equity fund of funds; however, I decided to take a position with the team I had been working with in the local retail brokerage. The main reason was that it was difficult to convince bankers and consultants that I was a better candidate for these types of positions than someone with an accounting or finance background and internship experience in their particular field.

I worked at the retail broker for just under two years, yet made a point of staying in touch with my contact at the fund of funds at which I had interviewed. I was intrigued by the mystique of working in alternative investments and was persistent in my pursuit of a position with this firm. I knew that even junior professionals at fund of funds had the opportunity to interact with successful senior professionals at major buyout funds, and that one can see a broad view of the markets and be exposed to different investing strategies including debt, venture capital, and natural resources. I was determined to work on the buy-side and I had had a great set of interviews with this group during the first go-around.

Fortunately, after 14 or so months, my contact at the fund of funds asked if I would like to meet for a round of golf. Given I was still drawn to the alternative asset classes and the buy-side, I accepted. During the round he informed me that the position I had originally interviewed for was again available, and if I was interested I could come in for another round of interviews.

I would advise candidates looking into private capital not to go to a fund of funds simply because you can't get into a direct private capital fund.

During this round of interviews the team focused on quantitative knowledge, skills, and understanding, as well as culture fit. I tried to demonstrate my entrepreneurial drive by speaking to my experience with the student-run fund I had founded during my college days. I also tried to demonstrate my social abilities and team skills. Coming from a science background my quant skills were not as much in question; however, the team was interested in how effective I was in Excel.

So to say the least, the interviews were intense. In addition to the time I spent with my contact at the firm on the golf course (he was definitely gauging my interest), there were four solid rounds of interviews during which I met all of the investment professionals as well as the CEO and CIO of the larger organization. Some of the questions were more personality/lifestyle focused and there were several "what would you do in this situation?" type questions. There was also a fair share of quantitative questions such as "What is the weighted average cost of capital?" and "What is the fee structure of a GP?"

One of the specific concerns this firm had was around lifestyle and location. They were not located in a city and had recently lost a junior professional for just this reason. They were also concerned about my accounting skills, as my background was nonexistent in this area. To help appease some of the accounting concerns I showed them some of the complex mathematical work I had done in the physics lab. Although this was not accounting, it helped them grasp my ease with Excel and understanding of sophisticated mathematics. For a case study, I was given an excerpt from a private placement memorandum and a quarterly report and asked to build a simple spreadsheet including cash-on-cash multiples and IRRs. There was a foreign exchange component to this exercise that I was later told tripped up a lot of candidates.

The long and short of the story is that things worked out. I was brought on as an analyst and promoted to senior analyst in just over a year. Interestingly, the senior analyst position is the same position for which the firm typically hires people coming from two-year investment banking or consulting programs.

Today, a lot of what I do centers on my ability to judge people and strategies. In essence my group is betting not only on the historical performance of a certain team but the ability of that team to continue to produce results over their next fund cycle. In our position we try to judge fund managers and see how they add value to their companies. Ideally, when you're investing money for such a long time (10 years to well over 20 years), you want to be certain you're placing it with the right people.

I would not consider working at a fund of funds as a step down from working directly with a private equity group. Rather, I'd say it's a step in a different direction. What we do day to day is exciting and always different, spanning from investing in groups doing small growth equity in Central Europe to groups executing the largest global mega buyouts. I would advise candidates looking into private capital not to go to a fund of funds simply because you can't get into a direct private capital fund. Today, when I interview people, I need to feel candidates are genuinely interested in what we do on a fund level.

Although my career stemmed through an atypical background, the most direct and proven way to successfully break into the fund of funds world is through a traditional two-year investment banking or consulting program. There is no other clear-cut path.

Case Study 36: A Banker Joins a Hybrid Fund

This person had the banking skills, and also showed she could think critically about the market and specific deals.

■ ■ ■

I graduated in 2004 from a university in the South with a degree in business administration. Through an on-campus interview I got a summer analyst position at a bulge-bracket investment bank in New York and was placed in the health care group. I accepted an offer to return after graduation as a full-time analyst. At that time, I was not familiar with private equity and was even unaware that it was a common exit after investment banking.

I started looking for a job halfway through my second year in the analyst program, which was later than most of my peers, but I felt I needed the time to figure out what I wanted to do. In previous years, most of the analysts in my group went into more traditional private equity, but I was turned off by how long private equity associates spend analyzing individual deals. I knew that a PE associate can easily spend six months to a year performing primary due diligence on an investment opportunity, and that once the investment is completed, the same associate can spend the rest of her time at the fund working with the portfolio company.

I found that the people I met at funds that co-invest were generally friendlier and a little more laid-back than those at buyout funds. I also soon realized that, on average, there is a better lifestyle, though obviously this varies from firm to firm. Finding a place with a collegial culture was near the top of my list of requirements, and I found this to be more prevalent at smaller firms. There are large funds that do co-investing, but after working at a bulge-bracket investment bank, I wanted to work at a smaller firm in terms of number of people, where I felt I could make more of an impact in a less structured hierarchy. Although opportunities were available to me at buyout funds, I wanted to be more thoughtful about my job search and also tried to avoid the herd mentality that led most banking analysts to more traditional PE funds. I considered corporate finance positions, but found the pay cut too severe. Working at a fund that does co-investing did not require this sacrifice.

Positions at funds that co-invest come up more opportunistically than the more typical private equity jobs, and I quickly found that they do not necessarily hire on a set cycle. While it is probably beneficial to be ready earlier on, I found that it is not essential. Headhunters are the best way to find these jobs because outside of the few large funds, most do not have very public names. I interviewed at about 15 funds and turned down four job offers that I knew were not the right fit. At one fund that co-invests, I didn't feel I was a match for the firm's culture, and at another fund, I felt that the hierarchy was so entrenched that I would only be working for senior associates. It can be tempting to accept a job offer just to get the process over with, especially when the pay is attractive.

I began interviewing with the firm at which I am currently working in June of my second year, and the whole process took about a month. This was late by traditional standards since the two-year analyst program typically ends in late June, and it was hard to be one of the last analysts to accept an offer, even though I had turned down several. However, I was determined not to let the time pressure define my choice.

The interview process at my current firm included interviews with multiple people on three separate occasions. The first round was typical: I was asked questions about my resume and about my experiences in banking and in my internships. In addition to wanting to get a sense of my personality, they also wanted to see that I had the skill set necessary for the job. The second round of interviews included two case studies, which involved evaluating potential investments after having the opportunity to review financial models and read an overview of the businesses. This was the most difficult part of the process and tested my technical and analytical skills. The third interview was purely based on fit. I met with almost everyone on the private equity team. Especially at a smaller firm, it is extremely important to fit in with the existing team.

I found the interviews to be very technical, not only in that I had to speak in detail about my investment banking deals, but I was also challenged to analyze new information. I was given case studies, modeling tests, and accounting quizzes. Funds that co-invest are looking for the same level of technical skill in associates as are buyout firms, and also the ability to think high-level about opportunities, more from a consulting angle. Overall, the process and interviewers were similar to those at buyout funds.

For the most part, I found that it doesn't matter what investment banking group you come from, as long as you have good deal experience that you can confidently discuss. If you want to go to a mega buyout fund, it may matter more. It can also matter if the private equity fund has a sector focus.

Ultimately, I think I was an attractive candidate because I had the investment banking analyst skill set and showed I could take it a step further by thinking critically from a higher-level perspective. I showed a deep interest of co-investing and made it clear that I was not interested in a traditional PE fund. From the moment I

> *Ultimately, I think I was an attractive candidate because I had the investment banking analyst skill set and showed I could take it a step further by thinking critically from a higher-level perspective.*

walked in for the first interview with my firm, I had a good feeling that it was the right place for me. Although I tried to convince myself of this at other places I interviewed, some of which I received job offers at, it always felt like I was trying too hard to find reasons to accept the job. I chose my firm because I felt comfortable with and trusted the people. I also did a fair amount of checks on the firm, both while I was interviewing and when I got the offer, to confirm the company's reputation on the Street. I was very pleased with what I heard back and accepted the offer confidently.

I was accepted into a rotational program and will eventually work on fund of funds investing. Being that it is a relatively small firm, I work directly for a managing director with no one between us. This is essentially unheard of at any private equity fund. I was excited by the challenge, and it has worked out great.

I found that above all else, funds that co-invest want to make sure that you are really interested in what they do. It could get difficult to pursue this type of job search simultaneously with direct investing. Since the jobs require slightly different skill sets, it is better to focus on one. If you narrow down your search, both headhunters and interviewers will respect your dedication and it will show them that you are really there for the right reasons.

Chapter **IX**

FINDING THE RIGHT FIT

You might *think* you're fully prepared to pursue/accept an opportunity at a private equity fund, but there's probably more you can do to increase your chance of success. Even if you have first-rate finance and deal/project skills, you could still end up continually getting turned down for positions, pulling yourself out of contention for others, or left with offers that may not be appropriate for you. And, in each case the common denominator is most likely the issue of fit (or the lack thereof). In this chapter we give some of our guidance on how fit relates to your job search, since we believe finding the best fit can be a springboard to a flourishing career.

If you've been reading this guide closely you will have noticed several mentions of *fit*. Maybe you came across these observations: "To me, it is very important that a candidate *fit* in with the personality of my firm" (Insider Tip, Chapter III); and "Strategy-wise, I believe it's important to target the right funds given your background. You shouldn't waste your time or the funds' time looking at places where there will not be a good *fit*" (Case Study 19). What exactly, you may ask, is fit and why is it so important to your search?

Securing a private equity position is about more than matching your skills with your future employers. It's about finding a place where your skills *and* your personality match those of the hiring firm. And, as you can see from these two quotes, fit is just as important to hiring firms as it is to candidates. Thus, our advice will hopefully prevent you from going down the wrong path and missing out on the right opportunity.

Glocap Insight

To find the right position in private equity it is important to do a thorough self-assessment. What are your interests? What drives you? What are your strengths and weaknesses? What does your experience position you to do? And what are your long-term plans, both professionally and personally? The answers to those questions will serve as a guide for where you want to focus your efforts.

TARGETING THE RIGHT FUNDS

Selecting a private equity fund is a process analogous to selecting a college, which commonly has two main phases: First you research and decide which schools to apply to; and second, after your application is accepted, you have to choose one to attend. We believe this analogy can serve as a model for guiding your PE search. First we discuss targeting the right funds, which will help kick-start the process of analyzing fit for those beginning their search. Once you have offers, the next section, "Evaluating Your Choices," will help you narrow your options so you can pick the place where you are most likely to thrive.

Self-Assessment

When initiating a search, we recommend conducting a self-assessment to help come up with key criteria that will help identify a potential group of funds where you think you could fit in best. The first part of this exercise will help you determine what your relative strengths and weaknesses are. This will narrow down what firms could have interest in *you*, and you'll be in a better position to make an intelligent decision about which to pursue. As part of this task you should be asking yourself questions such as:

- Am I good at financial modeling?
- Do I have specific industry expertise?
- Do I have hands-on exposure to operations?
- Do I think strategically?
- Am I very research intensive?
- Do I like to network and develop business?

With the answers to those questions in hand you should turn your attention to the different types of funds that you *want* to pursue. From what we've seen over the years, there are several factors that will help narrow the field. These include:

- The investment approach of the fund. Some funds work very hands-on with their portfolio companies, others are more execution intensive.

- The stage of investing. By now you should know that working at a VC fund is very different from working at a later-stage growth fund or a buyout fund.
- Whether a fund is industry-focused or more of a generalist fund.
- The size of the deals and the deal teams.
- Compensation.
- Geography.

After a brief look at these factors you should be able to eliminate some additional funds (or at least types of funds) that do not meet your criteria. For example, if you know you don't want to do health care investing or you can't see yourself living in Texas, it doesn't make sense to consider firms in either of these categories. Or if you can't ever see yourself at a five-person, $200 million fund (or, in contrast, at a $10 billion fund with 100 people), you will be doing yourself (and a recruiter) a favor by removing a firm of that size from consideration.

If there are still some funds that you are less certain about, it's probably better to keep them on your list than spend too much time thinking whether they should be eliminated. The time to dig deeper is when you have offers on the table, and we go through a more thorough evaluation of how to do that in the second section when your diligence will be more intense. However, having a manageable list is important as it will allow you to conserve your energy and stay focused, and that will ultimately allow you to perform better in your interviews. Otherwise, you may find yourself trying to convince a health care VC fund to hire you one day, a real estate buyout fund the next, and then a general growth equity fund after that, and ultimately you will have a tough time being generally persuasive to any of them. If you recall, the author of Case Study 11 says: "I would advise that when targeting PE funds, people should target a narrow subset of funds in which they fit. Taking a shotgun approach will not work."

EVALUATING YOUR CHOICES

If you have one or more offers in hand, it's time to embark on deeper diligence to find your best fit, because where you take your first role, for better or worse, does set your career in motion (just like the college you went to and the first job you took out of school). Therefore we recommend you take the time to choose a place that you truly believe will offer you the best experience.

Going back to the example of when you applied to college, the first part of that search may have led you to target three small liberal arts schools in rural New England, two large universities in the Midwest, and two engineering schools on the West Coast. These were all varied institutions, but you had a sincere interest in each of them when you applied. When you were accepted to some of them you had to weigh all the variables, not just the size of the schools and geographic location. Given that it was such an important decision, you probably did a thorough evaluation to get a grasp of which school would be the optimal fit for you and thereby help you best get where you wanted to go. You might have talked to alumni and current students and looked into the professors, the academic departments, the sports programs, and the overall culture of the student body to help you choose which school to attend. Wouldn't it be smart to put the same effort into deciding which PE offers to accept?

Glocap Insight There are usually no right or wrong answers when it comes to finding your best fit. For example, as it pertains to selecting a college, some people simply prefer big-city schools while others prefer a rural campus. Both have trade-offs, but neither is necessarily better or worse than the other. Beyond analyzing the trade-offs in relation to your preferences, there is no magic formula to help you choose the place where you will fit best (be it a school or a PE fund).

In private equity there is a common set of factors that everyone has to consider, but candidates prioritize them in different ways. To help you make a choice, let's look in more detail at some of the variables mentioned in the previous section and consider the pros and cons of each. It will then be up to you to rank them according to your personality and preferences. When candidates come to us with a choice to make, we advise them to take a step back and ask themselves, "Where do I want to be in 5, 10, 15 years? And which path will be the best step to get me there (or at least leave me with the most options)?" Indeed, many funds may ask you this as well.

Fit is always important, but its importance increases as you advance in your career. For example, if you are finishing business school and are deciding which offer to accept, you are making what could be a career decision, so you should think even more about fit than pre-MBAs who generally have windows of natural transition ahead of them. That's because, whereas earlier in your career you were still *thinking* about your 10-year plan, once you have your MBA it's time to start *implementing* it.

What Is the Fund's Reputation?

Before we get into the different fund variables, we recommend all candidates look out for some universal warning signs. In general, most funds that you will come across are legitimate and doing relatively well enough to have gotten to where they are. However, because we've seen enough examples of people getting into situations that are less than they bargained for, we want to alert you to some potential problems.

A fund that has a bad reputation and is falling apart is obviously one that should be avoided, but that's an extreme case. Two more common signals to look out for are if a firm has had fund-raising troubles and if senior professionals have recently left the firm (this could have happened while you were interviewing or right before, and you wouldn't have known unless you were plugged in). In fact, anytime people have left a fund for reasons other than the natural end of their commitments, it should at least raise some caution.

If you come across a fund with these signs you should do some extra research. Why did the senior people leave? Were they squeezed out? Why is fund-raising slow? There could be a valid reason, and if there is, you should find out what it was. On the flip side, if a firm has raised new money and has had a great retention rate, you should probably have little to worry about.

One of the best ways to research the reputation of a fund is to speak with the firm's current associates or those who used to work there. We have found that associates who are rotating out into business school are especially helpful and are usually candid about their experiences. They may also have a handle on other firms, so don't limit your questions to where they worked. We suggest you also take a look at the business schools they are going to, as that reflects on the reputation of the fund—are they the same ones you would be interested in attending? It's always a good idea to check the industry publications to see if the firm has been in the news lately.

If you can't find out about a firm's reputation from people who have worked there, other good people to turn to for insight into how a fund is perceived by the PE community are investors in PE funds (such as a fund of funds or an endowment), bankers who cover the industry (financial sponsors), or even recruiters—for many strong candidates we are happy to (and do) give advice even if we didn't ultimately help them with their specific offers.

Is the Fund Doing Deals?

Clearly, the best place for you to grow and enhance your skills would be at a fund that is actively closing high-quality transactions. Before accepting an offer, make sure you know when the investment period for the current fund runs out (the life of a fund is typically 10 to 12 years, with the initial 5 to 6 years used to deploy capital and the remaining years focused on harvesting the investments); how many deals on average the fund closes; how much uninvested capital (often called *dry powder*) a fund has; and whether any attempts have been made to raise new money. Then do a careful comparison of the funds at which you have offers.

Maybe you're choosing between two well-known $1 billion funds. One is in its fourth year and has about $100 million left to invest, and the other just raised its fund. Joining the older fund may not give you as much exposure to new deals. Any new deals may be add-ons to existing investments, and chances are you could spend a lot of time working with those portfolio companies as well as raising money for the next fund—either can be worthwhile, but it may not be what you signed up for. At the newer fund you would probably mostly work on new deals, which may be what you had in mind.

Be careful and don't just think that doing deals is enough, because simply putting money to work is not the endgame. Your goal should be working on high-quality deals, as the success of the transactions you've been involved in will influence how you are perceived. We've received calls from people looking to make a lateral move out of a firm where fund-raising has stalled, because they don't want to get stale not doing deals for three years. Taking the right measures now could help you avoid the same situation.

Fund Performance

A fund's performance is important both in an absolute sense and vis-à-vis its peer group (meaning, for example, funds that were raised at the same time). A fund that has consistently performed well will have an easier time attracting new investors than poorer-performing or start-up funds. Nevertheless, look into why it performed well. Was it one amazingly successful investment, or several? What are the chances that it will continue to perform well? Are the same people around who made it successful?

You may like the idea of joining a start-up fund, but do you have the appropriate risk tolerance? Since there is no fund performance to look at, you should focus on the track records of the senior people. It is their reputation that will carry the fund.

Investment Approach

The investment approaches of funds can run the gamut. Some focus on achieving value by finding a good deal at a good price and therefore concentrate on the financial and structuring aspects. Others may focus more on the value they add value post-investment and concentrate on improving the operational aspects of companies. Most funds would probably say they do both, but since the ball is in your court we recommend you look into what you prefer and where you like to be on that spectrum. Do you enjoy diving into numbers and modeling complex deals? If so, you might want to join a fund that will continue to enhance those skills. Maybe you prefer a more active role with port-folio companies. You can sometimes get a good indication about a fund's investment approach by looking at the backgrounds of the investment professionals. Some funds can be weighted toward former ex-consultants or people with operations backgrounds and will therefore tend to be more hands-on, while others that have a larger number of former bankers might be more focused on the financial aspects of deals.

Stage

The previous chapters went over the skills required by early-stage venture capital, later-stage growth equity, and leveraged buyout funds (for a refresher, take a look at Chapter I). As someone with multiple offers in hand, you should figure out if one of them is from a fund that says it invests in companies at more than one stage. In such a situation you should get a better understanding of the target allocation to the various investment stages. This will help you define what you really will be doing.

For example, you may want to do extra research on any fund that does some growth equity along with LBOs. Growth equity can involve more deal sourcing; however, if that is a primary part of the job but you wanted the LBO deal experience, you may not be right for this fund, and vice versa. Both buyout and growth equity funds can offer great career-track platforms, and there are top firms in each category, so it will be up to you to figure out what opportunity fits best with what you want to get out of it for the long term.

Industry Focus

Industries come in and out of vogue. Part of the choice you have to make is whether even to target an industry-specific versus a generalist fund. When considering industry focus, think about the pros and cons of specialization. If you become specialized in one industry, you will be attractive to some funds but less so to others. In our experience, focusing on a specific industry can make it tough to diversify into new areas (in Chapter V we pointed out that post-MBAs have a tough time switching industries), but it can be helpful when trying to get an edge. You may have more options if you are a generalist, but may find it difficult to join an industry-specific fund later on. We have seen candidates succeed choosing either path, but you should at least be aware of the implications of each option.

Deal Size/Deal Team

Both the size of the deals that a fund does and the size of its deal teams are generally dictated by the overall size of the fund. As you would expect, the general rule of thumb is that larger funds do larger deals and have larger deal teams, while smaller funds usually do smaller deals with smaller deal teams. There are trade-offs to each.

There are more layers of professionals working on larger deals, but then again, even as a member of an eight-person team, you would be getting exposed to complex transactions with a lot of moving parts and that, in itself, would be a unique learning experience. You may, for example, play a role in a $10 billion LBO of a company with 10,000 employees spread across 20 divisions in six countries. The deal could have several different capital tranches and a complex set of ownership to evaluate. Even being a part of a large team could still result in tremendous learning.

However, if you are working on a large deal you will likely have less access to portfolio companies and their top management, and may have less interaction with senior investment professionals at your firm. Since the larger deals can sometimes be done as club deals with other major LBO funds, you could find yourself working with four other LBO shops and have responsibility for only a fraction of the deal. Therefore, while you would be involved in a mammoth deal, you should question how much you would be learning and from whom.

Generally, smaller deals are less complex and have fewer moving parts. In a smaller deal you won't come across $2.5 billion debt facilities (a $50 million equity investment with a $30 million mezzanine piece would be more likely). However, the smaller deal teams (it could be just you and one other person) can mean more responsibility in executing the investment, and more involvement with portfolio companies and the senior management of your fund. You could even be traveling with a partner and dealing directly with the CEO of a company when the partner can't, and therefore learning how to run a business as well.

As with the other variables discussed in this chapter, there are no right or wrong answers. You must decide which place will be the best experience for you. If the sizes of the deals are similar, you might want to go to the fund with the leaner teams. Such a situation could occur if you have offers from two $1 billion funds that do control buyouts and have performed well.

Thinking about the size of the fund that you enjoy is also important because firms may begin labeling you as a smaller fund person or a bigger fund person depending on where you work. This will come into play if you decide to make a lateral move down the road. Keep in mind that there is a general bias toward hiring people to do the same size deals that they have done in the past.

Geography

Geographic preference is more than picking a fund in a city where you want to live. Of course, you shouldn't go to a fund that is in a city where you don't want to be. But you should also not assume that one fund is better than another because of its physical location. There are definitely $500 million funds in smaller cities that are more reputable than $500 million funds in major financial centers. If you join a reputable firm in a smaller city, you will still be marketable to funds in other geographies later on.

We've been asked by candidates with multiple offers if they should take what they think is an A– opportunity in a major city or an A+ one in a smaller locale. If you are truly open to any geography, we will stick to our theme that you should go after the best learning experience and therefore shouldn't let where you will live get in the way. You should look carefully at the brand, the people, and the reputation of the funds where you have offers. Even if your friends haven't heard of a specific fund, if top-caliber people are there, industry pros should give you credit for a strong learning experience.

Compensation

How you are compensated naturally plays some role in whether you accept a position, but we continue to stress that finding the best place to advance your career in the long term should be as important as the money that you will make in the short term. The idea is that finding the best platform will give you the best prospects for long-term compensation.

We think candidates have a healthy mind-set when they tell us they want to be compensated fairly and that they are seeking an environment where they will be learning the most, and thus advancing the fastest. These are the candidates who tend to realize that being somewhere where they will be cultivated as a strong investor can be the ideal form of compensation. If you can earn a lot while you learn, then you've found a good place. Alternatively, it may not be worth it if you end up at a firm where you are earning a lot but may not be getting as much out of the experience.

Some candidates can probably afford to take a risk and go to a start-up fund that is being run by top people, even if at the beginning it doesn't offer as much cash, as long as it is a place where you can grow and over time receive a percentage of the carried interest. (See Chapter XII for a more detailed discussion on carry and compensation.)

Chapter **X**

THE RESUME

Preparing a top-notch resume is a necessary but not sufficient requirement to securing a private equity job. Recruiters, and in fact most anyone in a hiring position who has looked at hundreds of resumes, are extremely adept at sizing up candidates very quickly based on what they see and read in a resume. This chapter discusses the role of your resume, gives detailed suggestions about what we think should (or should not) be included, and makes suggestions on the general structure and content. Appendix B contains 15 real-life resumes that correspond to case studies appearing in Chapters III through VIII.

A primary purpose of the resume is to help you come across as compelling enough for a firm to want to initiate a dialogue with you. Therefore, in our opinion, your approach when putting one together should be to present a thorough and accurate picture of yourself and what you have done, with the goal of landing an interview. You should at all costs avoid using excessive (and unnecessary) embellishment or over-the-top phrases that could harm you (see "The Personal Section" in this chapter). With that in mind, as long as you present yourself well and stay within the norms of accuracy, your resume should serve you best.

We evaluate thousands of candidates each week and look for well-presented resumes with an easy-to-read format, simple fonts, and *zero* typographical errors. Even one typo, confusing format, or poor use of grammar could be reason enough to separate one qualified candidate from another. Some schools, such as Harvard Business School, have adapted a standard resume outline for their students that presents an easy-to-read summary of a candidate's education and work history. We think this consistent look helps readers focus on the content of the resume without the distraction of different formats.

As recruiters placing individuals into high-end positions at PE/LBO and venture capital funds, we work off the initial assumption that every resume we see will be of higher quality, especially given the caliber of professionals we presume we are dealing with. As we examine each resume further, the basic content including any additional accomplishments and the way they are presented will play a large role in how we determine the attractiveness of a candidate. For example, a candidate will come off as attractive if he has a solid academic performance, good work experience, and a well thought out, clear career progression. That same candidate will appear even stronger if the academic and work experiences are supplemented with additional achievements and, of course, if those are presented well on their resume.

ELEMENTS OF AN EFFECTIVE RESUME

Keeping in mind the main goal of the resume, we don't want you to miss out on an interview simply because you omitted something or worded it poorly. From our perspective, if you have a solid academic and professional background, with a combination of banking, consulting, and/or private equity, you should draw some interest as long as you have put together a quality resume that reflects that background. Candidates without the traditional background will probably have to go the extra step to make sure their resume stands out (without lying or embellishing, of course) and gives them a needed leg up to differentiate them in the PE hiring process.

Following are some general suggestions, based on common inquiries we receive, of what we think should be considered when constructing a resume.

Be Honest

We cannot stress enough that you are who you are and your resume is not a place to pretend to be someone else. That means not listing things you have not done or embellishing things you have done. Expect that the claims you make in your resume will be verified. This includes test scores, GPAs, work experiences, and athletic accomplishments. Some firms ask for transcripts or graduation degrees; almost all ask for references and will check them. Putting something in that doesn't belong is simply not worth the risk.

Deals Matter

Highlight and list your deals and projects. Remember that anything you list is fair game to be discussed, so don't list something that you didn't work on or that you are not prepared to talk about. You should break all deals down individually and list your responsibilities along with the size of the deal, the structure used, and the status—has the deal closed or is it pending?

Since not everyone is familiar with company names, you should be clear about the industry in which you have done deals. If you're at a PE fund you should take this one step further and describe your current fund by mentioning its name, size, the stage of deals on which it focuses (it can be multistage), and the industry focus if there is one. If you have very extensive deal experience we suggest including a separate deal sheet as an addendum to your resume.

Special Responsibilities

In addition to listing your work experience, it's important to list any other special responsibilities you have had along the way. Maybe you led a team of analysts, did some special work for the chairman of your company on an internal project, or represented your company overseas. Perhaps you were tapped by upper management to be involved in recruiting or training. In our opinion, any of these could indicate that you were considered a leader and a trusted representative of the firm, and will help you stand out from our perspective.

Avoid More than One Page

We are of the school of thought that a nice crisp resume is usually one page, especially for anyone with 10 or fewer years of work experience. We have seen very senior people squeeze their experiences into one page, so we think you should be able to as well. The exception to this rule is if you have specific additional information—such as a deal sheet, a list of patents you were granted, papers you have published, and so on. (This is especially true with academics and PhDs). These can be included as a supplement.

Don't Forget the Months

Although other guidelines suggest otherwise, we think it's beneficial to always list the month and year you started and ended a position. If you left a position in December 2007, but your resume just says "2007," someone reading your resume in January 2008 will not know if you have been out of work for 10 days, 10 weeks, or 10 months.

Objectives

Not all resumes need to include a stated objective. If you have a background that is common for the position you are pursuing, an objective might be redundant. An objective can be more helpful for someone whose background may seem like a further stretch for the role they want (this may be someone who is changing careers or industries). In such a case an objective should address why your skills are applicable for the particular position you are targeting.

Cover Letters

Although cover letters usually go hand-in-hand with resumes, we don't feel they are always necessary. If you are sending a resume directly to a hiring firm we wouldn't discourage including a cover letter. However, if you are working with a recruiter, a cover letter is not necessary because most of the recruiter's role is to assess your skills, and they will frequently do their own write-up about why you are appropriate for a specific role.

Grades, Test Scores, and Recognitions

It's safe to assume that GPAs and test scores are relevant for your entire career. Always list GPAs to at least one decimal point. Some individuals with high GPAs sell themselves short by not including it at all because they heard it does not matter once you are more senior or post–business school. List GMAT and SAT scores if they are good to great. We might recommend holding off if they were very low. For MBAs, business school GPAs are not worth including, but top class distinctions such as a Baker or Arjay Miller Scholar from Harvard Business School or Stanford's Graduate School of Business should be mentioned.

What about High School?

High school information should generally not be included unless it is pretty significant—for example, valedictorian of a 500-student graduating class, or class president. Some graduates of prep or private schools may list their schools, as ties among alumni can be strong. Listing a major accomplishment or leadership position such as being captain of a varsity team, newspaper editor, or member of a championship team is acceptable, but the listing should be brief.

The Personal Section

We suggest you include a personal section on your resume. This is one area where it is acceptable to be a little more creative. List some of your true hobbies, interests, and accomplishments. However, avoid the temptation to include things because you think people will want to read them—avid crocodile wrestler, drag racer, or base jumper—unless you really do those things. Firms and recruiters can see through that and size you up pretty quickly.

Golf, hiking, fly fishing, coaching soccer, playing piano, tutoring, photography, ballroom dancing, judo, and traveling are all pretty descriptive and neutral. Being a contestant on college Jeopardy or a child actor is also interesting and probably worth including. Wine tasting, reading spy novels, driving the Amalfi Coast, avid Cincinnati Reds fan, are all fine but approaching the limits. Smoking *fine* cigars while drinking single malt whiskey, playing with your two *beautiful* children, saying you enjoy intellectual political commentary, or watching ESPN are probably over the top and could potentially hurt you.

Language/International

Language skills and dual citizenship may be included in the personal section. However, if you are really pushing for an international career you could list these in a separate section, adding levels of proficiency—for example, native French speaker, fluent in German and business German, conversational in Mandarin.

Some Other Dos and Don'ts

- De-emphasize older, less relevant work experience (i.e., summer jobs unless with brand-name firms or jobs during college).
- There is never a need to write "references available upon request." In the realm of private equity recruiting, it is assumed that you can present several references.
- In the current world of e-mail, don't worry too much about paper stock. In most cases, if a hard copy of your resume is needed, it will be printed from a computer. Since recruiters will e-mail your resume on to clients, we recommend you make sure the document doesn't have passwords or fancy formatting that can get lost in older versions of software.
- Whatever contact information you include is fair game, so make sure whatever you list (e-mail, mobile phone, work phone, home phone) is in working order and that it is safe for a recruiter or firm to use.

SAMPLE RESUMES

In Appendix B are a series of 15 resumes of candidates from varying backgrounds who all secured private equity positions. As indicated at the top of each resume, these correspond to the case studies earlier in this book. We have slightly altered these per the requests of the candidates who were gracious enough to allow us to reprint them. We feel the resumes provide a good glimpse of what makes certain candidates attractive to private equity funds because, except for the modifications, the resumes are similar to how they appeared when the candidates landed their PE interviews. Resume 6 is particularly short because this person got into PE directly out of undergrad and didn't have an extensive work history.

We recommend you look at all of the resumes in this section, regardless of the level of the candidates or the path they took. But we suggest you make an extra effort to look for a resume from someone who is at the same entry point as you and compare your resume to theirs, both for style and substance. Also, take a look at what makes each person stand out. Sometimes it's their personal experiences, other times it's their academic or career accomplishments.

When you look at the resumes, focus on how they describe work experiences and what they include in the personal sections. To help you out, each resume has a section at the top called "Recruiter's Perspective," in which we highlight key points that jump out at recruiters and hiring firms when scanning the resume. Some resumes also have notes under "Pluses." These are not the ubiquitous action words that many resume guides suggest using; rather they are specific highlights that give the candidate added attraction in the eyes of our recruiters.

Rankings of undergraduate institutions on each resume come from *U.S. News & World Report's* list of America's Best Colleges 2007. The business school rankings are from *BusinessWeek's* 2006 ranking of best MBA programs. (Note: this ranking is done every two years.)

Chapter **XI**

THE INTERVIEW

At this point, you've read our insight into the hiring process, learned about the importance of fit, and should be able to put together a strong resume. But the most crucial part of the process is still ahead—the interview. Even if you are a top banker or consultant and know your deals and/or projects inside and out, you should be aware that a large part of business is still about the human element and one-on-one interaction. You may have all the skills to be a top PE investor, but if you don't perform well in your face-to-face interviews, you may never get a chance to showcase them on the job at a PE fund.

No matter when you try to break into private equity, we can almost guarantee that your interview process will be exhausting and thorough—and that holds true regardless of the size of the fund at which you're interviewing, the stage at which it invests, or the role for which you're being considered. To help you prepare and avoid any surprises, this chapter reviews the types of questions, the subjects that will be covered, and the structure and timing of interviews.

Throughout this guide we've emphasized that firms are looking to hire superior candidates who can help their funds earn solid returns while also protecting the firm's brand and reputation. Even a smaller fund will want its own star. Remember, the professionals who launched these funds worked hard to get where they are. They are proven achievers and top performers, and they want the same caliber of professionals working for them. The way they size you up in interviews is not too different from the due diligence they do on their own investments. In essence, they want to know if you will be a good investment for them—in terms of both time and money.

The interview is your chance to prove that you have more than just the technical skills to excel in the role. Most industry veterans will tell you that private equity is about more than just the numbers and that there is a human element that plays a big part in making successful investments. Because many deals (and business in general) are still based on relationships and trust, firms will need to be comfortable in the knowledge that you can handle senior-level relationships, such as being put in front of the CEO of a company, or running a call with a banker or lawyer.

LATER-STAGE PE/LBO INTERVIEWS

Later-stage PE interviews will have a mix of quantitative and qualitative elements, with the extent of each depending on the level (pre-MBA interviews will predominantly focus on quantitative aspects, while more senior roles will have an additional qualitative aspect). Most funds are collegial, close-knit groups and are looking for someone who will work well with them in a collaborative environment. They will use the interviews to get a feel for whether they would want to work with you and how well they think you will interact with professionals at the firm, their vendors, and executives at their portfolio companies. Therefore your maturity, communications skills, presence, and leadership all play a significant part in the people side of the business.

The Interview Rounds

The type of firm at which you are interviewing and the time of year will generally determine the pace of your interview process. As noted in previous chapters, there is a cycle to interviewing at both the pre- and post-MBA levels. Candidates with brand-name/bulge-bracket experience are pursued aggressively early in the cycle by the larger PE funds with predetermined hiring needs (April through August of the first year of their analyst program for pre-MBAs; early in the second year of business school for MBAs or, for some, even before they return for their second year).

In the case of pre-MBAs, the funds will seek to meet as many of the top candidates as they can and quickly advance the best ones to the next round. If a fund is not based in your local area but is interested in meeting candidates in your city, it may fly a few members of its team in to conduct interviews in person. It's best to be flexible around their calendar, as they may not make another trip for first-round interviews and your one window of opportunity could close. Some funds may also conduct first-round interviews via telephone or video conference if a face-to-face meeting cannot be arranged (we offer some guidance on phone interviews later in this chapter). First-round interviews for MBAs could be on or close to campus. Later rounds will typically be at the fund's offices.

Glocap Insight

The interview cycle affects how quickly you may be expected to respond to an offer. Private equity firms that interview earlier in the cycle can either give candidates the luxury of a week to accept an offer, or force their hands and demand a more immediate answer. If you get an offer later in the cycle, more frequently you may have only up to a few days to make a decision, because at that point the candidate pools are thinner and hiring firms don't want to be left without backup options.

As we explained in more detail in Chapters III and IV, in addition to the top bulge-bracket pre-MBA analysts and the top-pedigree MBAs, each year other very strong analysts and MBAs get into high-quality PE funds. These candidates will most likely get interview traction with PE funds that recruit later in the season. These funds have less predictable hiring needs and, thus, choose to wait until they have more clarity with respect to their hiring needs, which is frequently later in the hiring cycle and closer to when you can start. For both pools of candidates, interviews may be on more of a rolling basis.

If you are a pre-MBA or a current MBA and are interviewing later in the cycle, most PE firms will wonder why you have not been hired yet. They may ask you point-blank why you're still available. The reasons can vary, but you should be prepared with a clear story as to why you are still in play. Maybe you were out of the country, were stuck day and night working on deals, or had turned down offers for various other reasons (for example, the investment stage may not have been to your liking, the geography was wrong, or your gut simply told you it wasn't the best platform). Perhaps you made it to several final rounds but didn't receive any offers. All of those are valid reasons and responses. However, if you went on 10 first-round interviews and were not invited back for any second rounds, this raises caution flags. Recruiters and employers will try to sniff out why that was the case, and you should be prepared with a good, confident answer.

In general, interviews at PE/LBO funds should stretch out over three to four rounds (sometimes there can be as few as two rounds for junior roles). The early rounds of most pre-MBA interviews will include a mix of penetrating questions to determine quantitative (modeling) and qualitative (big picture/strategy) skills. If you're invited back for later rounds, there will probably be more of the same questions, but they may come from different people. Often these rounds become a test of endurance to see how well you can stay engaged and provide consistent and intelligent answers.

The middle rounds are frequently used by firms to narrow down the group of candidates according to best fit. For example, clients that use us for pre-MBA recruiting may have 20 candidates in for first rounds, 10 back for a second round, and 5 finalists for a final round (of which they may hire one to three people). The middle rounds are also when candidates may decide whether to continue interviewing at a specific fund.

Insider Tip ▷

From a Senior Associate

In interviews I generally look for traits that will enable candidates to excel within our environment, because, while our fund may be large, there are really only a few senior managing directors and myself. The ability to learn quickly, to prosper without much supervision, and to execute efficiently are highly valued. These abilities are not limited to the type of investment bank one may have been trained at; instead, they are specific to individuals and their ability to communicate their strengths and skills to others.

Unlike pre-MBAs, current or post-MBAs will not necessarily be interviewed by junior professionals, at least not in early rounds. Instead, you will most likely initially be interviewed by professionals at your same level or more senior. There is a chance that you will be asked to meet one or more junior investment professionals in one of the middle rounds. This may be part of the screening process, so we would suggest not letting your guard down if it happens. We have seen people get dinged because they talked down to someone.

The later rounds are when candidates should expect to meet many partners of the fund (if not all of them). In a large firm this may mean just the partner(s) in the industry group with which you are interviewing. Once you meet the partners you should be beyond most of the quantitative hurdles, so you can expect the interview to be more conversational and qualitative in nature (how you think about investments, etc.). But don't be surprised if you are still asked a few technical questions to spot-check your knowledge and see if you are prepared.

Partners may also want to re-affirm your interest in them. If you've gotten this far it's probably because everyone else you've met thinks you have the hard skills to do the job and that you can fit into the team and represent the firm, and they have probably told the partners as much. This last step is your opportunity to show the partners that they were right and that you belong with the firm.

The "Why PE" Question

You would think we would not have to tell you, but you will very likely be asked, "Why do you want a job in private equity?" For those who have already worked in PE, the question may be amended slightly to, "Why are you pursuing a *career* in PE?" In fact, you can expect almost all the professionals you meet during each of the different rounds to inquire about this in some form. For many funds a logical follow-up question would be, "Why do you want to work at *our* fund?" The funds want to see that you are genuinely interested in private equity, that you have the right motivation for wanting to be in the industry (and at their firm), and that you can express that in a cohesive and articulate way. These are such obvious questions, but you would be surprised how many people bomb them.

We've heard of pre-MBAs answering the "Why PE?" question with responses like, "Everyone else in my analyst class is doing it, so I thought I would too"; "I thought it would help me get into business school"; and "I want to be on the buy-side." The answer they were more likely hoping for is that you have a passion for investing and that you want to apply your skill set to working hands-on with companies, building businesses and creating value. The following quote from Case Study 3 exemplifies this point:

> Go into interviews with confidence and determination. Show them that you know *why* you want to be in private equity and, more specifically, *why* you want to work for them. These are all extremely small organizations where every person is an important member of the team. It's similar to an athletic team with only a handful of members: Come draft day, they want to know that you will be a good draft pick for them.

Deal Skills

Your financial knowledge and deal skills are always going to be important, and you should be able to address both intelligently. The extent to which you will be asked about your deals (including your specific role on the deals) can vary for pre-MBA, current MBA, and post-MBA candidates. We discuss those entry points separately here.

Pre-MBAs will be expected to know specific financial models they built and what the variables and drivers were. At this level, PE/LBO funds are known for asking modeling-intensive questions relating to valuation. We frequently hear that candidates are asked how to calculate *free cash flow*. Although this calculation is done by most banking analysts every day, we found that many candidates still have trouble doing it on the spot.

The funds will also want to know that you can put together complex models that come up with accurate valuations and that you understand how all financial statements interact. You should be ready to first walk your interviewers through how you construct a model and then be ready to put one together as part of the interview process (though this would not likely happen until a middle round when the hiring fund is more interested in you). In most cases, candidates are informed in advance when there will be a modeling test. In those cases it's possible you will spend a few hours at the fund's offices during your interview, often in a separate room, building a model (you will probably be given a computer, a couple of 10ks, and whatever else you need). Your performance on this exercise could help determine if you advance to final rounds and meet the partners. In certain cases, it could also be the final indicator of whether you ultimately are given an offer.

From a Partner at a PE Firm

The biggest mistake made by people interviewing for PE jobs is that they don't take a view. When you are asked, "What do you think about this investment opportunity?" you have to have an answer. Your view may be wrong, but that doesn't matter if it is well thought out. That's what investing is all about.

Although in most cases pre-MBAs will not be expected to know more than what they did on a particular deal, you can set yourself apart by being able to discuss more dimensions of the deal. For example, knowing why the deal made sense and what the value drivers were could differentiate you from other candidates. If you worked on a merger, you should know why the companies merged and be able to explain the big picture behind the deal. But be careful. At the end of the day, you're being interviewed for a position that will require intense modeling work, so having A+ answers to the "why" questions will not make up for B+ modeling skills.

Although Case Study 14 appeared in the post-MBA chapter, there is some valuable advice about pre-MBA interviewing, most notably the modeling questions:

> I interviewed at about 15 to 20 firms. They all pretty much asked the same questions: How do you get to free cash flow? Walk me through an LBO that you worked on. How would you model it? They grilled me on my deals, asking if I thought they were good ones—basically anything on my resume was fair game. I think this is a weak point for people with banking backgrounds. They are used to burying themselves in the models. They have to learn to take a step back and judge the entire deal. Some gave me quantitative brain teasers, and all asked, "Why do you want to go into PE?" I would also add that since the PE firms don't train you, they will expect that you got your training from your analyst program, and they will test that during the interviews.

For further proof of the lengths to which PE firms will go to test your modeling skills, take a look at what the author of Case Study 1 had to say. In his case, some of the modeling questions even came from partners. As you may recall, this person began pre-MBA interviewing in late summer and in the space of a few weeks had his offer in hand:

> I would advise other banking analysts interested in PE to be sure they want to do it well before the recruiting period comes up. You've got to go after it hard, so you better want it and do your homework, especially when it comes to preparing for interviews. It sounds obvious to say that you better know your LBO models and your deals inside and out, but it's true. On my interviews I was grilled pretty hard by the partners.
>
> The firm that eventually extended me an offer had me meet just about everyone that I would be working with, which meant about 12 to 15 people. About half of them asked me about my work and the others just wanted to get to know me and see if I would fit in with the firm. All the other firms asked me pretty technical questions. They asked me to walk them through an LBO model. Some would show me an LBO model and say, "Let's say the depreciation changes by $1 million—talk about how every line in your model changes."

For current MBAs and more senior post-MBAs, the finance/modeling questions will probably not be as intense. If you worked previously in PE you may be asked some basic questions to test your knowledge, but for the most part the funds will assume that you have the quantitative skills to do the job. If you secure a position at this level you will probably not be directly putting together as many models, but you will have to understand the models that others produce. Instead, candidates at this level should be well versed in discussing several aspects of the investment, including origination, due diligence/valuation, negotiations/structuring, interaction with management, and any operational/strategic work that went into deal.

If you are a current MBA with previous PE experience, you will probably be quizzed about your past deals and your responsibilities (even though your last deal experience was more than a year ago). Funds will specifically probe to see how you stack up against your peers and that you had a better understanding of deals. At this level, a key focus of the funds will be to gauge your partner-track potential, which can include skills such as comfortably interacting with senior management, having deal-sourcing ideas and skills, and understanding deal strategy. They want to know what you learned, from whom you learned it, what your deal team looked like (for example, was it just you and a partner on deals?) and what your specific responsibilities were.

Personality Matters

Although we spoke at length about fit in Chapter IX, we feel it's important to point out again that interviews are when your personality and your potential to fit in with the culture of a fund come out. You may have had a good enough resume to get an interview, but your ability to fit in—and the hiring firm's impression of whether you will—becomes a big determining factor in whether you will get an offer.

It's easy to determine from a resume if a candidate has the pedigree and relevant deal skills required. As recruiters, the majority of our time is spent assessing the qualitative skills and personality of candidates to determine whether they should be introduced to our client. After that, a lot of our effort is spent assessing whether we think a candidate will integrate with the hiring firm. Even though some funds may control billions of dollars in investments, they are relatively small organizations compared to most companies. For example, billion-dollar funds can have as few as a dozen investment professionals, and even the very large ones with several billion dollars in assets under management may only still have 100 people. Thus, the partners and other investment professionals will want to feel comfortable working and interacting with you on a regular basis.

In addition to simply interviewing you, we estimate that 10 to 20 percent of firms go as far as giving candidates personality assessment tests—the Myers-Briggs Type Indicator and the Caliper Profile are two examples. These tests, which most often are given after the final round, are designed to determine personality types that help hiring firms assess fit within different team environments and serve as a double check against potential conflicts. We have found that the hiring firms that use these tests put a lot of weight on the results, and your performance can weed you out even after you have met everyone you need to.

Case Studies/Tests

Case studies/tests are frequently part of the interview process. If you know what's in store you could find ways to prepare (such as building a model); however, many PE firms want to see how you react on the spot. The cases/tests are usually designed to measure your thought process to see how insightful and resourceful you are, and sometimes also to assess how you work under pressure. Therefore, we warn you to expect surprises.

We heard of one PE fund that put a candidate in a room with a stack of industry publications and gave him a couple of hours to identify some investment leads and then to present an argument as to why they were good investments. In either instances, you may be given a few days to review a business plan and put together an analysis and valuation as part of a PowerPoint presentation that you will present to a mock investment committee (see Case Study 17).

Do Your Homework

It goes without saying that all candidates should research the firm and the professionals they will be meeting. Initially, that means knowing in detail what the fund does. This may be obvious, but funds still complain to us that candidates come in unprepared for the initial interviews. We think at a minimum you should know the fund's size, how long it has been around, the stage at which it invests, and its investor base. You should also familiarize yourself with recent investments the fund has made. While you're looking at the portfolio companies, it wouldn't hurt to select two or three of them and assess, in your opinion, why they were good investments for that fund and how they fit together with the fund's investment strategy. You should be up-to-date with what is happening in the larger markets and have some investment ideas so you can also be prepared for any on-the-spot case studies.

Beyond knowing about the fund, it's important to be familiar with the backgrounds of the investment professionals, including the schools they attended, where they're from (if you can research that beforehand), and the consulting firms, investment banks, companies, and so on, at which they worked prior to joining the fund. Knowing their professional backgrounds can give you some insight into the style of interviewing that you can expect (consultants and bankers are each known for asking specific types of questions relating to their own type of training). Most funds have detailed web sites, so getting this information should be relatively painless. Not having it is almost inexcusable.

To reaffirm what we are saying, take another look at the interview advice in Case Study 9 from someone who beat the odds and entered PE directly out of undergrad:

> Before interviewing, I networked with alumni from the firm, who gave me a sense of what to expect. Most private equity firms have web sites where they give extensive information on their investments and the backgrounds of the people. I walked in with info on every person, thoughts on potential areas for investment, and opinions and questions on recent deals the firm had done. That gave me a lot to talk about in meetings and I think probably stuck out. Finally, having a clear, credible story on why I wanted to be in private equity was critical, and being able to back it up with experiences on my resume showed I was serious.

Insider Tip ▷

From a PE Principal

You'd be surprised how many candidates come unprepared to an interview at my firm. We will often ask, "What's an investment we've made recently and why do you think it or its industry is interesting, or not?" The stuff is right on our web site, but people don't look. As a banker the same person would never go to a client meeting unprepared. It is a pleasure to interview someone who is well prepared, because it makes for an interesting meeting and because you know they will bring that same approach to the job.

Interviewing for a Sourcing Role

Some funds (mainly growth equity and certain venture capital funds) bring on junior or mid-level professionals to focus predominantly on deal sourcing. These positions—which generally require extensive cold-calling and networking for deal flow and thus focus less on valuation/modeling skills—have become more popular as the competition for quality deals has increased.

We usually recommend that candidates interviewing for these positions try to identify a few private companies that would be good investment opportunities and be prepared to talk about them in the interview—this is almost always a direct question that you will be asked. You could also be asked to prepare a 10-minute presentation, complete with slides, which could be given to companies, explaining why they should partner with the fund at which you are interviewing. This, of course, is also a test of how much you know about the fund, its past investments, and its strategy (see Case Study 13 for the story of someone who secured a sourcing role at a growth equity fund).

Some Additional Advice for Current MBAs

There are several aspects specific to MBA interviewing that are worth highlighting. In Chapter V we pointed out that the hiring market separates MBAs into two camps—those with and those without previous PE experience. Not surprisingly, the process and questions asked during interviews for MBAs with and without prior PE experience differ as well. Following are some specific points for MBAs to keep in mind.

If you have prior PE experience and want to return to the same type of investing you were doing before business school, you can expect a pretty straightforward interview. For example, if you did middle-market consumer LBOs and want to continue on that path, you should know exactly what to say. But if you want to change fund profiles, you need to effectively explain why the transition makes sense for you and how the hiring firm will benefit from your past experience. For example, if you were doing domestic tech investments and want to do cross-border manufacturing deals, you will have to be convincing as to why that is the case.

The same goes for any major change in stage of investment. For example, if you have venture experience, why would doing investing in LBOs now make sense? You should also be ready to explain the thinking that went into the choice of your summer position during business school, since the reasons behind your decision can often provide insight into your long-term planning. Case Study 15 gives a good look at one person's MBA interview experience:

> Most of the interviews were pretty similar, and I would say that people should be prepared. Only one firm gave me a case to read and prepare notes. The rest had me walk through my background and asked about what deals I had worked on, why I wanted to work in PE, and why with that specific firm. The fact that I had worked at a hedge fund in the summer but was seeking a job in PE also came up at every interview. Some also asked questions like, "If you had money to invest, where would you put it?"

In general, if you are not returning to your pre-MBA PE firm, you can expect to be asked why that is the case. You should have a solid, unwavering, nonabrasive answer prepared to share in interviews. Simply answering by saying "The fund is not hiring anyone" is fine, but if others at your level are being brought back, you should be able to address why you were not one of them. If both you and the firm ultimately agreed that there wasn't a long-term fit, you should avoid sounding disgruntled. If you specifically say it was your choice, the funds will dig deeper to make sure. Also, if you can't explain why you are a better candidate than when you entered business school, you will not impress your interviewers. Conversely, if you do well at conveying how you have grown into a better investor, then the odds will be better that there will still be a spot for you.

If you are a current MBA and don't have PE experience, you obviously cannot rattle off previous successful investments you were a part of, so if you do get an interview, your investment judgment, financial knowledge, and deal skills will be examined instead. There's no hiding the fact that you don't have a PE background, so you will have to work extra hard to convince a fund that you created value in the past and can do the same for them. One way to do that is to describe a situation in which the value you added helped lead to the success of a project or deal. Maybe you helped launch a new product, turned around a troubled division, and/or got a deeper understanding of business, management, and operations issues. Also, since many firms put a premium on leadership and success, make sure to cover any superior achievements you've had, whether they are professional, athletic, academic, and so on.

VENTURE CAPITAL INTERVIEWS

If you read Chapter VII, you know that venture investing is very different than later-stage PE/LBO investing, so it's natural that the interviews will be, too. These differences were pointed out well by the author of Case Study 31, who interviewed at both types of funds:

> There was a stark difference between the interviews at buyout and VC funds. The buyout partners grilled me on financial matters, asking me the different ways that I might structure a deal, what different sources of funding I might use, and when I would use one over the other. Venture capital firms asked more goal-type questions than skill-testing questions. I was asked why do you want to be an investor? What stage of investing do you like? What types of companies do you like? I know one venture fund that gave candidates an assignment to evaluate a company by coming back with a PowerPoint presentation and model.

The Process

Similar to PE/LBO funds, the interview process at VC funds typically lasts about three to four rounds, but the pace of the process from first to last round can be different for pre-MBAs versus post-MBAs. At the pre-MBA level, candidates can expect a quicker and more structured interview process since the VC funds that do hire at this level frequently compete for some of the same bankers and consultants as the PE/LBO funds, and therefore have to also match their timing. At the post-MBA level, the hiring is typically done with a lot less urgency. In fact, in Chapter VII, we pointed out that VC funds rarely actually *need* someone at this level, and that can make interviews play out for several months.

The experience of the author of Case Study 33 gives some good insight into post-MBA interviews (he joined his VC fund after nine years in operations):

> The interview process took about six months and the firm seemed in no hurry to bring someone on. I met with everyone on the investment team and was asked things like what did you learn while at the start-up? What areas do you think are promising to invest in? How would you evaluate investment opportunities?

Early-stage VC funds usually have fewer professional layers than PE/LBO funds. Thus, regardless of your level, you could spend most of your time meeting partners, and it's a good bet that each will ask you similar questions, mainly to assess your understanding of technology combined with business/commercial instincts. Venture firms are also known for using case studies in the mid to later rounds (we discuss those more later).

For post-MBAs, interviews in the mid to later rounds could include evaluating a live deal or even visiting a potential company with the deal team. By going to this length the VC fund is testing you out as a member of its investment team and seeing how you would perform in such a situation. As with the overall private equity industry, venture capital is still very much a people business and, given its own tightly knit culture, it's not uncommon for your final culture check to include a dinner with the firm's partners, which may also involve significant others.

Know Your Interviewers

Just as we mentioned earlier in the PE/LBO section, we suggest all candidates—pre-MBA and post-MBA—prepare for VC interviews by learning as much as possible about the funds and the investment professionals whom they will be meeting. In most cases, the fund's web sites can provide a lot of what you need, but you should supplement that information by speaking with people in the business, including other venture capitalists and even recruiters. Being familiar with the investment professionals and the partners includes knowing where they went to school and where they worked prior to venture—for example, do they come from a banking, consulting, or operations background?

Given the availability of information, it's inexcusable not to be fully informed about the fund, including knowing the industry in which it invests and its major investments—ideally both the winners and the losers.

The "Why VC" Question

Initially, possibly as early as the first round, VC funds will ask why you want to be a venture capitalist and why you want to work at their particular fund. That may seem obvious, but you should have an answer ready. As described in Case Study 32:

> The most important thing is to be passionate about venture investing. You should not be in it for the money and should definitely not come off as if you are. If you are passionate, curious, and excited then you will want to learn the science and finance. And the passion should not just be for venture—it should be for venture, biotech (in my case), and being an entrepreneur.

We've heard of people answering the "Why do you want to work in venture?" question by saying something like, "I want to take companies public." That may be what grabs the headlines, but it's not necessarily what an associate would be doing. Another mistake would be to say that you want to do complex modeling and valuation work (remember, early-stage VCs don't utilize those skills as in-depth).

A VC fund might prefer to hear that you have a deep passion for technology or life sciences and that you want to apply yourself to develop further into a strong investor. The fund will want to feel your enthusiasm for new products and ideas that could reshape a specific industry, and be convinced that you will work tirelessly within their firm to develop those ideas and products into successful companies.

Other Questions

You will be asked what you did in past jobs and how those experiences will help you be a strong investor. The VC funds might be less worried about the specific mechanics of what you worked on, but they will want to know your thought process regarding formulating an investment thesis and where you believe there are opportunities. Since a good part of your job will be evaluating business plans, they will want to know how you recognize value in start-up companies. A more probing question might be how you would determine the value potential of a specific company or business plan in the absence of financial statements. As a follow-up you could be presented with the following question: "If you're given a stack of 25 business plans, what would make one jump out at you?" You may even be asked something like, "If you had $1 million what would you do? In which industry would you invest?"

Your interviewers will also want to see that you understand the sector in which the fund invests and that you have thoughts on where that market is headed. Ideally, you will even have ideas about companies in the industry with which you previously worked that could be interesting investments. Don't be surprised if a fund specifically tests your industry knowledge. For example, if you say you know software, you might be asked to identify an enterprise software company worthy of investment.

After assessing your industry expertise, VC funds will also want to see that you are familiar with the players in the specific industry and whether you have a network to

From a General Partner at a VC Fund

When we interview we look for people who are excited about entrepreneurship. If you don't have that, you will not have the motivation to do well. We want someone who takes initiative and wants to know what the big disruptive technologies are. We want people who think ahead of the curve. I always ask candidates where they see investment ideas, and if they hem and haw through their answer they're not going to make it.

access interesting companies. Needless to say, if you are not very familiar with other companies in your area of expertise, we recommend you get caught up with them. Also, as we explained in Chapter VII, you may have the deep industry expertise that funds find attractive, but if you are not familiar with the terminology used in the venture community you could appear weaker on a relative basis than others who are more comfortable with the parlance. If that is the case, we recommend you learn the meaning of terms such as *Series A and B* financings, *up and down rounds*, *pre- and post-money* valuations, *Angel funding*, and so on.

In addition to asking about your investment ideas, many funds will want to see that you have had the confidence to invest on your own. Along those lines, you will more than likely be asked what investments you've made in the public markets and to explain the thought process behind them. We've even heard of funds asking questions such as, "If you had all your life savings invested in one stock, which would it be and why?" Again, they want to see what you look for in a company and how you evaluate investment ideas. At the very least they want to understand your ability to assess risk/return and that you have confidence to act on your thesis.

Case Studies/Tests

Formal case studies can be a significant part of many VC interviews. As either a pre- or post-MBA, a large majority of your time will be helping the partnership source, screen, and qualify new deals and this will, of course, involve reading business plans. Case studies, which are designed to replicate that work, can either be written or verbal and could be take-home or an on-the-spot presentation. We know of VC funds that present candidates with a company that it had considered as a possible investment. In such a situation, you may be told what issues and/or reservations the fund had with the company, and then you will be asked how you would evaluate it. The fund wants to see if you think like an investor. You may get to take the business plan home with you and be told to come back in 48 hours with a more thorough presentation. The VCs want to see that you are a good thinker and problem solver in a relatively aggressive time frame.

GENERAL TIPS

Following are a few miscellaneous suggestions that we recommend everyone keep in mind, regardless of your level and whether you are interviewing at an early-stage venture capital, growth equity, or a leveraged buyout fund.

Phone/Video Interviews

Some funds may conduct the first one or two rounds of interviews over the phone. In this case you should prepare in the same manner as if they were in person. These funds know they will not decide to give an offer to a candidate based solely on this type of interview—but most are willing to eliminate candidates based on this screen.

If a fund likes you, it may take the initiative to fly you to their offices for in-person meetings, or commonly it might leave it more open-ended by saying something akin to, "We really enjoyed speaking with you. Let us know the next time you will be in town so we can meet in person." Such as response generally means that the plane ticket will be on your dime (see *Out-of-Town Interviews*). As a side note, phone interviews can have additional relevance for deal-sourcing roles since they can mirror the actual role of calling companies and being persuasive.

Out-of-Town Interviews

We've found that someone who is really interested in a position and is given a soft invite for an out-of-town interview (meaning the firm has said it will not pay for your travel but is willing to meet you if you are in the same city) will find a way to make that meeting happen. To us, the more resourceful candidates distinguish themselves by finding creative ways to get in front of a firm in another location (many clients use that as a natural selection tool to see who is more driven). Some ways candidates can be creative include re-routing a return flight from a business trip, making a point to be in a specific city to see family, visiting friends, or combining a trip with other interviews.

Since there are still no guarantees that funds will not cancel at the last minute, there is some inherent risk in just showing up—but having to assess that element of risk is perhaps a good screen for a future investor. In our view, a blind trip for the interview is not usually wise, unless you truly are prepared for it to be cancelled; and if that happens, you cannot feel burned or complain.

Dress Code

Even though most PE firms are known for being business casual, our advice is to always play it safe: When in doubt, wear a suit. For women that means a full suit with jacket and either pants or a skirt. You will never be penalized for being over-dressed, but you could lose points for dressing inappropriately. We'd also caution men about their selection of neckwear. We're not saying that a certain tie will get you the job, but you probably have one in your wardrobe that should be avoided.

The only time we would say that it is acceptable not to wear a suit is if a recruiter tells you that it has been cleared with the firm where you have an interview. And even in that case, we recommend you avoid wrinkled clothes or rolled-up sleeves. Keep it clean and conservative. We have never heard of earning points for creative dressing in a PE/VC interview, but we have heard of points being deducted.

Always Be on Your Best Behavior

Some firms go out of their way to wine and dine finalist candidates (this is especially relevant with pre-MBAs). We know of one that will fly you to their offices for a Friday interview and have you stay the weekend so you can see if you would like living in that city, and we have heard of other firms doing similar things. It should go without saying, but we'll point out anyway that you should always maintain a level of professionalism during interviews, group dinners, and casual outings sponsored by the hiring firm.

You should basically assume that you are on a 24/7 interview. Therefore, avoid saying something too casual or initiating discussions on controversial topics (such as politics, religion, etc.). Definitely do not drink too much and, of course, watch your language. The professionals interviewing and hosting you are not your friends (at least not yet) and you should not act as if they are. Believe it or not, each year we get feedback from clients that a candidate fell short on an imminent offer for some of these reasons, so playing it safe is usually the best default option.

Chapter **XII**

COMPENSATION

Compensation is no doubt at least part of the allure of working in private equity, but we hope you've identified other facets of the profession that are equally appealing. Since profits in private equity are realized over the life of a fund—often 5 to 10 years—don't expect to hit pay day early on. For most professionals, the first few years of compensation will be driven mainly by base salaries and cash bonuses. Don't get us wrong, you can do well with your annual base salary and bonus, but in PE the big money comes further down the line in the form of carry when a fund is successful and is bringing in profits from its investments.

We see many candidates very focused on securing the highest dollar amount possible. In our opinion, however, a higher offer from one fund doesn't necessarily mean it is the better opportunity. Each year, we see candidates turn down a higher short-term cash package for various trade-offs, including a better promotional track, more professional growth, increased responsibilities, or, of course, upside potential in terms of equity. Our general belief is that if a candidate is joining a smart team with quality mentorship and a strong investment platform, that candidate's compensation should work out in the end just by sticking with the fund through the long-term investment cycle.

Senior professionals at all private equity firms frequently tell us they want people who understand the longer investment cycles of PE and are ready to put in the work to reap the benefits down the road. If you truly want a long-term career in PE, you have to exude that mindset, because staying with a fund and building up equity—known as *carried interest*—are the best ways to accumulate wealth (we offer a more detailed discussion of carry later on). If you look at any ranking of top earners in private equity, those at the top of the list are not there because they have high salaries. Of the professionals on the 2007 *Forbes* list of the 400 richest Americans, at least 20 are there based on fortunes made from leveraged buyouts. We can safely assume that their fortunes were earned because they produced tremendous, consistent value over long periods of time by having the patience and discipline to make successful investments and reap the high equity returns.

Keep in mind that private equity is not for those who are very focused on maximizing earnings in the first couple of years. If you get restless about making money at your current PE fund and think the solution is to make a lateral move, be careful. Chances are you will have to prove yourself again to reestablish goodwill with the new firm. In some cases, that could mean taking a step back in compensation. We have seen some people benefit economically by making a switch, but have also seen others who did not fare as well and would have been more ahead if they had stuck it out longer at their original firm. Either way, you should know how your compensation could be affected if you do change firms.

PRIVATE EQUITY VERSUS HEDGE FUNDS

Since private equity and hedge funds compete for some of the same talent, it's important that you understand the compensation structure of each type of firm. In Chapter I, we explained that PE funds are not affected as much by short-term fluctuations in the public markets as are hedge funds. In contrast to PE, which is more of a long-term equity game, hedge funds are marked-to-market each year and bonus calculations are more closely tied to annual profits.

VENTURE CAPITAL

As we pointed out in Chapter VII, venture capital is different in many ways from later stage PE/LBO, and that extends to how VC funds pay as well. Total cash compensation at VC funds (especially traditional early-stage) is generally lower than it is at similarly sized PE/LBO funds. It should be noted, however, that VC funds, on average, can sometimes pay higher base salaries than some PE/LBO funds, and in general those salaries usually represent a larger portion of total compensation.

That's not to say you can't make a lot of money in venture capital. Although total compensation will be lower during your initial years (before you become partner), there is no question that venture capital offers great prospects for long-term wealth creation (assuming investment success) that can be equal to or even greater than that of PE/LBO and hedge funds.

FUND OF FUNDS

Overall compensation paid by funds of funds is generally lower than that paid by similarly sized PE/LBO funds. Base salaries at funds of funds account for an even larger percentage of overall compensation than they do at VC funds. Over the past few years we have seen growth in total compensation at the larger funds of funds, with the main driver being the changing investment mix of the larger/hybrid funds. As these funds expand their direct investing activities to include co-investing and secondary investing, they continue to put more of a premium on candidates with direct investment skills.

To find candidates with these skills, funds of funds have had to compete more with later-stage buyout funds, and in so doing have had to raise compensation. In such a scenario, compensation at funds of funds more closely mimics the more bonus-heavy compensation structure of later-stage private equity funds.

COMPENSATION TRENDS

Over the past year, we have found that the increases in PE compensation were driven primarily by the larger average fund size and by the intense competition for top talent both among other PE/LBO funds and from hedge funds. These factors are especially evident given the recent record-breaking fund-raising. Not surprisingly, the influx of new cash has increased the need for talented professionals, while the increased management fees generated by the larger funds have allowed these funds to pay up for that talent. Hedge funds have also been targeting the same candidate pools, putting additional upward pressure on compensation. Although the increase is most prevalent among the mega PE/LBO funds (those with several billion dollars in assets), it has trickled down through the rest of the industry.

Table 12.1 gives a breakdown of average base salaries and bonuses at later-stage private equity, venture capital, and funds of funds (see Chapter I for a definition of each type of fund) across all fund sizes, as presented in the 2008 *Private Equity Compensation Report*, published by Glocap Search. Looking at specific fund sizes not mentioned in Table 12.1, the report notes that total average compensation for senior associates (those fresh out of business school) at later-stage PE funds with $2–$5 billion in assets under management came in at $356,000 in 2007–2008. Total average compensation for senior associates at large venture capital firms ($2 billion and above) was $276,000. Given the continued market turbulence and the anticipated slowdown in new deals, we've been seeing signs that increases in compensation could potentially level off.

Examining some outlier data points gives an idea of the upper bounds of some compensation ranges (remember, these figures apply to only a very small subset of candidates). For example, in today's highly competitive market, mega PE/LBO funds (those with several billion dollars in assets under management) may offer top-tier MBAs annualized total cash compensation packages of $425,000 and higher, while superstar pre-MBA associates (those hired out of two-year investment banking and consulting programs) are being offered packages at these firms that can in a few cases total nearly $300,000 or more in their first year at their funds.

Table 12.1   Compensation Breakdown by Job Title (All Fund Sizes)

		PRIVATE EQUITY	VENTURE CAPITAL	FUND OF FUNDS
Analyst	Average base salary	79k	76k	71k
	Average bonus	78k	48k	39k
	Total cash compensation	157k	124k	110k
Associate	Average base salary	96k	107k	90k
	Average bonus	105k	59k	55k
	Total cash compensation	201k	166k	145k
Sr. Assoc.	Average base salary	149k	131k	138k
	Average bonus	160k	76k	66k
	Total cash compensation	309k	207k	204k
VP	Average base salary	186k	177k	166k
	Average bonus	242k	117k	93k
	Total cash compensation	428k	294k	259k

Source: *The 2008 Private Equity Compensation Report*
Note: The data does not include compensation from carried interest.

CARRY

Those striving to break into the PE industry should understand the role of *carried interest*. Carried interest is the portion of fund returns that is paid to the general partner, which, as we pointed out in Chapter I, can range from 15 to 30 percent of profits (20 percent is most common). This is the general partner's fee for carrying the management responsibility plus all the liability for providing the needed expertise to successfully manage investments.

There are many ways to calculate this profit share (in dollars, points of fund carry, or percent of fund carry) and to account for it. Carried interest is an integral component of overall compensation and, similar to receiving stock grants in a company, the vesting schedules can vary; ranges are generally three to eight years. As the industry has matured and become more institutionalized we have noticed that the percentage of overall carry earmarked for non-partners has steadily increased. Whereas we estimate that 5 to 10 years ago, about 85 to 90 percent of the carry was held by the partners, in today's market, we believe 75 to 80 percent is more common (in a firm that is built out and has multiple PE funds).

Anecdotally, of the non-partner carry pool, it seems that close to one-half is allocated to the next generation of leaders (usually at the principal level). Also, from our experience, approximately 85 to 90 percent of funds offer newly minted MBAs a percentage of carry.

Chapter **XIII**

WORKING WITH A RECRUITER

Although there are some candidates who successfully land an opportunity in private equity on their own, many find that working with a recruiter who specializes in private equity is also beneficial, regardless of how they eventually obtain their position.

A large part of what we do as recruiters is reaching out to candidates who have the relevant backgrounds for the types of searches we work on. If you are a first-year pre-MBA analyst at a well-known investment bank or consulting firm, or if you are in the first year at a top-ranked business school and have previous private equity experience, you can expect to get calls from a recruiter when the PE hiring season begins. For top pre-MBA analysts, that could be as early as January or February (before you complete your first year), and for MBAs it could be the second semester of your first year. Those star pre-MBA candidates may get calls from multiple recruiters. Either way, it will be up to you to decide if the recruiters who are calling have the opportunities you find interesting. But if your phone doesn't ring right away, it doesn't mean that you're out of luck. You can simply be less visible—either in a smaller geography or a less-recognized banking or consulting program—in which case it could take recruiters longer to find you. Because of this, you may want to reach out to recruiters yourself.

We're often asked by candidates how we decide who to invite in for a meeting with us. We typically first meet candidates whose resumes reflect the appropriate work experience and other relevant components sought by our clients (e.g., school, test scores, GPA, etc.). While meeting these candidates we can then determine if their non-resume variables (e.g., personality, demeanor, communication skills, etc.) could make them a potential match, and if so we would look to introduce them to our client. Therefore, the best way to get in front of us is to have the relevant industry experience at a solid organization (investment banking or consulting for pre-MBAs and private equity for post-MBAs) and a high level of achievement across the board, especially from both undergraduate and graduate levels (if applicable).

If you don't have the relevant industry background that a PE recruiter is looking for, then securing an interview with that recruiter will be tougher. In this situation we'd strongly suggest utilizing your personal network (get recommended to the recruiter by somebody we know and respect) or persistence (to a point). In our case, a personal recommendation carries a lot more weight if it comes directly from someone we know well in the PE world. For example, rather than an e-mail from you saying, "Joe said I should give you a call," it would be helpful if Joe e-mailed us with, "I know someone who I think you should meet. His background may not be perfect, but he's a great guy, knows his stuff, and I think he could have what it takes to be an investor."

Glocap Insight   Depending on the level of position and the competitive landscape, we estimate that approximately 30 to 50 percent of PE professional roles are filled by recruiters. In an industry such as PE there historically has not been a shortage of high-quality professionals, and therefore a recruiter is often hired not only to find candidates who can do the job but, more importantly, the *highest-caliber* candidates, while also screening for the optimal fit.

TIPS FOR WORKING WITH A RECRUITER

Following are some tips for getting the most out of working with a recruiter.

Make the Intro

Introduce yourself briefly—this can be by e-mail or phone (for Glocap you also could register a confidential profile on our web site). If you have a top-tier background and/or can get a high-end recommendation to a recruiter, you are more likely to hear from someone sooner. A recruiter interview will most likely start with a short description of your background, and you should highlight your major strengths. Explain why you are looking to leave your current position and note your potential job interests. Do not restate your entire resume. If applicable, mention how you got the recruiter's name (referred by a colleague, etc.).

We'll Call If We See a Potential Match

Professional recruiters will usually try to respond to a direct inquiry from you at least as a courtesy. The response could be via e-mail or a quick callback. You'll likely receive a call as well if your background is a good match for a particular client with whom the recruiter is *currently* working. If the recruiter doesn't have any present opportunities to discuss with you, they might still want to connect to learn more about your background for future reference, or will simply hold on to your information until a search opens that does match your background.

No Practice Interviews

If you are presented an opportunity, be honest about your level of interest. If it's your dream job or your qualifications match the job perfectly, explain that to the recruiter—it could help them better market your background (assuming they agree there is a potential fit). If you haven't heard of the firm or need to contemplate the opportunity further, feel free to ask for a few days to research and think it over. Do not take the interview for practice, informational purposes, or other reasons besides a sincere interest in employment with that firm. It is better to take the time up front to think about it and decline the interview than to go for other purposes, since recruiters are very sensitive to not wasting their client's time. If you decide to pass on an interview, briefly explain why and perhaps have a follow-up conversation with the recruiter to further hone in on your job search interests.

Recruiters as Resources

Think of recruiters as a valuable resource. They may have additional insight into a particular firm and position, which could help you evaluate the opportunity and prepare for an interview. A good recruiter who spends enough time getting to know you as well as their client is in a great position to assess the all-important fit. Recruiters are usually immersed in the market, so, as we explained in Chapter IX, a recruiter could be a good source of information about how a fund is perceived in the market. We are happy to give advice to many candidates even if we do not place them.

Feedback

After a client interview, let the recruiter know how your meeting went and if you're still interested in the position or would like to bow out of the process. Be specific about how the opportunity does or does not meet your interests. It's fair to ask if the recruiter has received feedback as well. Most recruiters will share constructive feedback they've received from the client, but please, don't shoot the messenger!

Keep Us in the Loop

Stay in touch with your recruiter, especially if your search criteria may have changed, if you're approaching final rounds at another firm, if you were recently promoted, or if there were other important changes to your profile and/or status in general.

When checking in with a recruiter, be specific. If you'd like to inquire about the status of a certain opportunity, note the firm's name or job/reference number. Try to avoid merely touching base in a general way—this usually adds little to no value to the recruiter or your job search.

Know What You Want

Most successful candidates focus on what they want. It's okay to have job interests in several different areas, provided your skill set really does extend that far, but try to tier your interests and identify which opportunities are most interesting and fitting for you.

Don't Play Hard to Get

Be responsive. If you're contacted by a recruiter, make a point to follow up as quickly as possible. If you're slow to respond, they may think you are uninterested, out of the market, or even difficult to represent. Remember, you need to make a good first impression on the recruiter in order to be introduced to their client.

Hiring Firms Have the Final Word

Clients (the hiring firms) are the ones who pay recruiting fees. As such, they can define as narrowly as they please the set of resumes and backgrounds that they are interested in seeing from a recruiter. The question is not whether you can learn the job, but rather if you have the background that the client is looking for. While you may be a 75 percent fit for the role, someone else could be a 98 percent fit and you just may not stack up competitively enough. In other cases, even if you do check all the boxes, there may be others applying for the same position who also check those same boxes but are even more qualified.

No Attitude, Please

Remember that you are one of many candidates with whom the recruiter is working. You can certainly feel confident about being a strong candidate, but having an attitude that conveys, "You will make money off of me," is not a good way to get the attention you want. A wise recruiter knows that a great candidate can also be a potential future client. When working with a recruiter, your job search is a collaborative effort!

Chapter **XIV**

ON THE JOB: WHAT TO EXPECT

Up until now this book has focused on dispensing advice in the hope of improving your chances of landing a position at a private equity fund. Given the amount of energy and commitment involved in the job search, we felt it important to also inform you about what lies ahead once you are working at a PE fund and what the transition to your first role may be like. This chapter draws heavily on testimonials from professionals already working in private equity. Whether you have accepted an offer to begin work or are still in the early phases of your search process, the firsthand accounts presented here provide useful insight into the reality of what it's like to work in private equity.

The commentary in this chapter should underscore the fact that your initial position in private equity, be it at the pre- or post-MBA level, will be different in many aspects from any previous work experience you've had, whether that was in banking, consulting, or another industry. Private equity is a high-profile, high-intensity industry that invests large amounts of capital on behalf of LPs that demand results. As a principal investor, performance is the ultimate barometer of your success. Your primary purpose, whether directly or indirectly, will be to help your fund produce above-market returns for its LPs by sourcing new deals, executing live ones, and, often at the same time, working to grow your fund's portfolio companies.

EXPECT MORE RESPONSIBILITY

No matter where you are working, you can expect to be given more responsibility than what you have been used to, which includes playing a major role in investment decisions, interacting with partners of the firm and CEOs. To one pre-MBA associate at a mega buyout fund, the biggest challenge of his first year was juggling the core technical work with the new investment responsibilities:

> You are responsible for both modeling and analysis work and management meetings on top of that. It's a challenge to have all of that responsibility. In one moment you are way down in the weeds modeling a deal, and the next you are being asked to come up and have a view of the bigger picture. It's one of the best features of private equity, but it can also be hard. It's challenging, but also rewarding.

Concurrent with added responsibilities will be the need to be more assertive and proactive. As a principal investor, even associates interact with key service providers and vendors and work directly on deals with bankers, lawyers, and accountants. It's not uncommon for junior professionals to independently manage calls with senior bankers and partners at law and accounting firms (you are now their client). A recent business school grad who had no previous private equity experience noted that when he joined a mid-market buyout fund he got right to work:

> I was managing real deal processes, meeting with CEOs and management teams on day one. Whereas as bankers you're working *for* them, now *they* are in essence working for *my* firm. If I don't like a deal I can kill it, and people will listen.

For some, being given more responsibility can mean stepping out of your comfort zone. One pre-MBA who joined a mid-market fund from a consulting program points to the following scenario:

> Once I was working with the VP of marketing [of a portfolio company] to develop a road map for the company. While I could check back with my firm for guidance, I was given the project to run with, and the company's growth may have been dependent on what we came up with. That can be a lot to digest. Another time I was working to integrate two of our portfolio companies. I had to be able to work with VPs on both sides. Here I was, this 20-something, working with people in their 40s who have been in business for many years. You want to earn their respect, but at the same time you have to be assertive because you own their companies. That's different from when you were a consultant and they hired you. In this role all eyes are on you. This can be uncomfortable for someone who has been on the job for five months, but it is typical of the type of responsibilities you are given early on.

EXPECT TO THINK LIKE AN INVESTOR

Unlike being an adviser, where your firm may have worked on a new deal or project each month, in private equity you're usually committed for the life of the deal. As a principal investor you will be investing millions (in some cases billions) of dollars of *your* firm's capital, and you will have to be comfortable forming your own investment theses around that. As one pre-MBA associate with a banking background noted:

> Early on, an MD got off the phone and asked me what I thought of an investment idea. I was dumbfounded. That would never happen in banking. And he wasn't just being

nice. The people who hire you know you're smart; that's why they hired you, and they want to hear your opinion. In meetings you must be ready to voice your opinion. In banking you were *supposed* to be quiet. Here, you are *encouraged* to speak up. In fact, you'd better.

In general, most candidates with banking backgrounds felt their modeling skills prepared them for the technical portion of the job. However, getting used to formulating their opinions on deals, at least at the beginning, took some time, as this former banker pointed out:

> Banking is more transactional. You do a deal, kick it out, and move on to the next one. Private equity is more relationship driven, even at the junior level. In my case, I lacked some polish that I didn't really know I would need. I thought I would come in here and be doing deals and it would be easy. In banking you work hard, but the processes became rote and eventually you don't have to think much about what you are doing. At my private equity firm, on day one I was given a memo and asked what I thought. I had never made a judgment call before, and here I was being asked to make a decision and for my input on which lenders to call, and so on. I quickly found out that there is a lot to think about.

Perhaps not surprisingly, consultants, who were used to presenting recommendations from their analysis to clients, felt more comfortable formulating their views on investments and working with portfolio companies. One noted that the growth strategy work he did as a consultant was similar to the type of interaction he had with his fund's portfolio companies. Another former consultant said his training prepared him to quickly understand a company and a market, and that helped him when judging potential private equity investments:

> My consulting background gave me the ability to talk with CEOs and to understand the market in which they worked. It allowed me to be able to discover a compelling market and a compelling market opportunity. As a consultant I was always talking to clients about their product, who the competitors were, and what the competitors were doing. I was used to speaking to customers, potential customers, management teams, analysts, and bankers to get a full picture of the company and its prospects. Bankers were usually talking only about financials. As a consultant, many times I was brought into deals and asked my opinion and was trying to solve problems for clients, so I was prepared for that aspect of the work.

EXPECT LESS MODELING, MORE DUE DILIGENCE

To the surprise of many, building financial models does not occupy as much time as they thought it would (although many commented that when models are constructed they are often more complex and detailed). Instead, the due diligence you conduct will be deeper and more involved. If your firm has exclusivity on a deal or is closing in on a final bid deadline, your life can be consumed by that single deal.

Remember, the goal is to determine whether your fund will invest a significant amount of capital. You will be looking at how your fund as an owner can enhance profitability and improve management, and you are not likely to find all the answers to those questions from having your head down in Excel models all day and night. The due diligence is comprehensive and involves getting out of the office to visit companies as well as talking to management teams, industry experts, consultants, etc. It's about learning to ask the right questions and figuring out what drives a business. As one pre-MBA associate notes:

> In private equity you do more analysis and due diligence. You're taking a deeper dive into a company in which you are considering investing, and it's not just financial diligence. You are looking into every aspect of a company, including its management team, its insurance, its products, competitors, and so on. The level of analysis is nothing like investment banking. You take a completely different approach. At a PE fund you have to have the mind-set that this is our money and we're going to have to live with our decision for a long time, so there is fiduciary responsibility of being in PE. That leads to a much more thorough diligence process.

Although the due diligence must be exhaustive, the time you have to research a potential investment can vary. And while bankers, who were used to a quicker transaction pace, may find they have more time to complete the due diligence, individuals from nonbanking backgrounds may feel more challenged. One candidate who joined a mid-market fund with a corporate/industry background said he was caught off guard by how quickly the due diligence had to be completed:

> Coming from industry did prepare me. I was ready to do detailed due diligence and that skill set translated nicely. The difference is that at a PE fund you have to do due diligence relatively quicker and sometimes based on less information. In corporate/industry you may have 3, 6, or even 12 months to research a new product and have a larger budget with which to do that research. In PE, where you may be competing against other funds for an acquisition, you can't take as long to come up with an answer for your managing directors.

EXPECT MINIMAL TRAINING

Few PE funds provide more than informal training. By and large you will be expected to arrive on day one ready to handle most facets of investment work, and that means armed not only with the skills that you demonstrated in your interviews, but also with an attitude that shows you want to get ahead. One director at a multibillion-dollar fund noted that it's important that new entrants be honest about what they know and don't know, adding:

> The senior people are willing to help, but you have to take the initiative to ask questions and learn what you don't know. That means coming in with an attitude that shows you are ready to learn and work hard. If you don't know something, that's fine, we can teach you, but you won't make it if you have a bad attitude (for example, being lazy and immature and not composed during management meetings). The people who hire you know you can do the job. Now they want to see you take initiative and show an eagerness to learn and to get better.

Some without banking backgrounds felt the need to brush up on their modeling skills. Knowing what he lacked, one consultant took matters into his own hands:

> I had knowledge of the domain but no core finance background. I had built models before, but hadn't built complete three-statement financial models. With that in mind, after receiving my offer and before I was scheduled to start, I signed myself up for a financial modeling course. I think I would have been asked to do this if I was performing poorly after I began, but I felt it was better to do it before I started. We do growth equity and don't do many three-statement models. I had done mostly income statement models and return models based off revenues and earnings, but I felt I needed to shore up my skills to be ready.

EXPECT A LESS STRUCTURED WORK ENVIRONMENT

In addition to lacking much formal training, the environment of most private equity firms is less institutional and not as structured as you have been used to. An advantage of this type of environment is that you will have more exposure to senior people. At the same time, however, you will be expected to work more independently to get up to speed. One pre-MBA associate noted that he is often on a deal with only a principal and a partner and has to work well on his own to meet their expectations in a timely fashion. He added that "no one is sitting on top of me, breathing down my neck." Of the reduced supervision, he notes:

> Private equity is more about deploying capital and developing returns and less on developing people, and you have to be aware of this. You're on your own and may have no weekly meetings with your supervisor. Your managing director doesn't really check in with you on a consistent basis, so you are often left to manage your own time. To me, it was surprising. I was expecting a little more focus on professional development. I think this is typical of most pre-MBA positions—especially at mid-market funds that are less institutionalized and there is less of an emphasis on professional development.

A consultant who joined a mid-market fund as an associate added:

> I came from a large organization that had a very structured environment. Coming into a shop like this is very different. It is so unstructured that you have to create your own path and have to be a lot more proactive. I am typically working with a VP. I have a lot of freedom and am always encouraged to ask for help. For me the change was not a shock, but it's something to adapt to—at a big firm you are part of a big team.

To one business school graduate who had an investment banking background but no previous PE experience, the benefits of working at a less structured firm were clearly apparent:

> I went from a large investment banking organization with thousands of people that was not very entrepreneurial, to a small mid-market PE team in which the bottom line is shared by everyone. It's very much a team approach. We have meetings with everyone in the firm once a week and there is no bureaucracy. The hours are better

and don't compare to the ridiculous hours of banking where there was too much work done because no one owned a project. Here the teams are small so they have to be a lot more efficient.

In a firm with a looser structure, junior professionals can find themselves reporting to one or more partners at the same time. One pre-MBA associate who joined a smaller buyout fund from a corporate background explained that:

> In a corporation you may have one boss, but in PE you may find yourself working simultaneously on two or three deals for two or three different partners. Each partner feels his deal is the most important. You may also find yourself working on one deal for two or three partners and each may have his own bias and needs. You have to be able to handle each situation.

At times, the structure of the firm will mean that everyone has to pitch in, even with some of the more administrative tasks, as this MBA who went from a bulge-bracket bank to a mid-market PE firm pointed out:

> You will be asked to do a lot of things that you might not have done in a bigger firm. You may also have to figure out things for yourself. If you need something photocopied or a presentation put together you may have to do that on your own. That may take many people by surprise. In I-banking we had an entire graphics department with printers and binders to help put presentations together. Although we don't do many presentations in my PE firm, when we do we have to fend for ourselves. Having a good attitude is important, as is being flexible. You are all working for the common good of the firm. It's like owning your own business—when a situation comes up, you will have to put the fires out yourself.

GENERAL PREPARATION TIPS

Following are some additional observations and tips gleaned from the many private equity professionals with whom we spoke. As with the others mentioned earlier, these should also help you better prepare for a transition into PE.

- *Read about the industry and get up-to-date on deals in the market.* The more you know about the market going in, the less you will be caught by surprise. One pre-MBA associate who had a corporate background notes that being aware of active deals—whether mid-market, lower mid-market, or large capitalization—will help new entrants acclimate themselves to the specific market they will cover. "If you know you are going to follow companies in a specific sector, it would be a good idea to get a sense of where publicly traded companies in that sector are valued, as that will help give you an idea if potential investments are being priced fairly," he notes. (See Appendix A for a list of news publications and free e-mails.)
- *Get into the investment mind-set.* To sharpen your investment instincts, perhaps start thinking of the companies you like and about developing an investment

thesis quickly—why a company is (or is not) a good investment. One pre-MBA said, "You want to get to the point where, within an hour of reading an offering memorandum, you will know what you have to find out about the business that would make you invest in it. Your mind-set should be, buy it, grow it, and exit it. You will have to figure out how you can help the company triple or quadruple sales and then how you can sell it." If you haven't started your new position yet, you should be asking yourself about transactions you are working on: Does a deal make sense? Would you buy it? Is it a good investment? Why would you buy it?

- *Get to know the standard deal process and documentation.* A good way to get familiar with what the work will be like is to speak with friends or other professionals you know who are already working in private equity. They can give you insight on the resources they use to conduct due diligence and what their investment process is like, and may even introduce you to some of the standard documentation you may come across on a day-to-day basis, such as investment memos, confidentiality agreements, and various legal documents. One pre-MBA associate notes that the documentation involved in deals was new to him:

> Reading legal documents was a shock to me. Even though you have lawyers at your disposal, if you've never read a term sheet, an asset purchase agreement, or a loan document, I suggest you become familiar with them, as you will want to be able to read and understand them yourself.

- *Be aware of what else it takes to succeed.* In addition to perfecting the skills you will need to perform your daily tasks, you should be striving to build your deal expertise and should become acquainted with the talents that will help you move up in the industry. For many, that can begin with learning how to manage a deal, and building relationships in the deal community (lawyers, bankers, consultants, accountants, etc.) that will help you develop an ability to source new investment opportunities down the road which is a highly valued and usually requisite skill for being a partner. As one pre-MBA notes, "You need to be thinking, every time you get involved with a company, I should be getting to know these CEOs and bankers because that is how I will be successful in bringing in my own deals."

Appendix A

RESOURCES

There are many publications and web sites that cover the private equity industry. These are always a good resource and can help you stay abreast of fund-raising efforts for both existing and newly formed funds, as well as hiring updates. A lot of the newsletters and web sites have job listings, but reading about new funds can be an equally effective way to find out about potential opportunities. Similarly, stories about people being hired and moving from one fund to another can give insight into the backgrounds sought by specific funds or, better yet, leads about potential vacancies. These stories could also help you research funds at which you have interviews.

Buyouts
www.buyoutsnews.com
Bi-monthly magazine from Thomson Financial.

The Deal and *The Daily Deal*
www.thedeal.com

European Venture Capital Journal
www.evcj.com

FINAlternatives
www.finalternatives.com
Free independent source for news on the alternative investment industry.

Financial News Online
www.efinancialnews.com

Private Equity Analyst
www.privateequityanalyst.com
Weekly subscription newsletter.

Private Equity Central
www.privateequitycentral.net

Private Equity Hub
www.pehub.com
Interactive forum for the PE community.

Private Equity Insider
www.peinsider.com
Weekly subscription newsletter.

Private Equity Online
www.privateequityonline.com
Free daily e-mail.

Private Equity Week
http://hosting.mansellgroup.net/enablemail/
   ThomsonNewLetter/HostedWires/NewsLetters/
   july13-06.htm

You can sign up for PE Week Wire, a free daily
   update.

Private Equity Wire
www.privateequitywire.co.uk
Free daily e-mail.

Venture Capital Journal
www.vcjnews.com

SUGGESTED BOOKS

PE/LBO

Baker, George P., and George David Smith. *The New Financial Capitalists: Kohlberg Kravis Roberts and the Creation of Corporate Value.* New York, Cambridge University Press, 1998.

Bruck, Connie. *The Predators' Ball: The Inside Story of Drexel Burnham and the Rise of the Junk Bond Raiders.* New York: Simon & Schuster, 1988.

Burrough, Bryan, and John Helyar. *Barbarians at the Gate: The Fall of RJR Nabisco.* HarperCollins Perennial, 1991.

Higgins, Robert. *Analysis for Financial Management.* New York: McGraw-Hill/Irwin, 1984.

Rickerstein, Rick, Robert E. Gunther, and Michael Lewis. *Buyout: The Insider's Guide to Buying Your Own Company.* New York: American Management Association, 2001.

Stewart, James B. *Den of Thieves.* New York: Touchstone, 1991.

Venture Capital

Amis, David, and Howard Stevenson. *Winning Angels: The 7 Fundamentals of Early Stage Investing.* Financial Times Prentice Hall, 2001.

Aspatore Books Staff. *Inside the Minds: The Ways of the VC.* Aspatore Books, 2003.

Bartlett, Joseph W. *Fundamentals of Venture Capital.* Madison Books, 1999.

Gompers, Paul A., and Josh Lerner. *The Money of Invention: How Venture Capital Creates New Wealth.* Harvard Business School Press, 2001.

Lerner, Josh. *Venture Capital and Private Equity: A Casebook.* Boston: John Wiley & Sons, 2000.

Stross, Randall E. *eBoys.* New York: Ballantine Publishing Group, 2000.

Wilmerding, Alex. *Deal Terms: The Finer Points of Venture Capital Deal Structures Valuations, Term Sheets, Stock Options, and Getting Deals Done.* Aspatore Inc., 2003.

Zygmont, Jeffrey. *The VC Way.* Basic Books, 2001.

DIRECTORIES AND GLOSSARIES

Galante's Venture Capital and Private Equity Directory
Asset Alternatives Inc.
http://www.fis.dowjones.com/products/galante.html

The Directory of Venture Capital and Private Equity Firms
Grey House Publishing
www.greyhouse.com/venture.htm

Glossary of Private Equity and Venture Capital
vcexperts.com/vce/library/encyclopedia/glossary.asp

vFinance Venture Capital Resource Directory
www.vfinance.com/ventcap.htm

Private Equity Database
http://www.privateequity.com

The PSEPS Venture Capital and Private Equity Directory
http://www.private-equity.org.uk/

Stern Private Equity Club
New York University
http://pages.stern.nyu.edu/~spec/index.html

Center for Venture Capital and Private Equity Finance
Stephen M. Ross School of Business, University of Michigan
www.bus.umich.edu/CVP/index.html

Tuck Private Equity Club
Tuck School of Business, Dartmouth
http://mba.tuck.dartmouth.edu/pages/clubs/peclub/index.html

ACADEMIC AND BUSINESS SCHOOL CLUBS

Wharton Private Equity Club
http://wga.wharton.upenn.edu/club_info.asp?ID=24&CuID=1&CuTy=Professional

Harvard Venture Capital and Private Equity Club
http://www.hbs.edu/mba/studentlife/clubs/venturecapitalprivateequity.html

Yale School of Management Private Equity Student Interest Group
http://students.som.yale.edu/sigs/private_equity/

OTHER RESOURCES

American Venture Network
www.avce.com
Publishes American Venture *magazine*
www.americanventuremagazine.com

Private Equity Info
www.privateequityinfo.com
Subscription-based source for information on private equity firms—their investment interests, portfolio companies, and professional biographies.

Has a regularly updated database of firms and contacts.

Private Equity Intelligence
www.preqin.com
Information on products and services for private equity funds, venture capital funds, funds of funds, investors, and advisers. Contains fund performance, investor profiles, fund-raising, and research and consulting information.

REGIONAL U.S. VENTURE CAPITAL AND PRIVATE EQUITY ASSOCIATIONS

Connecticut Venture Group
www.ct-venture.org

Dallas/Fort Worth Private Equity Forum
Contact: pfh1521@aol.com.

Evergreen Venture Capital Association
www.evca.net

Florida Venture Forum
www.floridaventureforum.org

Illinois Venture Capital Association
www.illinoisvc.org

Long Island Capital Alliance
www.licapital.org

Mid-Atlantic Venture Association
www.mava.org

Missouri Venture Forum
www.missouriventureforum.org

Minnesota Venture Capital Association
www.mnvca.org

New York Private Equity Network
www.nypen.org

Venture Investors Association of New York
www.viany.org

Rocky Mountain Venture Capital Association
www.coloradovca.org

San Diego Venture Group
www.sdvg.org

Venture Club of Louisville
www.ventureclub-louisville.org

Western Association of Venture Capitalists
www.wavc.net

Young Venture Capital Association
www.yvca.net

Young Venture Capital Society
www.yvcs.org

NON-U.S. VENTURE CAPITAL AND PRIVATE EQUITY ASSOCIATIONS

Australia Venture Capital Association
www.avcal.com.au

Austrian Private Equity and Venture Capital
  Organisation
www.avco.at

Belgian Venturing Associations
www.bvassociation.org

Brazilian Venture Capital Association
www.abvcap.com.br/

British Venture Capital Association
www.bvca.co.uk

Canadian Venture Capital Association
www.cvca.ca

China Venture Capital Association
www.cvca.com.hk

Czech Venture Capital Association
www.cvca.cz

Danish Venture Capital Association
www.dvca.dk

Emerging Markets Private Equity Association
www.empea.net

European Venture Capital Association
www.evca.eu/

Finnish Venture Capital Association
www.fvca.fi

Association Francaise des Investisseurs en Capital
www.afic.asso.fr

German Venture Capital Association
www.bvk-ev.de

Gulf Venture Capital Association
www.gulfvca.org

Hong Kong Venture Capital Association
www.hkvca.com.hk

Hungary Venture Capital and Private Equity
  Association
www.hvca.hu

Irish Venture Capital Association
www.ivca.ie

Israel Venture Association
www.iva.co.il

Italian Private Equity and Venture Capital
  Association
www.aifi.it

Japan Venture Capital Association
www.jvca.jp/en

Malaysian Venture Capital Association
www.mvca.org,my

Netherlands Venture Capital Association
www.nvp.nl

New Zealand Venture Capital Association Inc.
www.nzvca.co.nz

Norwegian Venture Capital Association
www.nvca.no

Poland Equity Investors Association
www.ei.com.pl

Philippine Venture Capital Investment Group
www.philvencap.com

Associação Portuguesa De Capital De Risco
www.apcri.pt

Russian Venture Capital Association
www.rvca.ru

Slovak Venture Capital Association
www.saef.sk

Singapore Venture Capital and Private Equity
  Association
www.svca.org.sg

South Africa Venture Capital and Private Equity
  Association
www.savca.co.za

Spanish Venture Capital Association
www.ascri.org

Swedish Venture Capital Association
www.vencap.se

Swiss Private Equity and Corporate Finance
  Association
www.seca.ch

Thai Venture Capital Association
www.venturecapital.or.th

Turkish Venture Capital Association
www.turkvca.org

Appendix B

SAMPLE RESUMES

Resume 1

Profile
Pre-MBA:
Bulge-Bracket Hire
(see CASE STUDY 1)

Work Experience

Bulge-Bracket Investment Bank, New York, NY   *July 2004–Present*

Analyst

- Designed and manipulated integrated financial models to evaluate various financing and acquisition scenarios
- Performed corporate and asset valuation analysis using discounted cash flow, comparable trading, comparable transaction, and leveraged buyout methodologies
- Developed financial projections and detailed operating models for clients
- Worked directly with the client in a one-on-one setting in order to properly model assets for potential Master Limited Partnership (MLP) formation
- Analyzed transactions to determine accretion/dilution impact and credit implications
- Modeled MLP transactions and performed analysis including G.P. valuation, incentive distribution rights (IDRs) and cash parity under an IDR reset
- Prepared presentations and marketing materials including board presentations, rating agency presentations, due diligence presentations, roadshow presentations, and investor presentations
- Interacted with senior bankers, client management, and lawyers on a daily basis

  Selected transactions include:
    - ~$160 million IPO
    - $113 million common unit offering
    - $130 million common unit offering
    - $1.1 billion of Series A Notes
    - $230 million common unit offering and $275 million of Senior Notes

Regional Bank, New York, NY   *Summer 2003*

Intern, Public Finance Department

- Built a comprehensive database of debt issues, issuer credit characteristics, credit enhancement, and liquidity facilities
- Analyzed the trading of municipal securities after issue, determined the extent of bank's access to retail accounts through institutional intermediaries, and performed industry research

Boutique Investment Bank, New York, NY   *Spring 2002*

Analyst

- Performed industry research, compiled industry and company overviews, and performed financial research
- Performed valuation analysis, created pitchbooks, analyzed and compiled financials, and composed a memorandum for a debt offering

Education

Top 10 Undergrad   *2000–2004*

Bachelor of Arts in Economics, 2004

- Graduated summa cum laude with a GPA of 3.89 and a major GPA of 3.87
- Journalist for independent weekly newspaper
- Phi Beta Kappa Society, Golden Key National Honor Society
- Psi Upsilon Fraternity, Entrepreneur's Club

High School, 1996–2000

- Graduated 3rd in class of 400
- SAT: 800 Verbal/770 Math
- National Merit Scholarship Winner, Advanced Placement Scholar with Distinction
- Member of Varsity Tennis team for four years

Interests

Baseball, basketball, golf, tennis, skiing, music, reading

Profile
Pre-MBA: Getting In from a Consulting Program
(see CASE STUDY 3)

EXPERIENCE

MAJOR CONSULTING FIRM, Analyst   2002–2004

- *Growth strategy.* Developed a national business growth strategy for a telecom regional bell operating company to achieve an additional $3.5 billion in annual profitability.
- *Market entry strategy.* Formulated a comprehensive enterprise mobility strategy for a Fortune 25 IT services company.
- *Mergers and acquisitions.* Evaluated potential acquisition targets for a leading data storage device company as part of a broader full potential project.

SOFTWARE COMPANY, Founding Employee and Business Development Manager   2000–2001

- *Product/market strategy.* Drove product line from concept to execution. Led cross-functional effort to articulate strategy, create collateral, model pricing, and orchestrate sales efforts.
- *Strategic sales and channel development.* Led sale of $1 million software/services contract. Negotiated strategic channel relationships. Facilitated acquisition of Series B venture financing.
- *Alliance development.* Executed and managed over 20 strategic partnerships with leading technology providers, system integrators, and channel resellers.
- *Team-building.* Ignited early recruiting efforts and helped to drive critical growth as a founding employee.

MEDIA/BROADCASTING COMPANY

Production Assistant/Technology Correspondent   Fall 1999

- *Technology reporting.* Spearheaded, wrote, directed, and produced an investigative news package on the emerging technology and Internet sector in Asia.
- *Industry analysis.* Supported anchors and reporters by providing key industry knowledge and insights for their tech-focused stories.
- *Executive interviews.* Led research efforts, developed questions, and participated in interviews of luminaries like Microsoft's Steve Ballmer.

LEADING INVESTMENT BANK, Financial Analyst   Summer 1998

- *Financial modeling.* Modeled profitability and optimized capital structure of a $400 million joint venture in the transportation industry.
- *Capital structure analysis.* Examined financing covenants impacting the capital structure for major telecom company resulting in a $3 billion credit facility.
- *Risk assessment.* Analyzed and modeled critical risk factors and their associated financial impact on a multibillion-dollar offshore oil and gas projects.

EDUCATION

Top Five University

M.S., ENGINEERING   June 2002

- Concentration in Technology Management/Entrepreneurship with relevant coursework, including Strategy in Technology Based Companies, High Tech Marketing, Computer Networks, and Change Management.
- Research Associate
- GPA: 3.97/4.0; GRE: 2210

B.S. with Distinction, Engineering   March 2000

- Executive roles in various student organizations.
- Major GPA: 3.99/4.0; Cumulative GPA: 3.88/4.0

SKILLS/INTERESTS

- Proficient with SQL, Access, C, HTML, and Excel financial modeling.
- Spoken Mandarin Chinese.

Resume 3

Profile
Pre-MBA:
Getting In from a Regional Bank
(see CASE STUDY 4)

Experience

Mid-Market Investment Bank
Financial Analyst, Leveraged Finance Group

- Originated, structured, and executed syndicated loans and high yield transactions for leveraged buy-outs, mergers, acquisitions, and recapitalizations
- Created offering memoranda, management presentations, rating agency presentations, and road show presentations
- Executed internal analysis for senior credit underwriting process, including memoranda for initial screening, commitment committee, and sales force marketing
- Performed detailed historical and projected comparative financial analysis to evaluate company credit quality, industry trends, and capital markets trends
- Awarded 3rd year offer

Selected Transactions:

- Regional Manufacturer
  - Sole lead manager on $100MM senior subordinated note offering to fund $175MM acquisition
  - Sole lead manager on $150MM senior secured credit facilities to complete recapitalization

- Restaurant Operator
  - Sole lead manager on $200MM senior subordinated note offering to fund $300MM acquisition

- Technology Services Provider
  Sole lead manager on $150MM senior secured credit facilities to complete recapitalization

Education

Ivy League University   1998–2002
B.A. in History
- Awarded university scholarship for academic achievement
- Senior Honors paper
- 4-time varsity letter winner in baseball

High School   1994–1998
- Top 5% in class with 3.9 GPA
- Elected captain of baseball team

Leadership

University Varsity Baseball   1998–2002
- Two-time conference champion

Regional Alumni Club   2003–2004
- Elected President of 300-member regional alumni club

Investment Bank Training Program—Mid-Market Investment Bank   2003–2004
- Assisted in creation of new LBO model for firm's Investment Banking platform
- Developed extensive case study to instruct incoming and future analysts about financial modeling and the execution of the underwriting process

Profile
Pre-MBA: **Getting In from a Mid-Market Bank—Late Cycle**
(see CASE STUDY 6)

EXPERIENCE

Mid-Market Investment Bank   2003–2005
Financial Analyst—Investment Banking, Corporate Finance Group

This middle market investment bank provides investment advisory, fairness opinion, solvency opinion, valuation opinion, restructuring advisory, and portfolio management services to over 1,000 clients ranging from closely held companies to Global 500 corporations.

- Performed extensive modeling and quantitative valuation analyses, including leveraged buyout, discounted cash flow, accretion/dilution, and merger analyses; constructed integrated stand-alone and pro forma financial models. Completed covenant flexibility, borrowing base availability, cash flow, and debt instrument analyses for clients on both financing and M&A transactions
- Conducted due diligence, analyzed potential synergies, and sensitized financial models
- Conducted industry research (market size, market share, industry trends, competitive landscape, customer trends) to both market companies and determine the correct market niche and possible arenas for expansion
- Project experience includes:
  - Advisor on the sale of a large franchisee of a national car rental agency
  - Advisor on an accelerated sale process for a defense electronics company with a preemptive offer by a large conglomerate
  - Engaged by a private equity sponsor for the sale/recapitalization of a courier services business
  - Advisor on the sale of a privately owned defense electronics company
  - Advisor on the sale of a privately owned semiconductor capital equipment company
  - Engaged to raise a senior and subordinated debt for a public apparel company
  - Advisor on the management/equity sponsor buyout and the associated financing of a Las Vegas casino
  - Advisor on the sale of an HVAC/refrigeration company
- Prepared financing and strategic alternatives presentations to clients in a range of industries, including apparel, real estate, and technology
- Ranked as the top analyst in class and received the highest ratings for learning ability and modeling skills

Private Equity Firm   Spring & Summer 2003
Analyst Intern—Generalist Group

This firm is concerned primarily with mezzanine investments in high growth but low technology industries.
- Conducted thorough analysis of transactions to analyze returns on specific investments and assess fund performance to date
- Assisted the Chief Operations Officer in reconciling accounts and past transactions, and identifying potential investment opportunities within the current portfolio
- Completed industry and company analyses within various sectors which included transportation and apparel

Private Equity Firm   Summer & Fall 2002
Summer Analyst Intern

Focuses on special situation investment opportunities within various industries, exclusive of the high technology and telecommunications industries.
- Conducted quantitative and qualitative due diligence on public and private companies for the purposes of evaluating potential investment opportunities, authoring comprehensive company and industry analyses
- Conducted extensive research within the paperboard, cosmetics, and specialty chemicals industries
- Created stand-alone LBO and merger models and evaluated various capital structure and financing alternatives on potential investments
- Performed discounted cash flow and accretion/dilution analyses and performed comparable company and M&A transaction analyses
- Prepared information packages and presentations for prospective clients

Venture Capital Fund   Spring 2002
Research Intern

This seed venture capital firm concentrated on investments within the nanotechnology sector
- Researched potential sources of intellectual property within certain accredited universities conducting research in the nanotechnology sector
- Corresponded with and evaluated various technology transfer offices to evaluate potential co-investment opportunities

EDUCATION

Top 30 University—School of Business   1999–2003
B.S. degree in Business Administration, Emphasis in Corporate Finance, Magna Cum Laude
- Cumulative GPA: 3.85/4.00; Dean's List: 1999–2003
- Presidential Scholarship for Academic Achievement

High School   1995–1999
   SAT-I: 1520 (Verbal: 780; Math: 740)

ACTIVITIES

Fraternity, Ski Club   2000–2002, 1999–2000

Resume 5

Profile
Pre-MBA: An Accountant
Gets In—Later in the Cycle
(see CASE STUDY 8)

EXPERIENCE

MAJOR ACCOUNTING FIRM   NEW YORK, NY

Associate, Corporate Finance—Transaction Structuring Group

- Advised investment banks, private equity firms, Fortune 500 companies, and other corporate clients on the financial accounting and reporting, regulatory aspects and tax implications of complex financial transactions. Involved in the structuring of mergers and acquisitions, off-balance-sheet financings, leveraged buyouts/recapitalizations, dispositions, joint ventures, leasing transactions, and financial derivative products.

- Worked on-site at a client in Europe to assist in the structuring of the sale of a $1.6 billion equity investment in a local telecommunications subsidiary to a Fortune 100 company.

- Spent three months in Asia investigating the events which led to a $2.6 billion loss incurred by a major Asian commodities trading corporation.

- Analyzed business development strategies that would enable a Fortune 100 company to enter a new line of business while achieving desired balance sheet and income statement presentation results.

- Assisted in the structuring of the leveraged recapitalization of a home products corporation that would provide substantial accounting and tax benefits to a large private equity firm.

- Provided a pooling-of-interests analysis for a foreign company on the acquisition of a U.S. corporation.

EDUCATION
1992–1996

IVY LEAGUE

Bachelor of Science in Economics. Graduated cum laude with a dual concentration in Finance and Entrepreneurial Management.
Finance/Management GPA: 3.7/4.0, Cumulative GPA: 3.6/4.0.

PERSONAL

Worked over fifteen hours per week for seven semesters to help defray educational costs.
Enjoy golf, running, swimming, music, and traveling.

Profile
Pre-MBA: **Directly Out**
of Undergrad—An Exception
(see CASE STUDY 9)

EXPERIENCE

11/97–5/99　　**Intern,** Start-Up Tech Company, Palo Alto, CA

Developed marketing strategy for angel-funded 3D graphics software tools start-up.
Produced marketing materials and company publications. Sold software through cold-calling
and trade shows; efforts led to sales to multiple marquee customers.

6/98–9/98　　**Intern,** Consulting Firm, London, England

Evaluated and drafted recommendations on potential leveraged buyout transactions for a
$650 million private equity fund managed by the firm. Conducted interviews of customers,
competitors, and industry experts. Performed public company and comparable
transaction analyses.

EDUCATION

9/96 – 6/99　　**Top Five University**

BA in History (4.0 GPA) with honors and University distinction awarded June 1999.
Elected to Phi Beta Kappa. Departmental honors thesis accepted with high honors.
GMAT: 740.

3/98–6/98　　**Overseas University,** England

9/95–5/96　　**Johns Hopkins University,** Baltimore, MD

SKILLS AND INTERESTS

- Avid surfer, rock climber, and skier
- Elementary German speaker

Resume 7

Profile

Pre-MBA: From Industry into a Healthcare Fund

(see CASE STUDY 11)

EXPERIENCE

Major Biotech Company   2001–2003

Manager, Strategic Planning Group

Responsible for financial and strategic planning for novel cancer therapy product.

- Financial Analysis:
  - Created financial model to forecast future cash flows based on multiple clinical development plans.
  - Performed valuation and sensitivity analysis.
  - Presented financial analysis to senior management.
- Market Research:
  - Led team in quantitative assessment of new markets in order to identify future growth opportunities.
  - Developed U.S. pricing strategy.
  - Identified target physician segments for sales force to call on at launch using primary research.
  - Co-led efforts with brand team to develop global positioning statement and key launch messages.
- Managed MBA summer intern.

Manager, Business Development Group

Promoted to Manager within 17 months of hiring and was the only manager without an MBA or other advanced degree.

- Evaluated market opportunities and built valuation models for over ten business development assessments.
- Managed due diligence process and provided recommendations on whether or not to pursue deals.
- Worked on deal team to in-license development rights for an early stage cancer product.
- Expanded international forecasting capabilities through the development of a global financial model.
- Developed competitive intelligence as a core competency for three other brands.

Software Company, San Francisco, CA   2000–2001

Business Analyst

- Worked in product marketing, corporate development, and sales for an early stage software company. Acquired in fall of 2001.
- Conducted competitive market analysis of 100 private companies in the software/technology sectors.
- Provided strategic recommendations on acquisition targets to the Board of Directors.
- Created new product line and developed branding, pricing structure, and client database.
- Received award for sourcing the most sales meetings of all employees through cold calling.

EDUCATION

IVY LEAGUE   1996–2000

B.A. in Human Biology with Academic Honors
- Courses: Corporate Finance, Accounting, Statistics, Genetics, Immunology, Vaccine Development, and Organic Chemistry.

LEADERSHIP ACTIVITIES

VENTURE PHILANTHROPHY FUND, San Francisco, CA   2001–2003

Engagement Manager
- Led diligence team to identify and invest $50K into two non-profit organizations for this venture philanthropy fund. Provide ongoing strategic and operational support to the fund's grantees.

NON-PROFIT   1998–2000

Founder and Director
- Founded regional site of national non-profit health care organization, with 300 volunteers, 10 full-time staff and offices in four U.S. cities.

INTERNATIONAL DEVELOPMENT ORGANIZATION   Summer 1999
- Principal Investigator. Directed 10-person field research team to evaluate the sustainability of a regional community health program.

MEDICAL RELIEF ORGANIZATION   Summer 1998
- Emergency Medical Technician. Traveled with 4-person medical team to provide public health infrastructure to remote villages.

ATHLETICS

Captain of semi-pro four-person adventure racing team   2000–2003
- Earned consistent top-ten finishes in 24-hour, 70+ mile adventure races.

Recruiter's Perspective
- Extensive industry experience at brand name company
- Solid summer experience
- Strong GPA
- Top undergrad university
- Company founder reflects entrepreneurial/ management skills

Pluses
Presented product to senior executives...Drove product launch in Europe...Led networking infrastructure development...Filed for patents...Led international team of 30 developers.

Experience

2001–2003	**Microsoft Corporation**	Redmond, WA

Program Manager/Software Design Engineer

Defined the strategy, design, and implementation of Microsoft's next-generation communication and entertainment product.

- **Business and Product Strategy**
  - Presented product to MS senior executive staff and key industry influentials.
  - Defined core thinking behind brand strategy and long-term business plan.
  - Drove product launch in Europe.
- **Software Development**
  - Led networking infrastructure development for Microsoft's peer-to-peer application.
  - Designed, implemented, and distributed a peer-to-peer file system (patented).
  - Filed for 5 patents as inventor.

Summer 2000   **Telecom Company**

Program Manager/Software Engineer

Architected audio content management system. Filed for 2 patents as inventor.

Summer 1999	**Microsoft Corporation**	Redmond, WA

Software Design Engineer

Designed and implemented a core component of the Microsoft consumer operating system.
Ranked in the top decile of Microsoft's interns.

1997–1999   **Online Game Company**

Senior Designer/Founder

Designed and implemented the internet's largest online text-based MMOG (60 thousand total users, 500 current users). Led an international team of over 30 developers.

Education

1997–2001   **Ivy League University**

Bachelor of Arts degree in Computer Science, Magna Cum Laude. GPA 3.8/4.0.

Interests

Complex systems/machine learning, finance, running, creative writing, electronic music, photography.

Resume 9

Profile
Post-MBA:
Returning to Your Pre-MBA Firm
(see CASE STUDY 14)

Education
2003–2005
TOP 5 BUSINESS SCHOOL
Candidate for Master in Business Administration degree, June 2006.

1995–1999
TOP 5 UNDERGRAD
Bachelor of Arts with Honors in Economics. Focus on international development.
Women's varsity sport.

Work Experience
Summer 2004

MANUFACTURING COMPANY
Operations Intern

- Conceived and executed improvements to address fulfillment of missing, wrong, and damaged parts. Designed and implemented associated company-wide IT modifications, and developed productivity improvement plan with $200,000 annual savings.

2001–2003
Top-Tier, Multibillion LBO Fund

Evaluated and executed equity and debt investments in the U.S. and Europe for large private equity fund. Developed operating models, restructuring models, and valuation analyses for leveraged buyout and distressed debt investments. Authored and presented investment memos to investment committee.

- Transaction A. Conducted comprehensive business, financial, and industry due diligence. Coordinated legal, accounting, and other advisory teams. Executed $400 million of new high-yield and asset-backed financing. Worked with management to assess potential raw material sourcing strategies and identify near-term follow-on acquisitions.

- Transaction B. Drafted and negotiated transaction documents, financing agreements, and management contracts. Completed bank and high-yield debt refinancing. Worked closely with senior and middle management to determine growth strategies and implementation plans for new products. Developed long-term budget, identified acquisition targets, and evaluated strategic partnerships and marketing plans.

- Transaction C. Evaluated a variety of strategic alternatives for portfolio company, culminating in $2 billion take-private transaction. Executed refinancing of $500 million of senior notes.

1999–2001
INVESTMENT BANK A
Restructuring Analyst (December 2000–July 2001)
Mergers & Acquisitions Analyst (July 1999–December 2000)

Summer 1998
INVESTMENT BANK B
Financial Analyst—Consumer Group

Summer 1997
Researcher-Writer—France and Europe Guides

Personal
Fluent in French. Enjoy comedy films, playing sports, and traveling. Citizenship: U.S. and U.K.

Profile

Post-MBA: **Returning with Narrow Geographic Preferences**

(see CASE STUDY 15)

Education

2004–2006   **TOP 5 BUSINESS SCHOOL**

Candidate for Master in Business Administration degree, June 2006. Recipient of Scholarship for demonstrated leadership and values. Member of VC & Private Equity Club.

1996–2000   **TOP 25 UNIVERSITY**

Bachelor of Business Administration degree, *summa cum laude*, in Finance and Business Economics. Minor in Accountancy. GPA 3.84/4.00.

Experience

Summer 2005   **ABC CAPITAL GROUP**
Investment Analyst

Responsible for evaluating investment opportunities for a $750 million value-oriented hedge fund.

- Analyzed opportunities in consumer products, shipping, media, and education through a combination of fundamental analysis, management interviews, and industry research.
- Conducted in-depth industry analysis. Recommendations led to several investments.

2002–2004   **LBO Fund**
Private Equity Associate

One of 25 investment professionals managing $6 billion of private equity capital.

- Responsible for transaction execution, structuring investments, financial modeling, conducting due diligence, managing external advisors, securing debt financing, reviewing contracts and recruiting executives.
- Completed $190 million leveraged buyout of pharmaceutical company. Actively involved in securing the debt financing package, negotiating agreements and conducting extensive due diligence. Closely evaluated products and markets, discovering substantial undeveloped value in key products resulting in over $15 million in incremental EBITDA.
- Identified attractive healthcare segments and networked with potential CEO partners. Proactively pursued investments in generic pharmaceuticals, specialty pharmaceuticals, medical products, hospitals, and managed care. Evaluated over 50 healthcare investment opportunities independently and in conjunction with partner-CEOs
- Led six-month proactive industry effort in the Medicare HMO industry. Built relationships with dozens of prominent managed care executives.
- Worked closely with management teams of portfolio companies to review add-on acquisitions and improve business performance.
- Created investment thesis for a consolidation in the active pharmaceutical ingredients industry.
- Actively involved in Associate recruiting. Led recruiting efforts during the 2003–2004 season.

2000–2002   **Mid-Market Investment Bank**
Investment Banking Analyst

- One of 10 M&A investment bankers advising on over $4 billion in transaction volume per year.
- Top ranked analyst in first and second year.
- Advised food company on $700 million acquisition.
- Advised company on its $100 million sale to telecom company. Achieved purchase price 60% higher than originally anticipated.

Community   Founded community business association for high school students designed to develop business skills. Activities included mock investing and entrepreneurship projects.

Personal   Climbed Mount Kilimanjaro (19,300 feet). Avid basketball player. Enjoy international travel (Europe, Southeast Asia, and Africa).

Resume 11

Profile

Post-MBA: A Pedigree Returns after Testing the Waters

(see CASE STUDY 16)

Experience

2001–2004   **LARGE PE FUND**   NEW YORK, NY

Associate. Responsibilities included evaluating new deals, leading business and industry due diligence, raising debt financing to support transactions, negotiating financing and transaction agreements and monitoring portfolio companies. Industry experience includes Media & Telecom and Industrial & Consumer.

- **Selected transactions and portfolio coverage:**
  - $150 MM equity investment in a $1.4BN LBO.
  - $3 MM equity investment in digital cable network. Target investment of $20 MM.
  - $40 MM mezzanine investment in owner/operator of mid-market TV stations.
  - $35 MM equity investment in broadband services provider. Served as a Director.
  - $25 MM equity investment in acquisition vehicle in the B2B publishing space.
- **Other:**
  - Formed investment thesis and identified investment candidates in digital cable.
  - Actively reviewed investment opportunities in the business process outsourcing (BPO) space.

1995–1997   **ABC SECURITIES INC.**   NEW YORK, NY

Analyst—Leveraged Finance Group. Performed valuation and credit analysis for leveraged buyouts of companies in the media, industrial, and consumer services industries. Presented to internal credit committees, drafted securities offering memoranda, and worked with syndications desk to structure and sell underwritten debt securities. Consistently ranked at top of my class.

- Lead-managed several senior and subordinated debt issuances for various acquisitions.
- Nominated by senior management to serve on internal analyst leadership council. Devised improvements to the investment banking analyst program.

Other   **INTERNET COMPANY (June–July 2000)** Member of the team responsible for launch of new product category. Created and presented category business plan to senior management team.

VC FIRM (August 2000) Reviewed early stage investments in BPO, call center and software services industries for $160 million venture capital fund.

OFFICE OF CONGRESSMAN (July–August 1997, Washington, DC). Organized small-business conference in Congressman's home district.

Education

1999–2001   **TOP 5 BUSINESS SCHOOL**

Master in Business Administration degree.

1991–1995   **TOP 10 UNIVERSITY**

Bachelor of Arts degree in Economics. Dean's List. Received Dean's Awards for student leadership. Selected by peers to speak at graduation exercises.

Personal   Lived in India, Japan, and Hong Kong. Interests include world affairs, entrepreneurship, and golf.

Service   Captain—MS Walk Team, raising $50,000 to find a cure for Multiple Sclerosis.
Captain—United Way Campaign, raising $250,000 for various United Way charities.

Profile

Post-MBA: **Going after the Opportunity in Person**

(see CASE STUDY 21)

Experience

Summer 2001	**BULGE BRACKET Investment Bank**	Tokyo, Japan

Associate, Investment Banking Division/Equity Capital Markets

Hired directly by senior executive to assist in helping local associates and analysts to develop a broad repertoire of industry skill sets, including valuation, presentation techniques, work ethic, and morale.

1998–2000	**Analyst, Mergers & Acquisitions**	New York, NY

Executed and marketed a variety of M&A transactions. *Offered an Associate position.*

Selected Transaction Execution Experience:

- Senior analyst on a team advising leading Latin American telecommunications company in the formation of a $4.0 billion joint venture with other regional companies. Complex technical analysis involved valuing many disparate assets within four segments (mobile, cable, CLEC, and Internet) from four different countries.

- Lead analyst on a team advising European company on a $500M bid for Latin American iron ore producer. Managed day-to-day activities, reporting directly to a Vice President. Responsible for extensive client interaction, significant due diligence, complex valuation analysis, detailed minority shareholder buyout scenarios, and an understanding of relevant country takeover regulations.

Education

2000–2002   TOP 5 BUSINESS SCHOOL

Master in Business Administration degree, June 2002.

1994–1998   TOP 100 UNIVERSITY

Bachelor of Science degree, *magna cum laude*, in Business Administration. Finance and Economics concentration.

- 1996–1998: Elected captain of school's development ski team.
- 1995: Overseas University: Completed summer program.
- 1997: Completed a 2-month summer seminar on Finance and International Business in England.

Personal   Fluent in Polish. Proficient in Spanish. Internationally ranked alpine ski racer (1990–1998). Enjoy adventure sports.

Community
- Assisted a $2BN Foundation in developing its private equity diversification strategy.
- Worked with a European city's bid to host the Winter Olympics.

Resume 13

Profile
Post-MBA: Taking a Pre-MBA Role as an MBA
(see CASE STUDY 22)

WORK EXPERIENCE

6/03–8/03   **BULGE BRACKET INVESTMENT BANK**   San Francisco, CA
Summer Associate, Investment Banking (Offered permanent employment)
- Executed $1.1bn secondary offering for major hardware company, including diligence and positioning.
- Evaluated strategic alternatives for a leading semiconductor company on a retained assignment.
- Analyzed debt restructuring options for a regional radio/TV company and a large clothing company.
- Advised a late stage telecom technology start-up on options regarding a sale of the company vs. an IPO.

7/99–7/02   **MID-TIER M&A BOUTIQUE**   San Francisco, CA
Analyst, Global Technology Group, Investment Banking   *New York, NY*
- Executed M&A and corporate finance transactions, including diligence, valuation, positioning, document drafting, and financial analysis.
- Established firm's client presence in the U.S. software sector, including screening, establishing contact, and developing client relations with over 100 software companies.
- Co-head of West Coast Analyst recruiting and active participant in Associate recruiting.
- Started as the only analyst of the San Francisco Technology Group, supporting up to 7 senior bankers.
- Ranked at the top of the analyst class.
- Informally offered associate position—elected to attend business school.

6/98–9/98   **THE ABC INDUSTRIAL COMPANY**
Intern/Analyst, Strategic Management Center (Offered permanent employment)
- Researched data and created Excel model on the worldwide bearing industry to resolve antitrust issues.
- Constructed a "toolkit" manual to systematize company's acquisition processes.

EDUCATION
8/02–6/04   **TOP 5 BUSINESS SCHOOL**
Master in Business Administration with Distinction
- Awarded 1st and 2nd Year Honors.
- Elected Treasurer of Squash and Tennis Club and of Volleyball Club.
- GMAT: 770.

9/95–6/99   **TOP 5 UNIVERSITY**
Bachelor of Science in Physics with Distinction and Minor in Economics
- GPA Overall: 3.98; GPA in Major: 3.92; GPA in Minor: 4.24 (A+ = 4.3).
- Phi Beta Kappa inductee.
- Member of Varsity Team (NCAA Champions in 1996, 1997, and 1998).
- Recipient of Student Scholar Athlete Award, 1997.
- In-depth course study: Physics, Mathematics, Economics, Pre-Medical (Chemistry, Biology).

OTHER
- High school valedictorian
- Fluent in Excel, Word, Access, and PowerPoint.
- Enjoy tennis, volleyball, football, hiking, skiing, and social dancing.

Profile
VC: A Traditional Pre-MBA VC Hire
(see CASE STUDY 31)

Education	1998–2002	**Top 50 University**

- B.S., **Electrical Engineering**
- GPA: 3.6
- SAT: M—800, V—800
- Spring 2002—Japan (Study Abroad)

Work Experience 2002–2004   **Major Consulting Company**

ASSOCIATE CONSULTANT

Strategic and management consulting. Served clients across retail, automotive, construction products, travel services, and real estate.

- Real Estate Investment Trust, Full Potential Diagnostic
  - Identified and collected data on several property performance metrics across portfolio of large multifamily REIT.
  - Used multivariable regression to compensate for market/asset differences between properties.
  - Identified over $100M in revenue enhancement opportunity through internal benchmarking.
- Glass Manufacturer, Growth Strategy
  - Conducted a bottom-up market sizing and segmentation of the glass industry to guide client in making sales force and product development investment decisions.
  - Identified up to $34M in potential revenue growth opportunities within client's existing product and geographic footprint.
- Travel Services Provider, Growth Strategy
  - Performed win/loss analysis to understand client's relative ability to win proposals in different industries. Insights used to refocus sales force toward selling to selected industries.
  - Developed cash flow forecasting model to assess client's ability to meet revolver terms given varying operating or financing scenarios.
- Auto Parts Manufacturer, Portfolio Strategy
  - Created financial fact base comparing profitability of client's product lines produced in nearly 30 manufacturing facilities globally.
  - Fact base used for best-demonstrated practice analysis and determination of core products and processes.

Summer 2001   **Investment Bank**

INFORMATION TECHNOLOGY INTERN

- Created a project management application for the network infrastructure division using Java Server Pages with an Oracle database.
- Gained knowledge of the financial services industry through classes on derivatives and options and through ad hoc interaction with traders.

Summer 2000   **IBM Corporation**

INTERN

- Worked with four technical interns and one MBA intern to develop a location-based services strategy for wireless devices.
- Submitted two patent applications for a location aggregation framework developed during the summer.

Activities
- Junior Achievement
- Formula SAE Powertrain Lead (Build and race auto group)
- Symphony violinist

Honors   Chancellor's Scholar (Campus Honors Program), Mechanical Engineering Outstanding Scholar, National Merit Scholar

Resume 15

Profile
VC: A Consultant with a Law Degree Gets In
(see CASE STUDY 32)

EXPERIENCE

Major Consulting Firm, *Associate*, New York   Summer 2001; 2002–2004

Led complex strategic issue diagnosis and problem-solving, developed strategic recommendations, and managed client teams across multiple functions, including customer acquisition, operations, global organization, sales and marketing, and capability building. Specific examples include:

- Identified, developed, and piloted alternative pharmaceutical sales force models to reach underserved physician segments for major global pharmaceutical company
- Led development of European country strategy for major U.S. pharmaceutical company facing complex competitive challenges to its most important drug. Identified 35 million euros in incremental revenue through novel positioning
- Developed global R&D strategy for major pharmaceutical company. Wrote business plan to maximize the value of the biologics in support of the larger R&D efforts of the organization
- Built growth strategy for home equity business of major credit card organization. Identified $5-6 million in incremental revenue through customer acquisition strategies and better prioritization of internal resources
- Assisted client to identify opportunities for a start-up private equity fund focused on health care
- Conducted training for 2003 associates and analysts; actively involved in interviewing, recruiting
- Selected as Evaluator for National Business Plan Competition for Nonprofit Organizations; served on Nonprofit Leadership Group to encourage firm interest and commitment to nonprofit work

EDUCATION

TOP LAW SCHOOL, J.D., *cum laude*   June 2002

Activities:	Served as Course Assistant	
Internships:	Law Firm (London, England)	Law Firm (Tel Aviv, Israel)
	Law Firm (New York, NY)	U.S. Attorney's Office (Anywhere, USA)
	Attorney General's Office (Anywhere, USA)	Law Firm (Anywhere, USA)

TOP 5 UNIVERSITY, B.A., *cum laude*, in Economics and Philosophy   June 1997

Honors:	Distinction in the Major, Economics; Distinction in the Major, Philosophy
MILITARY	Served in infantry brigade of Israeli Defense Forces (Nov. 1998–Feb. 2000). Awarded distinction "Mofet Plugati" as most outstanding soldier during basic and advanced training and tour of duty
MEMBERSHIPS	New York Bar Association (attorney in good standing); Asia Society